W9-CEG-585

The Anatomy
of the
Catholic Church

THE ANATOMY
of the
CATHOLIC CHURCH

*Roman Catholicism in
an Age of Revolution*

Gerard Noel

DOUBLEDAY & COMPANY, INC.
GARDEN CITY, NEW YORK
1980

The author is grateful to the following publishers for permission to quote from their published works:

Orbis Books for Walbert Bühlmann's *Courage Church,* Copyright W. Bühlmann/St. Paul Publications, 1977.

Sheed & Ward, Ltd. for John Jay Hughes' *Stewards of the Lord,* Copyright 1970 by John Jay Hughes.

Dimension Books, Inc. for Dom Helder Camara's *Church and Colonialism,* English translation Copyright 1977 by Sheed & Ward, Ltd.

Library of Congress Cataloging in Publication Data

Noel, Gerard Eyre.
  The anatomy of the Catholic Church.

  Bibliography: p. 276.
  Includes index.
  1. Catholic Church—History—1965–   I. Title.
BX1390.N63   282'.09'04
ISBN: 0-385-14311-7
Library of Congress Catalog Card Number 78–22344

Copyright © 1980 by Gerard Noel
All Rights Reserved
Printed in the United States of America
First Edition

CONTENTS

For
Elizabeth

INTRODUCTION

FOR A WORK with such a title, this book may seem to be surprising in form. It differs from many previous treatises in attempting to be neither exhaustive nor even coldly objective. It looks at the Roman Catholic Church of today within a particular context, that of world revolution: and it seeks to explore those areas of Catholicism most relevant to the dilemma which this revolution poses, without forgetting the crucial but often neglected historical dimension. A candid study of the latter helps to dispel the modern myth that it is only now, in the late twentieth century, that the Catholic Church is being drawn away from its spiritual anchor by the currents of political and secular entanglement. Such entanglement was far more prevalent in the past, when Catholicism's sociotheological priorities were very different. Then, the Church spoke as a world power, in the language of organized religion, against the falseness of all "gods" but its own. Its voice was as powerful politically as that of any purely secular "empire." But it often failed to penetrate into men's innermost hearts. "Today the Church's mission is to testify against the profane powers that are laying claim to adoration. The witnesses killed today are those who refuse to offer incense to idols; they are those who stand up against false gods of wealth and power in all the forms of violence and falsehood with which they oppress and divide human beings. . . . The Church has entered an era new to it, a time for the renewal of structures, beliefs, laws, sacraments, a time not to reject the good grain with the tares but to discern the old and the new, what is dying and what is coming to birth through a return to its sources" (Bigo, *The Church and Third World Revolution,* pp. 300–301).

The "first revolution" of modern history was that of the eighteenth century against a surviving form of feudalism. It proclaimed "liberty, equality and fraternity," but succeeded in establishing, to some degree, only the first of these three. The "second revolution" was the socialist one against capitalism. It managed to establish a measure of "equality" where, previously, only the rich and influential few enjoyed an unearned inheritance of the earth. The "third revolution" is that of today. Signs of it appear in whatever part of the globe you happen to look. Its enemies are injustice and exploitation as brought about by man's greed. A minority of the world's people enjoy by far the largest slice of the world's sustenance and resources. This is the crowning in-

justice. The movement against it is unstoppable; but can it establish
what the other two revolutions failed to establish: fraternity? brotherhood? Call it what you will. It is here that Roman Catholicism becomes inevitably affected by this struggle.

Can a worldwide Church be neutral in such a situation? It must obviously support and promote justice—at whatever price. The Vatican
Council's Constitution on the Church in the Modern World stated
that "The joys and the hopes, the griefs and anxieties of the people of
this age, especially those who are poor or in any way afflicted, these,
too, are the joys and hopes, the griefs and anxieties of the followers of
Christ." But the Church finds—has found in the past—that its purely
verbal protests and other exhortations fall on stony ground and deaf
ears. Must it then join up with such revolutionary forces as seek man's
liberation from intolerable injustices—even if this means accepting violence, in some cases, as the lesser of two evils? If not, is it condemned
to stand aside and thus, having allowed others to "free" spiritually and
physically deprived humanity, be found, by posterity, to be more irrelevant than ever to the modern world in its actual situation?

Some would say that such questions are unreal: that the Church
must stick to its "traditional" role: that it must proclaim the truth,
that truth over which it was given exclusive guardianship by God himself. If it does this it has nothing to fear. One day men will follow.
Meanwhile it must keep its own "faith" intact and not capitulate to
those false "progressivist" prophets who come like sheep but inwardly
are ravening wolves.

What, however, *is* the real "traditional" truth as handed down in
(and conditioned by) the history of the Roman Church—a glimpse of
which is provided in the first section of this book? The Vatican Council has brought to light profound disagreement among Catholics themselves as to what this "truth" really is and how it is to be interpreted
today. The agony that such disagreement has produced, as analyzed
chiefly in the second section, is seen as little less than "traumatic" for
the Church at this tense moment in its life. The worst of the tension
may be passing, but the need for "readjustment" remains. The book
concludes with an attempted "prognosis" on the basis of the enormous
demands likely to be made on the Church as its center of gravity shifts
from the first to the "Third World."

That the ultimate answer to the Church's current dilemma can only
come to life in spiritual terms is one point, at least, on which all
believers, "traditional" or "progressive," would agree. For spiritual

renewal is a necessity for the people of God. The Church began with the coming of the Spirit. It can continue to do the work of Jesus its Lord only if the same Spirit is allowed by man to keep coming back in each new cycle of human development. It is thus that the book ends on the note of "Renewal."

Such are the main lines of inquiry which, by limiting the field to some extent, are intended to keep within manageable bounds this particular exploration of the "anatomy" of the Roman Catholic Church. The latter is frequently referred to in the text as merely "the Church." This is done purely for the sake of brevity and implies no kind of judgment on what constitutes that "Church" which embraces all Christians.

It should perhaps be added that the "revolution" which the Church is seen to be facing is not only a political and economic one. It is just as much intellectual, moral and social. There is, moreover, a widespread hunger for Faith in today's world; but there is a no less widespread distaste for dogmatism, moralizing, and purely conventional Religion. Should the Catholic Church, then, radically rephrase its theology or continue to expound it in terms meaningless to the majority of men, if sacred to a diminishing few? Should it accept the "new morality"—as rightly understood—or continue to champion what often turns out to be "unnatural" law? Should it, in short, accord full freedom to Faith even if this conflicts with some of its formerly most cherished concepts concerning the power of Religion?

The Catholic Church of today is in two minds as to which direction to take. This book attempts to illustrate some—but only some—of the areas in which its dilemma is particularly acute. It has not been possible to do full justice to the straightforward faith of the millions of ordinary Catholics, ministers or otherwise. Such faith is the backbone of a Church which, at its best, is uniquely impressive, and has, over the centuries, attracted the free response of faith of millions of men and women. But there is, of course, another side to the story . . .

PART ONE

GROWTH

CHAPTER 1

The Community That Became a Church

Ah, Constantine! To how much ill gave birth
Not thy conversion, but that dower
Which the first rich Father took from thee!

DANTE

Paradoxical as it may be, it is an historical fact that
imperfection is an essential part of the temporal church.
Christ lives on in the Church, but he lives as crucified. One
almost ventures to use a parable and to say that the
imperfections of the Church are the Cross of Christ. What
would become of us if human nature vanished from the
Church?

ROMANO GUARDINI

"In the course of its 2000-year history, the Catholic Church has only twice changed its stance. At first, it was a private fellowship surrounding Jesus. As it gradually became an international private cult, it was frequently confused with Judaism. From a persecuted sect, the Church became the official religion of the Roman Empire. As such, it Christianised and Romanised the barbaric Middle Ages of both eastern and western Europe. . . . Now the Church was returned to its original stance, a private cult of the Redeemer carrying his Good News to as many as it can persuade to believe. No longer the shaper of civilisations with imperial power at its command, Christ's fellowship must once more imitate the role of its Master . . ." (Day, *The Catholic Church Story,* Introduction).

Such a twofold change of stance is the key to an understanding of this Church's "anatomy" at a time of transition verging on metamorphosis. For the present reversion to an earlier position represents a clean break with much of what happened in between; and the events of the last fifteen years add up to as radical a change of stance as that of the fourth century A.D. What happened then?

The community of love founded by Jesus Christ became, at that stage, a powerful "church" in the modern sense of the word. It quickly went on to become a heavily structured establishment. The ultimate objective always remained man's salvation but the possession of new and powerful means for attaining this objective led churchmen along a perilous path, the path to absolute power. The very worthiness of the ends being pursued often rendered the means for achieving them of secondary moment. It became a tenet of terrible and inexorable logic that no greater evil could befall society than the dissemination of false spiritual teaching; heresy was treason. The Church, however, backed by an authority that became monolithic, had a mandate direct from God to save men from such an evil for the salvation of their souls. The fate of their bodies was necessarily nothing by comparison. Though man had a free will, objective error had, by definition, no rights and could never be tolerated. One day something like the slaughter of the Saracens, the butchering of Albigenses and the fires of the Inquisition was as inevitable as, for Nazism, was the "final solution" of the Holocaust.

All this was far in the future when Jesus was carrying out his ministry. Is it an exaggeration to say that he founded not a church but a community? Jesus himself hardly ever—perhaps never—used the word "church." The word readily occurred, however, to Matthew (the former civil servant) when making his crucial addition to the earlier description by Mark (Peter's companion) of Peter's profession of faith. In answer to the question "Who do you say I am?" Peter spoke up and said "You are the Christ." This according to Mark (8:29–30) was the end of the conversation except for Jesus' commands that they should tell no one. Matthew, however (16:18), adds the famous statement in which Jesus calls Peter the "rock" on which he will build his "church." It is this account—rather than those in Mark and Luke— which has been preferred and few quotations in the whole New Testament are more familiar to Catholics (and none more vital to papal claims) than this one.

The word "church," however, though foreign to the gospels, is frequently employed elsewhere in the New Testament to describe the body that began to emerge immediately after Jesus's death and resurrection. Was this yet a "church" in the sense of being juridically structured according to the various levels of hierarchical authority and with a distinction between clergy and laity? Evidently not. Rather, we are told, "the faithful all lived together and owned everything in common. . . . Day by day the Lord added to their community" (Acts 2:44 and 47). The community spread rapidly, first of all, during the "Judeo-Christian" period, through the network of existing synagogues; and then by means of the extensive lines of communication of the Roman empire. Where, if anywhere, was the nerve center of this growing body? To see the center as Rome involves reading history backward. Rome appears intermittently as the (not always effective) court of appeal in disputed cases but exercises nothing approaching universal jurisdiction. It is powerless to stop the proliferation of local beliefs and customs that have been springing up in the various churches.

What developed, in other words, was a community of communities or something like a federation of churches. The factor which produced unity without uniformity and authority without authoritarianism was that special and spiritual kind of community better described as "communion." The Greek word for this concept, *koinonia*, has become central to ecumenical thinking, especially in the efforts to work out a formula for reunion as between the Roman Catholic and Anglican communions of today. The men who, in the early church, had come to be known by certain names, such as presbyters, or elders, did not thereby set themselves apart from the others. All owed loyalty to all. The presbyters—in an atmosphere we would now call "charismatic"— did not form a privileged class. "The communities respected and honoured the charisms of each individual," as one writer put it in arguing that, for this reason, "the pre-Constantine period deserves our continued reflection" (Delespesse, *The Church Community*, p. 32).

Constantine changed all. The story of his impact on the Christian Church is as well known as it is fantastic and, at times, almost incredible. It is a story which "marks a turning-point in the history of the Church and of Europe. It meant much more than the end of persecution. The sovereign autocrat was inevitably and immediately involved in the development of the Church, and conversely the Church became more and more implicated in high political decisions" (Chadwick, *The Early Church*, p. 125). Constantine was a passionate unifier. His first task was to unify the empire itself by uprooting the usurper Maxentius from Rome. Though not yet a Christian (like many "converts" at that time he did not receive baptism until his deathbed) he did not, as had previous emperors, see Christianity as a natural enemy. He perceived it rather as a potential ally in the cause of internal imperial unity. He was also, if not profoundly religious, distinctly superstitious and ascribed his victory over Maxentius to divine intervention. Without abandoning his faith in Apollo and the Unconquered Sun, he adorned the imperial standards with the emblem of Christ. In later years he told of a vision he had seen on the eve of doing battle with the barbarians. The cross, he said, had stood athwart the midday sun inscribed with the words "In this sign conquer."

Constantine, in 312, marked his initial reconciliation with Christianity in spectacular fashion. To the Bishop of Rome, Miltiades (d. 314) he donated—along with a generous patrimony—a valuable piece of property. This was the Lateran Palace, destined to play a central role in the "imperial" life of the papacy. It came to incorporate a fine church, possibly adapted by Constantine from the existing great hall or "basilica" of the palace. Ultimately dedicated to St. John the Baptist, it thus became the prototype of those great basilicas which, as specially privileged churches, have come to dominate Roman ecclesiastical history. The era when Christians had to worship in private houses had gone forever. The Lateran Palace became the principal residence of the popes for nearly a thousand years as well as the headquarters of Church government and organization. It housed at the height of the Middle Ages what was arguably the greatest focal point of power over men the world has ever known. The basilica itself—"mother and head of all churches in the world" is to this day the episcopal seat of the Pope as Bishop of Rome.

The year after the gift of the Lateran, Constantine promulgated the Edict of Milan. Christianity by this edict was no more than "tolerated" along with other religions. It did not become the official state religion until nearly the end of the century, though it quickly became the recipient of considerable revenues, properties and endowments. But it did not, as Constantine soon came to see to his chagrin, possess sufficient uniformity of faith to be the desired instrument of cohesion within the empire. Such was his "reverence for the legitimate Catholic Church," as the emperor slyly told Miltiades, that he did "not wish to leave schism or division in any place." And so it was that the first of the Church's great "ecumenical," or universal, Councils was convened not by a Pope but by the emperor himself. Sylvester, the next Bishop of Rome, was not even present. Significantly it was not just a council of the Church but also a council of the empire. It was held at Nicaea, then a prosperous trading town by the Lake of Ascanius (now Iznik in northwest Turkey). Constantine had a palace there and he acted as host to three hundred bishops, almost all from the eastern half of his Empire.

Of the several disputed points of theology one dominated all others: Who was Jesus, and how could Christians come to understand and know him better? The same question is still being asked even more urgently, if in a different context today. At the time of Nicaea it centered on the elusive relationship between Father and Son in the formula of the Trinity and on whether or not Jesus could indeed be truly called God. "How could he be?" asked Arius (d. 336), the turbulent priest of Alexandria to the fury of his bishop. Had Jesus himself not made it clear that he was only God's Son, and that the Father was greater than he? Surely this meant he was something like God's "adopted" Son, though still the unique intermediary between the divine creator and all men. Besides, Paul had stated in his letter to the Colossians (1:15) that Christ was "the image of the unseen God and the first-born of all creatures." Even Tertullian (d. 230), the greatest mind among early Christian teachers, had given the Son a beginning in time.

What did the bishops of the Church think when they came together at Nicaea about this and other matters? Having made clear to them his concern not only for the unity of the Church but also for the combined unity of Church *and* State, Constantine sat back and listened to their disputations. But the process tried his patience. He had heard all this sort of thing before: endless arguments and counterarguments seeming to get no one anywhere. What was clearly needed—and what the Church lacked—was a formula of faith, that is a "creed," and an administrative framework capable of ensuring that such a formula was adhered to as the test of orthodoxy. But how, to clear a path toward achieving such an objective, did Constantine deal with the discordant voices in this great ecclesiastical "parliament" of his empire? He hit on a drastic but, in the event, extremely successful device. At the conclusion of the opening speeches, letters of petition and complaint were handed to the Emperor during an interval in the first day's proceedings. They amounted to a mass of memoranda in which, apparently, various bishops made accusations against each other. Constantine promised to deal with them but, in the end, handed back the letters unopened with the cunning observation: "God has raised you to the priesthood and given you the authority to sit in judgment, even over us. You cannot be judged by men." He then ordered all the letters to be burned. No one was to know of any disagreement among the Fathers of the Council.

Such tactics succeeded. Arius himself appeared before the Council but discredited himself. His eloquent opponent, the Alexandrian dea-

con (and subsequent bishop) Athanasius (d. 373) spoke for the majority. Arianism was definitely rejected. The assembly could then proceed to its main task of formulating a succinct statement of orthodox
Christian faith. This was the Nicene Creed which has lasted until today. On the question "who was Jesus?" it was stated that he was "very
God of very God, begotten not made." But the most important part of
the definition stated that Christ was "of one substance" with the Father
(by whom all things were made). Constantine himself was responsible
for the expression. To his great relief the Creed was accepted almost
unanimously by the Council on June 19, 325. The bitter controversy as
to who exactly Jesus was, had been, he felt, settled once and for all. In
fact it was only just beginning.

The Nicene doctrine of the Church was adopted as a law of the
Empire. Doctrinal agreement was complemented by unity in the fields
of worship and church administration. "Constantine wanted a per-
fectly dovetailed and inviolable organisation for the Church, the
model for which was to be the episcopal authority and the composition
of and relations between the communities" (Gontard, *The Popes,* p.
107). Such organization proceeded along the lines of those of imperial
Rome itself. The development was to prompt the picturesque over-
statement made many years later by Thomas Hobbes in a famous sentence: "The Papacy is not other than the Ghost of the deceased
Roman Empire, sitting crowned upon the grave thereof." The Latin
Church even took over such imperial terms as diocese, prefecture,
vicariate, consistory, and others. A papal representative was a "legate"
as he would have been in the time of Julius Caesar. When the Emperors discarded the title "Pontifex Maximus," the Popes took it over
as of natural right. But in signing bulls and other documents, Bishops
of Rome have, since the days of Gregory the Great, used as a title
more in accord with scripture and the community idea of Church:
"Servant of the servants of God."

One particular person, a contemporary of Constantine, was conspic-
uous by his lack of personal participation in these momentous events.
This was the Bishop of Rome or—with retroactive use of the title—
"Pope" of the day, Sylvester I (314–35). He was a wholly shadowy
figure as were all the bishops of Rome between Stephen I (254–57)*
and Damasus I (366–84). It was the latter who, after the removal of

---

* One of the few early bishops of Rome to attempt supervision over the
whole Church.

the capital of the Empire to Constantinople, enhanced the position of
Rome and began to lead the "papacy" out of the shadows. He made a
novel claim (in 382) to absolute "primacy" because of the powers
originally conferred on Peter and was the first Bishop of Rome to refer
to his see as the "Apostolic See." Rome, politically isolated after
Nicaea in the new imperial setup, took on increased ecclesiastical vigor
and independence. In fact "The pretensions of Constantinople had
propelled Rome, with sudden force, along the road to primacy; they
compelled it to gather together its earlier titles and combine them into
a single claim to be 'the exclusive inheritor of all, and more than all,
that the New Testament tells us of the prerogatives of St. Peter'"
(Barraclough, *The Medieval Papacy,* p. 24). What is particularly interesting in view of current ecumenical discussions is the view taken by
Damasus' illustrious contemporaries, St. Ambrose and St. Augustine,
on the meaning of papal primacy. They disagreed with the Pope's interpretation of it since Peter, according to Ambrose, had "a primacy
of confession not of office, a primacy of faith not of rank."

Unfortunately, however, rank and office were becoming as important to the emerging institutional church as confession and faith had
been to the first Christian community. To confession and faith must be
added—hope. For though Jesus' "little flock" (Luke 12:32) was initially very small it was the possessor of a magnificent promise. "It has
pleased your Father," he told them, "to give you the kingdom." This
kingdom, the Kingdom of God, was what Jesus came to give men in
order to change the world. The Church was the mere means for attaining this great end. "The Church is not possession of the kingdom, it is the struggle for it. But it is a struggle consoled by the promise that the gates of hell will not prevail against it" (*A New
Catechism,* p. 144). This then was the mission and mandate of
Christ's "Church," a word—*qahal*—often used in the Old Testament
for the People of Israel in the desert. This is also what Jesus meant: a
new people. But they were not to be left to wander in a desert. They
were to be taught and fed by certain individuals whom Jesus singled
out as heralds of an event, the coming of the Kingdom of God. Such
individuals were originally twelve in number. Each was called an apostle. *Apostolos* is Greek for "he who is sent"—an envoy. Continuity was
clearly necessary in some form if the new community was to survive.
Who, then, were the successors to the apostles?

It is Catholic teaching that Peter and the apostles passed on their
office as rulers to the "bishops," in its fullness, and to "priests" and

"deacons," in part. Such a "hierarchy" of ranks was, of course, unknown in the time of Jesus, but had become fairly clearly established by the early part of the second century. But the "primatial" rank of any one man took very much longer to emerge. The impetus given toward its final establishment by the Constantinian era and its aftermath was indispensable. A formerly embattled sect soon became a powerfully structured monarchical Church. The persecuted became the persecuting. The State Church became a Church-State. There was no room for nonconformity.

CHAPTER 2

The Church That Became an Empire

It might have been expected that the saviour of Christendom
[from Islam in 720] would have been canonized. . . . But in
the public distress [he] had been compelled to apply the
riches, or at least the revenues, of the bishops and abbots to
the relief of the state and the reward of the soldiers. His
merits were forgotten, his sacrilege alone remembered, and a
Gallic synod presumes to declare that [Charles Martel] was
damned.

EDWARD GIBBON

We all, prelates and clergy, have gone astray from the right
way, and for long there is none that has done good; no, not
one. . . . Therefore, in our name, give promises that we shall
use all diligence to reform before all things the Roman Curia,
whence perhaps, all these evils have had their origin.

POPE ADRIAN VI (1522–23)

THE STEADY PROCESS whereby the Catholic Church advanced toward
ecclesiastical imperialism was a constant blend of theory and practice.
The two influenced each other in an endless cycle of cause and effect.
In the best possible sense of the word the Church could, even from the
earliest days, look upon itself as a spiritual empire. It had a universal
mandate from Jesus Christ from whom, in turn, "all power" in heaven
and on earth had been given by the Father. Such "power" was
presumed to have been handed over to the Church. Its jurisdiction
could admit no limits whether national, racial or any other. Everyone
must be converted and come within the dominion of this supranational
body. Such was already the theory when the Church was given official
status by an effectively "worldwide" political empire. By the time this
political empire in the West had disintegrated, a new moral order had
been founded: the *Civitas Christiana* directed from ecclesiastical
Rome. All of its members belonged, in a sense, to a single nation. But

the process was a long one and happened only in very slow stages. And accompanying the political progress of the papacy was an astonishing ground swell of spirituality at every level, in the forms of monasticism, asceticism and popular piety. Astonishing holiness was at no time lacking in at least part of the Christian Church. Would this type of religion, based on conversion and conviction, alone be sufficient to plant the Faith in every land?

The official Church thought not. The taste of power, developed in the post-Constantinian era, pointed in much more ambitious directions. The weapons coming into the hands of an imperially backed state religion were immense. It was thus that a certain kind of Church model came to dominate Europe from about the fourth century until the Reformation. (After the Reformation it was transplanted by Spain and Portugal to the New World.) This Church model is best characterized by the term "Christendom." Catholicism had, it was felt, both a right and a bounden duty to establish a worldwide Christian domain. The reasoning was straightforward enough. As it possessed a monopoly on the means of salvation—and as everything was ultimately related in some way to salvation—the Church inevitably had authority over all matters whether spiritual or temporal. (See: Troeltsch, *The Social Teaching of The Christian Churches*, I, 2.) As time went on the "Christendom" model became susceptible of more precise analysis. "First, the organisational principle was total coverage of all territories; where people could be found, a Christian ruler had to ensure conversion, even if this meant the imposition of religion through force. The whole world was to be Christian: the message of Christ was universal. Secondly, the groups and sectors focused upon were all-inclusive, as the form was based on a monopoly of the faith. . . . A third factor of this model was the comprehensive relationship of the Church and society. As all matters were related to salvation, the Church was bound up with every phase of man's existence. Society itself was constructed from within the Church, on the Church's terms, and received from it express and direct regulation. Finally, the instruments used in exercising and generating influence were the webs of structures and groups which constituted society. Through a Christian ruler, the influence of the Church filtered down to all people. Structures made men Christian rather than the other way round" (Bruneau, *The Brazilian Catholic Church*, pp. 11-12). It was, then, a uniform and all-embracing Christendom which was the constant objective of the Catholic empire.

But insofar as this empire was Roman as well as Catholic it came, ultimately, to be concerned only with the "Latin" West.

The Church in the (Greek-speaking) East developed on different lines from almost the moment Constantine left Rome to establish Constantinople. He felt the "old Rome" to be too sullied by pagan associations to be the center of the kind of Christian empire he had in mind and after "New Rome's" inauguration in 330 he laid it down that at Constantinople no pagan rites should ever be performed. The Eastern ("Orthodox") Church moreover, had, from the earliest days, its own very clear idea of what constituted proper ecclesiastical priorities. It did not, as became the tendency in Roman Catholicism, look upon the Church as a worldwide organization in which each local body forms part of a larger and more inclusive whole. It followed instead the view of St. Ignatius, the great Bishop of Antioch at the turn of the first Christian century and the first man to call the Church "Catholic." For him the local community *is* the Church. He conceived of the Church as a Eucharistic society realizing its true nature only when celebrating the Supper of the Lord and receiving his body and blood in the sacrament. "The teaching of Ignatius has a permanent place in Orthodox tradition. Orthodoxy still thinks of the Church as a Eucharistic society, whose outward organisation, however necessary, is secondary to its inner, sacramental life" (Ware, *The Orthodox Church,* p. 21). The bishops of Rome, however, fighting for their heads with the eventual collapse of the Western empire during the barbarian invasions (fifth and sixth centuries) made greater and greater Church centralization one of their primary aims. In self-defense the Roman Pope was forced to assume a role never needed by the Greek Patriarchs of the East. He became an autocrat and absolute monarch. The general ecclesiastical pattern was (papal) "monarchy" in the West and (episcopal) "collegiality" in the East. The Greeks assigned to the Pope a primacy of honor but not the universal supremacy he came, more and more, to regard as his due. The Eastern Church, moreover, held that in matters of faith the final decision belonged not with the Pope alone but with a Council representing *all* the bishops of the Church. This claim corresponded with the normal means for settling disputed theological points during the first millennium of the Church's life. This means was "conciliar," that is, by way of Councils speaking for the entire Church. The first seven of these are particularly important since they established the dogmatic foundation of Christendom and counteracted the first great wave of "heresies."

All of these councils were convoked by the emperors and held in the
"East"—at Nicaea (twice), at Ephesus and Chalcedon and, on three
occasions, at Constantinople. None of them was attended by a Pope
who, however, sent representatives and generally confirmed the decrees that such representatives signed. Despite the appearance and
growth of divergencies between East and West—occasioned by political, cultural and linguistic as well as theological differences—all these
councils were considered as universally binding. And the Pope's position as of the fifth century had lost all semblance of its former shadow-
iness. Though, in great measure, owing its original ascendance to the
mere fact of Rome's political importance, it came later to possess a
much stronger moral claim to being a true spiritual rock. Recognized as much in the East as in the West was the purity of its faith in
the first eight centuries of the Church's life. While, during major doctrinal disputes, other patriarchates wavered, Rome almost always
stood firm. In the eyes of men who knew and cared, the Pope, as he
came to be called,* earned his claim to be the first teacher of Christendom, even if, to the Greeks, this had to mean first among equals.
Above all, papal and conciliar teaching were seldom at serious odds.
One notable occasion when they were was when Pope Honorius I
(625–38) was posthumously condemned as a heretic by the third
Council of Constantinople (681), the condemnation being confirmed
by the Pope of the day (Leo II). Honorius had agreed with the heretical "Monothelite" argument that though Jesus had two natures,
being only one person, he therefore had only one will. The council
replied that if he had two natures (one divine and one human) he
must also have had two wills. To maintain otherwise would be to im-
pair the fullness of Christ's humanity since manhood without a human
will would be a mere illusion. The dispute exemplifies the persistence
with which questions went on being asked, in one form or another, as
to the precise place in theology to be assigned to the person of Christ.
The question "Who was Jesus?" is, as already mentioned, being asked
more urgently than ever today.

Apart from a further Council of Constantinople in 869, later dis-
owned by the Greeks, there was a lull in conciliar activity until after

---

* The title "Pope" was ultimately derived from the child's word for father in
classical Greek. From the third to the fifth centuries it was applied to all
bishops, but more particularly after the sixth century, to the Bishop of Rome.
It was not universally recognized in the West as a Roman title until the
eleventh century. (In the East it was never recognized as such at all.)

the growing rift between East and West became official in 1054. Then, in the following century, no less than three councils were held, all at the Lateran Palace in Rome. After seven centuries of struggle the papacy had survived and brought light to the Dark Ages. In the twelfth century it was reaching the zenith of its power. Christian Europe had been born.

* * *

Far from lamenting that the early Christian community did not continue to spread slowly and laboriously through preaching and conversion, Catholics have, until recently, proudly rejoiced in its victory by more spectacular means. Such an outlook came to be characterized by the description "triumphalist," last personified among Popes by Pius XII (1939–58). One of its greatest champions in England was Hilaire Belloc who elaborated his theories in his key work on the subject, *Europe and the Faith*. "My object in writing," he stated (p. 94), "is to show that the Roman Empire never perished but was only transformed; that the Catholic Church which it accepted in its maturity caused it to survive, and was, in that origin of Europe, and has since remained, the soul of our Western civilisation." How had it happened?

Individual Popes had, from time to time, made giant strides forward. Leo I (440–61), called Leo the Great, carried the theory of papal supremacy to unprecedented lengths. A sort of prototype of Pius XII, he was, in spirit if not in birth, a Roman of the Romans. He brought to his office an inbred sense of authority and was obviously a man born to world power. He enjoyed it. He was the first Pope to take over the discarded heathen (imperial) title *Pontifex Maximus* ("supreme high priest"). Above all he saw St. Peter as something much more than the humble, chief shepherd among men to whom Jesus had said "He who is greatest among you shall be your servant" (Matt. 23:11). To Leo, Peter possessed nothing less than "princely authority." He was in fact "prince of the apostles." He was more. He was also a powerful prince of the Church. Leo elaborated such themes at some length in famous sermons which have survived. St. Peter, he concluded, through his successor as Bishop of Rome, "rightly rules all who are ruled in the first instance by Christ." The Church thus became a monarchy ruled by the Pope acting on Peter's behalf. His claim, moreover, to papal "plenitude of power" laid the foundations for even further developments later on.

Another Pope—the second of only three to be called "Great"—was

Gregory I (590–604). His intervention into Catholic and Roman history was dramatic. As a papal deacon he had led a procession of penance through Rome's streets to assuage divine wrath. The latter was popularly thought to account for the disease then dramatically affecting a city still reeling from the ravages of Vandals and Goths. Even worse than the pillaging had been the cutting of the aqueducts by the "barbarians." Rome was dying of thirst while water leaking from the breached conduits of the aqueducts turned the surrounding countryside into a vast malarial swamp. As the file of Roman penitents approached the massive mausoleum of Hadrian that stands near the right bank of the Tiber, Gregory had a vision. Above the vast fortress-like tomb he seemed to see the Archangel Michael with a flaming sword which he was putting back into its sheath. He took it as a sign that the plague would soon be over. This sepulcher of Hadrian, the emperor who had built the great wall around Rome, was thereafter known as the Castel Sant' Angelo and is one of the city's best-known landmarks. Many a Pope was destined to shelter behind its mighty walls, having made his way there by the underground tunnel from the Vatican.

The plague did indeed come to an end shortly afterward but not before the Pope of the day, Pelagius II, had died. At this moment of crisis it was Gregory who was the enthusiastic choice for Pope by the people and clergy of Rome. The distant government of the Byzantine empire, as it had now become, represented in the West only by an *exarch* (provincial governor) at Ravenna, was powerless to help the stricken Romans. The Church stepped in and the world became aware of an unfamiliar aspect of its potential power—the power of riches and possessions. Gregory was no stranger to such things but had given his own wealth away to join the Benedictine Order. His membership thereof made him the first monk to sit in the chair of Peter. He discovered that the Church's resources were enormous. She had grainlands in Sicily and Sardinia, forests in Brutium and Calabria and countless other possessions as far away even as Istria. She could do what was no longer possible for the weakened empire, namely charter vessels and bring grain to Rome from the islands. She could also do such things as ship lumber for the building of churches in Egypt and supply blankets for the monks in distant Mount Sinai. How had the Church become so rich? The first big material gains had come from the conversion and gifts of Constantine. But more recently had come a spate of generous benefactions from those who believed that gifts would help to contribute to their own salvation. This was a tradition which was to grow even more potent with the years, and to be a marked feature of medieval Catholicism.

Out of all this grew a complicated but extremely efficient Church government—far more efficient than the imperial one had ever been; and Gregory proved himself an able administrator. The papacy, perforce, took over powers formerly wielded by the state. The emperor might fume at such "usurpation" but it was the Pope who had the money to back his activities. These included successful military operations against the invading Lombards from the north and the Pope found himself negotiating the settlements that followed the cessation of hostilities.

He became a virtual temporal ruler, and has been called, for that reason, "the first of the medieval Popes." Such a role, however, was distinctly against his personal inclinations. He was primarily a visionary and evangelist. He was a great dispatcher of missionaries to far-off lands, his most famous being St. Augustine who came to England to become first Archbishop of Canterbury. Despite his patrician breeding and familiarity with wealth Gregory was genuinely humble. His preference for the title "servant of the servant of God" has already been mentioned. Ironically he made no extravagant claims for the Papacy. He reproved the Patriarch of Constantinople for assuming the title "universal patriarch" by asserting that none of the patriarchs, including even himself, could validly make such a claim. (Later Popes did not agree!) The fact remains that from Gregory's time onward the Popes "stood at the head of an efficient and highly organised bureaucracy. The papal notaries and *defensores,* the *arcanius* and *sacellarius,* the head and second-in-command of the financial offices, the *nomenclator* who assisted in dealing with petitions—all these constituted a civil service which by the late seventh century was probably the most effective administration in Western Europe" (Partner, *The Lands of Peter,* p. 10).

It was the next century, however, the eighth, that saw the most significant development of all up to this point. For it was then that the Pope's *de facto* temporal sovereignty became an established and officially recognized reality. As of the year 756—a key date—the Bishop of Rome became king of a territorial dominion which was to last for eleven centuries. The origin of this papal kingdom is associated with the appearance, about the middle of the century, of a fascinating document. Known as the *Constitutum Constantini* it appeared to be an extensive grant of territory to the Pope (Sylvester I) by the Emperor Constantine himself. It was supposedly a reward for baptism given to the Bishop of Rome before the emperor left for Byzantium in 330 and has become more famous in history as the "Donation of Constantine." The document had a crucial influence in the medieval period and served as the basis of some of the papacy's most extravagant claims. It was first used against the Lombards by the Pope (Stephen II) who was negotiating with the Frankish king, Pepin. As a result the Pope made his first accretion of temporal and territorial power, around Rome, in 756. But Constantine, according to the Donation, had given the Pope *imperial power* not only over the Lateran Palace but rulership over Rome and "all provinces, localities and towns in Italy and the Western Hemisphere." The "Donation" even included a handing over by the Emperor of his crown and imperial regalia, besides giving the higher Roman clergy the same protocol privileges and ornaments as patricians and consuls. The sudden "discovery" of such benefactions at a time (the eighth century) when the papacy was trying, in any event, to take the place of the old empire in Italy seemed little short of miraculous. Nevertheless the passage into history of the "Papal States," as they finally came to be called, was a stormy one. It was both helped and hindered by the great new political entity that was established throughout what was, geographically, Germany, namely the Holy Roman Empire. The indirect origin of the latter lay with Pepin's son, Charlemagne, whom the Pope crowned "Holy Roman Emperor" in 800. Western Europe, from then on, can be said to have become subject to the twofold government of "Throne and Altar." Charlemagne consolidated the great missionary efforts which had been going on in the farthest parts of Europe since the fifth century by his extensive conquests and settlements, notably among the Saxons, whom he Christianized with brutal efficiency. (The "Holy Roman Empire" as such was not established until 962 with the crowning of Otto I.)

As for the papal territories, their position did not begin to look impregnable until the eleventh century. By that time the Donation of Constantine began to be quoted specifically in papal documents and the Popes came to be seen as "successors not to Peter but to Constantine" (*Lands of Peter,* ch. 5). It was not, however, until the time of Innocent III (1198–1216) that the Papal States received their definitive foundation. And it was under this most notable of Roman bishops that the papacy entered onto the zenith of its power, a power so immense that it totally dominated the whole of the thirteenth century, being climaxed by the breathtaking claims of Pope Boniface VIII. In a papal bull of 1302 (*Unam Sanctam*), which has become perhaps the most famous proclamation of theocracy in world history, Boniface declared that the Church was the supreme power on earth. Its "worldly sword" could be wielded by such as kings and soldiers but only at the command of "the priest" and for the sake of the Church: "Whosoever therefore resists this power ordained by God resists God's ordinance. . . . We declare: because of the need for salvation every human creature is subject to the Roman Pontiff." In the exuberance of another occasion he is said to have exclaimed: "I am emperor!"

Even the scandalous divisions, disorder and decline that came after Boniface could not stop the most important development of all: the emergence of an imperial mold for the Roman Catholic Church which was so strong as no longer to depend exclusively on material and political power. It found, in the Middle Ages, a stronger support still in its spellbinding power over men's souls. The whole of Western European society having come under the aegis of the Church, every man and woman was conscious of the horrendous possibility of devouring flames for all eternity for disobeying this great body sent by God himself to rule the world. The "laity" accepted that the Church was the preserve of the clergy, who were immune from ordinary (civil) law and were the "natural" superiors in society. Worshipers in churches were mere spectators from afar when the liturgy was celebrated. The spirit of community had been lost, but relics and indulgences were available and rich men could pay for hundreds of posthumous "masses" for their souls. The fires of hell were meanwhile waiting for transgressors of Church law, and, as was believed, thousands of people were being devoured by such fires. The other side of medieval life is that of the flowering of cathedrals, universities and a remarkable degree of genuine spirituality and Christian heroism among ordinary people. Naturally it is more pleasant, today, to remember this aspect of medieval life rather than its darkest areas.

Would such vast power have been accumulated by the Church without the "Donation of Constantine," which was exploited for so long with such devastating results? The question is intriguing for, in the fifteenth century, this crucial document was found to have been a forgery. It was now too late, however, to turn back the clock. Even the Reformation did not, after the first shocks, temper papal claims. "He who reigns in heaven," began Pope Pius V in his bull of 1570 excommunicating Queen Elizabeth I of England, "to whom is given all power in heaven and on earth, gave the one, holy, catholic and apostolic church, outside of which there is no salvation, to be governed in the fullness of authority, to one man only, that is to say, to Peter, the Prince of the Apostles, and to his successor the Roman Pontiff. This one ruler he established as prince over all nations and kingdoms, to root up, destroy, dissipate, scatter, plant, and build, so that the Holy Spirit might bind together a faithful people, united in the bond of mutual charity, and present it safe and sound to the Saviour." The papacy, as is evident from these words, had taken its cue from the heady days of the fourteenth century when Boniface had proclaimed his imperial destiny in such ringing tones. But the "Chair of Peter" had taken a tremendous battering meanwhile. The ecclesiastical seesaw had been swinging about in crazy fashion and many of its occupants had gone overboard at the Reformation. Boniface had ended his days as a prisoner and the papacy had shortly afterward been "captured" by France. As soon as the long "Babylonian exile" in Avignon was over, the Great Schism occurred. No fewer than three powerful men at one time claimed to be the rightful Pope. One result of the chaos was the theory—known as "conciliarism"—that everyone in the Church, including the Pope himself, was subject to the authority of a legitimately constituted General Council. The principle was enunciated at the Council of Constance which (in 1415) brought the Schism to an end and elected Martin V as the one and only Pope. Martin, as soon as his "throne" was safe, repudiated the very "conciliarism" by means of which he had secured the papacy and declared that General Councils were subordinate to the Bishop of Rome.

This did not stop bishops in individual countries—after the Reformation—from wanting to be masters in their own homes, subject only to the Pope's jurisdiction in disputed cases. This movement for limited independence was known as Gallicanism. The papacy, according to the bishops, should resemble what we would now call a constitutional monarchy. Particularly resented were the exaggerated claims of Popes who had built steadily on the edifice of the early successors of Constantine and had come to call themselves "Vicars of Peter" and then, from Innocent III's day onward, "Vicars of Christ." Many of the bishops could not square such innovations with either scripture or even the (largely papalist) body of canon law which flowered from the twelfth to the fourteenth centuries. Such law, in the final analysis, had a decisively centralizing effect on the government of the Church and the most galling part of all to the majority of the episcopate was that their rival for power was not the Pope acting on his own. Rather, instead of consulting or being guided by the bishops in the course of a frequent conciliar dialogue as called for at Constance, the Pope was advised, and came to rely more and more heavily, on his own Court. Thus arose Church government by the "Curia." The faceless, unelected men who were closest to the Pope had the greatest say. This was not only convenient but vital when the Pope was constantly concerned with European politics. But it led to the internal "politics" of place-seeking at the Papal Court which has flourished ever since and goes on unabated to this day. The Pope, meanwhile, came to be credited by some with wisdom that was nothing short of "oracular," and some sort of definition about the Pope's special charisma would have come long before 1870 had it not been for the protracted struggle of the Gallicans. It was, ironically, the French Revolution that paved the way for the modern triumph of papalism, despite its initially shattering effect on the power of the papal empire. But the European revolutions of the earlier part of the nineteenth century brought back a new desire for authoritarianism. The papacy led the reactionary reshaping of Europe, and Pius IX, who had been elected in 1846, sailed home to the haven of "infallibility" on the crest of this tidal wave. This, however, left the bishops high and dry. They, as successors of the apostles, had been promised exactly the same "power" by Jesus as had Peter, whose successor was the Pope. But now the Pope had seemed to assume powers of judgment and jurisdiction that removed him completely from the bishops as a body or "college." There was a serious gap or imbalance at the "top" of the Church. Hence the plan, by the same (1870) Vatican Council (Vatican I) which had declared the Pope to be "infallible," to make a pronouncement concerning the "collegiate" position of the bishops alongside that of the Pope. But such a pronouncement never came. The royal troops, completing the political unification of Italy appeared almost at the gates of Rome. The Council was hurriedly disbanded. It was not until Vatican II, the Second Vatican Council of 1962, that the "collegiality" of bishops was finally discussed, along with the countless other burning topics that have given new life to the anatomy of the Roman Catholic Church today.

The traumatic personal effect on Pius IX of the loss of his temporal sovereignty over the city of Rome is nowadays scarcely credible. It is perhaps the crowning indication of the magnificence and majesty that had come to surround the papal mystique. The gates of hell, if they had not actually prevailed, had, in Pius' eyes, opened up on his very doorstep. It had happened only a few years after his famous gesture of defiance against the modern world in his "Syllabus of Errors" issued in 1864. "The Pope apparently believed that his spiritual power to excommunicate or to condemn doctrinal errors and the policies of secular governments might still prove influential as it had been in the past. Events were to prove him wrong" (Holmes, *The Triumph of the Holy See*, p. 145). It was rather as if the Bishop of Rome had said, on behalf of the Catholic Church: "Stop the world or we'll get off." The world, of course, did not stop and the papacy was ignored. Events thundered on until, exactly a century later, in November 1964, the Second Vatican Council promulgated its Constitution on the Church. It was a totally new look which said, in effect, "We want to get on again." But did the Church really mean what it said? Did it even say, on every occasion, exactly what it meant? Some Catholics were well content with a large but grey area of doubt on such matters. Not so Pope John Paul II who expressed a wish the very day after he was elected to grasp this particular nettle. On Tuesday, October 17, 1978, he issued what can be regarded as a "keynote" message, and is, for brevity, hereafter referred to as such. "We want," he said, "to insist on the constant importance of the Second Vatican Council. For us, it is a formal obligation that it be studiously put into effect. Is not the Council a milestone in the two-thousand-year history of the Church, and indeed in the religious history of the world? . . . First it is necessary to place oneself in harmony with the Council. One must put into practice what was stated, and what was 'implicit' should be made explicit in light of the experimentation that followed and in conjunction with emerging, new circumstances."

CHAPTER 3

The Fascist Phase

Silent night, holy night
All is calm, all is bright,
Only the Chancellor
Steadfast in fight
Watches o'er Germany by
Day and night,
Always caring for us.

NAZI VERSION OF *Silent Night*

First they (the Nazis) came for the Communists, and I did
not speak up because I was not a Communist. Next they
came for the Trade Unionists and I did not speak up because
I was not a Trade Unionist. Next they came for the
Catholics, but I did not speak up because I was a Protestant.
Finally they came for me and by then there was no one left to
speak up.

PASTOR NIEMÖLLER
(after World War II)

HAD THE CENTURY between the First and Second Vatican Councils
seen a gradual accommodation of the Church to the modern world
there might have been no need for Vatican II. The first half of the
century in question was taken up with lamentation of the loss of the
Pope's temporal power. And the second with the doleful consequences
of its nominal reassumption in 1929. The papacy, in other words, was
still involved with that world with which, allegedly, it has no direct
concern, that is the world of politics.

This involvement began in the fourth century from the time of Constantine onward. "Popes"—as they came to be called much later—
were elected not as Popes, but as Bishops of Rome. In the first three
centuries they were elected much as were other bishops. The clergy
and laity of Rome, as well as neighboring bishops, all had some part in

their election. From the fourth to eleventh centuries "election" to the Bishopric of Rome was a political affair with paramount influence being exercised by such temporal rulers as the Roman emperors and later the Ostrogoth kings of Italy. Even after the time of Charlemagne the "Carolingian" emperors attempted to control the selection of the Roman Pontiff.

Temporal rulers stopped at nothing to secure the appointment of their own chosen candidates. Coercion was freely used as was, on occasion, forcible deposition and imposition. It had been hoped that temporal papal power would make the affairs of the papacy independent. But the choice of Popes became instead a constant subject of the bitterest dispute between rival factions among the Roman nobility. Affairs built up to a climax as the first millennium of the Christian era approached its completion. Few Popes in the century following the death of John VIII (872–82) died peacefully in their beds. John himself was murdered. Stephen VI (896) was strangled in prison; Benedict VI (973–74) was smothered. John XIV (983–84) was done to death in Castel Sant' Angelo. John XII (955–64) an incestuous Satanist who had become Pope at eighteen, managed to escape death at the hands of others. He died instead of amorous excess while making love. He was succeeded by a layman, Leo VIII. The early years of the eleventh century saw the papacy seemingly on its way to becoming the family possession of the counts of Tusculum. In 1012 the head of the family had himself made Pope as Benedict VIII. (The practice of men not even in holy orders becoming Pope was still quite common.) Benedict was succeeded in 1024 by his brother John XIX and, in 1032 by his nephew, the fifteen-year-old Benedict IX. The Tusculan dynasty, however, came to an abrupt end when Benedict IX was bribed into abdicating by a rival aristocratic faction in Rome. In what direction could the Christian community look to be saved from drowning in a cesspool of debauchery and political intrigue? Certainly not to its bishops who were themselves almost all totally absorbed in the cares of politics, property and power. A spontaneous reaction came in the form of a new wave of blessed and purified monasticism which sent its cleansing rivulets through Europe. Its original sources had been the monastery of Cluny, an obscure village in a remote corner of Burgundy, but there were many other contributory streams.

Reaction higher up took the form of intensive administrative reorganization on absolutist monarchical lines. The big name here is that of Hildebrand, or Pope Gregory VII, whose centralization dominated the eleventh-century papal "reform." For him the path to reform was the strengthening of the Church and Christian society as a whole so as to enable it to enforce the truth. He thus paved the way for the sweeping actions and pronouncements of Innocent III and Boniface VIII. After them, however, further delineation of papal power was impossible for the time being. There were long periods during which it was difficult, at any given time, even to make sure who the rightful Pope really was. Until the danger was over of rival claimants deposing, anathematizing and excommunicating each other, the consolidation of the medieval papal empire hung fire. When the Schism was over the needs for more thoroughgoing reforms at every level had become pressing but were put off for so long that they were never tackled forthrightly from within. The Reformation from without changed all.

The eventual triumph of nationalism in Europe involved the papal church in a different kind of politics while, in the opening-up Western hemisphere, a new Catholic empire was being pioneered to join, and, to some extent, replace, the old.

"Gallicanism"—a product largely of nationalism—saw the local churches in the emerging national entities demanding some measure of independence from Rome. A new kind of seesaw was in constant motion until, as of 1870, a new problem came, more and more, to obsess the Popes. This, as already mentioned, was the "Roman Question." Without some temporal power and possessions, it was argued, how could the papacy function as the internationally respected nerve-center of a united worldwide body? The conviction that the loss of Rome meant that the "City of God" had been invaded by some sort of modern barbarians showed how far the imperially minded Church had succumbed to a materialistic concept of "mission." This central fact does not mean that the Church could not boast, as in every age, of numerous selfless heroes, martyrs and witnesses of the ancient faith. The Spirit never left the Church. But part of the Church often seemed oblivious to its promptings.

The "Roman Question" was supposedly settled by the Lateran Treaty of 1929 agreed between Pope Pius XI and the government of Mussolini. This ushered in a generation of effective if uneasy alliance between the Church and Fascism. So bald a statement of the situation has, in the past, seemed harsh to many. Harsher still, however, was the fate reserved for the statesman-priest Don Luigi Sturzo, the tragedy behind whose story is still largely unknown to most Catholics. In 1919 Sturzo founded the *Partito Popolare* (later developed as the Christian

Democratic party) which championed labor unions, universal suffrage, income tax and free education. The move had the approval of the Pope of the day, the far-sighted and open-minded Benedict XV. It marked the first return of Catholics to Italian political life since the loss of the Papal States. It was an auspicious moment, the more so as Sturzo was a vehement opponent of Mussolini. But he was also a prudent man who, though completely loyal, had no illusions as to the damage already done to the Church through the imperious papalism of past years. He was filled with natural horror at the mass exodus of Italian Catholics from the Church as a direct result of papal refusal to be reconciled to the new Italian state. He saw that the working classes had been almost totally lost. But he also remembered the fate of the original theoretician of Christian Democracy, Fr. Romulo Murri, who had viewed with alarm the concept of "Catholic Action." This had been prescribed for Italian Catholics by the Holy Office of the Vatican as a substitute for that direct involvement in political life which had been forbidden to them by the Church after 1870. Murri, however, could not agree to the imposition of a lay Catholic "political" structure whose "electoral" element would in fact be dominated by the Papal Curia. He was duly excommunicated and became a deputy in the new Italian Parliament. "He is better off outside the Church," Pius X remarked (incredibly!).

Sturzo, prudent though he was, knew the *Partito Popolare* could gain no real power without, initially at least, the support of the Socialists. By the time the crunch came the far-sighted Benedict had been succeeded (in 1922) by a Pope of very different caliber in Pius XI who was against any possible alliance with the Socialists. He was not impressed by Sturzo's campaign for social justice but looked instead (despite the callous murder of Mateotti and other Fascist atrocities) to Mussolini to restore to the Church some trappings of its medieval glory or, at least, something of the diplomatic grandeur it had lost by the revolutions of 1848. Sturzo's concept had to wait for Vatican II and John XXIII. The man himself went into a long and lonely exile after his party had been suppressed (in 1926) by the Fascist government.

The 1929 Lateran Agreement, while recognizing the new miniature Vatican City as an independent state and the former Papal States as part of Italy, made Catholicism the State religion. (In the late sixties discussions as to the accompanying Concordat's revision commenced but have not even after ten years reached final conclusions.) The 1929 event was greeted with euphoria in the official Catholic world. But nowadays many Catholics read with embarrassment the history of the new era that was foreshadowed. The implications and, indeed, actual consequences of it all have for long been glossed over. The very fact of the Church's new and costly involvement with politics is often denied. Largely forgotten is the assertion of Pope Pius X (1903–14) that "the Sovereign Pontiff, invested with the supreme magistrature, has no right to remove political affairs from the sphere of faith and morals." This echo of Innocent and Boniface made possible a kind of neo-imperialism in Church affairs which fed and grew strong on the anti-Communist platform. For the Russian Revolution produced a new enemy which threw the Church into the protective arms of Fascism and its allies. It was an aberrant period during which the Church failed to live by its own theoretical principles as to political entanglement, that is, not to become entangled. It is meant, while standing aloof from all political contacts, clearly and impartially to enunciate Christian principles and fearlessly to expose those who break them. The tragedy of the interwar Catholic Church in Europe was that it made no pretence to be in any way impartial in its political alliances. Fascism in Spain and Portugal were readily identified with the best interests of the Church while the Vatican's political preferences among schools of thought in France had become evident even before the First World War. As far back as 1898 a group called *Le Sillon* ("The Furrow") had been founded by Marc Sagnier, the French opposite number to Italy's Romulo Murri and the prophet of Christian Democracy in France. The French working classes had long become disenchanted with a Church that seemed in no way concerned about their human needs. The French Republic's anti-clericalist government reflected their views. But Sagnier aimed to show how it was possible to be a devout Catholic and a loyal Republican. He was determined that his society should promote social justice in freedom from the control of the bishops. It was consequently condemned and dissolved by Pius X, while its extreme right-wing rival, *Action Française*, was actively tolerated. The latter's leader, Charles Maurras, an atheist, was called by the Pope 'a doughty defender of the church and the Holy See' and Catholics, including clergy, were encouraged to join its ranks. *Action Française*, helped by the anti-Semitic current associated with the Dreyfus affair, became devoted to the restoration of the monarchy, the spirit of the *ancien régime*, and opposition to every kind of republicanism. The Christian Democratic movement was anathema to the *Action*

Française which, spurred on by papal approbation, grew more and more daring in its championing of the old order. Maurras, who had so shrewdly and eloquently, in his writings, reminded the Church of the long lost days of her greatest earthly glories, saw in the organizational aspect even of the modern Church the most convincing reasons for his support of the papalism of Pius X. But his support contained an undisguised element of contempt for the more humanitarian aspects of Catholicism. Such contempt, according to many, cried out for condemnation. The condemnation was long staved off by the conservative forces in the Vatican; and though it had actually been pronounced in 1914, the denunciation was only announced publicly in 1926. It was based primarily on the personally atheist views of Maurras who had by now become widely discredited and even sentenced to prison. So great, however, had Catholic support for the *Action Française* become that the Vatican condemnation stirred bitter controversy. The situation had long been further bedeviled by the passionate admiration of Maurras' movement by a Prince of the Roman Church in the person of Cardinal Billot. Billot, a heavyweight theologian of the old school, was an uncompromising opponent of democracy and any concession to progressive liberalism by the Church. Rather than revoke his stand, he decided, in the aftermath of Maurras' fall from papal grace, to surrender his scarlet "hat." Few cardinals in recent history have thus abandoned their title. The ghosts of Maurras and Billot haunt the Church and the Holy See to this day. The dissident group led by Archbishop Lefebvre carries on the same struggle under the guise of championing a return of the "Tridentine" (Council of Trent) Mass. This, in turn, has produced bitter controversy. Two separate issues have become fatally confused and the situation has been almost universally misunderstood both inside and outside the Catholic Church.*

Pius XI lived to regret his former faith in Fascism and died a disillusioned man. In the early days his only important brush with the regime was the issuance of the encyclical letter *Non abbiamo bisogno* in 1931. Its chief purpose was to protest against Mussolini's proscription of "Catholic Action." When Mussolini backed down, things went on more or less as before. Church criticism of Fascism was almost entirely restricted to specific matters where the state competed for the religious loyalty of Catholics rather than on broader philosophic, humanitarian or theological grounds.

* See below, Chapter 9.

The same pattern developed over Church relations with Nazism though on an infinitely more tragic scale. German Catholics, suspect as to their patriotism since their opposition to Bismarck's *Kulturkampf,* were as determined now to show their loyalty to the state as was Hitler to retain such loyalty. The Catholic bishops having originally endorsed the new regime, the Catholic Center Party voted for the measure allowing Hitler to rule by decree. Center and Catholic labor unions "voluntarily" dissolved themselves. Hitler, in return, agreed to a concordat with the Vatican guaranteeing Catholics freedom to profess and practice their religion and the independence of the Church. On paper nothing could have looked better for Catholicism. It seemed a triumph for the neo-imperialist system, with the Church retaining her privileges and maximum power while safeguarding her outward prestige and overall unity. For it must be remembered that the Catholic Church in Germany, along with the other Christian religions, enjoyed, as long as it retained the favor of the government, extensive benefits in the way of finance and property. Considerable public funds were provided for the Church while the status of the clergy and the educational system were legally protected. Was the Church, as personified by the Vatican, justified in preferring a totalitarian system that happened to favor the Church as a privileged body to that dreaded Communism which was its avowed enemy? A justification would have been hard to make on principle. The Vatican felt itself to be a victim of circumstances. The European Church was particularly strong in countries where not Communist but Fascist-type governments were in control. With such countries, however repressive of the individual, anti-Semitic or otherwise contemptuous of basic human rights, Catholicism even actively collaborated in return for protection for the institutional rights of the Church. Apart from Franco's Spain and Salazar's Portugal, the most notable examples are the "Clerical-Fascist" state of Engelbert Dollfuss in Austria and the "Arrow Cross" regime of Ferenc Szálasi in Hungary. Such is the mesmerizing effect politics can have on Catholic views of morality when "Church rights" are at stake. The Church, which tolerates no compromise or exceptions on matters of moral principle connected, say, with sex, found itself, when faced with the Fascist powers of prewar Europe, in a cruel dilemma. Should it gamble all on the firmness of its people's faith, or should it fall back on the conventional supports of organized Church power? It decided, in the end, to be pragmatic and give in as gracefully as possible, and take the latter course. This, however, was a time when there was no significant Catholic presence in any Communist country. Indeed, it was the spread of communism to countries where the Church was well-established and well-heeled that was so obsessively dreaded. The strongest political bulwark against such a danger was thought to be Nazi Germany and her natural or potential allies. (Since the absorption, after the war, of considerable numbers of Catholics behind the "iron curtain" the Church has been engaged in a prolonged and vigorous effort to reach accommodations with the various governments involved, in order to safeguard Catholics in the corresponding areas. Such *ostpolitik*— aimed at coexistence—had reached an advanced stage long before a Polish cardinal had been elected Pope.) Before the war, it was Germany which, quite naturally, posed the maximum problem for the Church. It was only very late in the day—too late in fact—that it was realized that an historic miscalculation had been made. Pius XII did, finally, reveal what had perhaps long been his true mind about Nazism. He did so in a speech to his College of Cardinals when he thundered that Nazism was "a Satanic specter . . . the arrogant apostasy from Jesus Christ, the denial of his doctrine and of his work of redemption, the cult of violence, the idolatry of race and blood, the overthrow of human liberty and dignity." But this was in June 1945. Nazi Germany had surrendered to the allies. Hitler was already dead.

Things had been very different ten years earlier. Somewhat innocent conservative churchmen had then felt hopeful that Nazism, if approached with diplomatic understanding, would grow out of its worst excesses and bring about the desired regeneration of the country. Hitler, for his part, felt confident that Christianity would eventually die by default and played his cards accordingly. The concordat with the Catholic Church was a major step forward and greatly increased the prestige of the "New Order." By sanctioning the liquidation of religious political parties and the barring of clergy from politics, it became a landmark in the consolidation of the totalitarian state. The initiative having passed to the Nazis, they found themselves able to violate the concordat with increasing frequency and impunity. The Church, on the other hand, thrown on the defensive, felt that any breach of the concordat from their side would lose them the privileges they were still guaranteed on paper. The Vatican-Nazi agreement thus gave no practical protection to the Church from attack while undermining such Catholic resistance as there was.

Eventually, perilously late in the day, Catholic churchmen in Germany began to show alarm about the "new heathenism" in their midst. Some began to realize what only became too clear to most after the war: that communism, an avowed enemy, tended to bring out the best in Catholicism in terms of heroism, defiance and deepened faith. Nazism, on the other hand, was to bring out the worst, in terms of pre-occupation with privileged status, superficial safety and protected property rights, but only at the expense of fatal compromise on funda-mental principles. An effective protest early on might have stemmed the tide. But by 1937 Hitler's confidence was already well-established and he knew that the majority of Catholics backed him. The eventual alarm of the German bishops demanded some sort of response from Rome. It came in the form of the encyclical *Mit brennender Sorge* of March 1937, drafted with the help of the Vatican Secretary of State, the former papal nuncio in Germany and future Pope, Eugenio Cardinal Pacelli. The first major Church document to criticize Nazism, it was smuggled into Germany and read from every Catholic pulpit on the Sunday before Easter. All this happened before a single copy of the papal letter had fallen into Nazi hands.

The encyclical protested against oppression of the Church. It urged Catholics to resist the idolatrous cult of race and state, to take a stand against the perversion of Christian doctrine and morality, and to remain loyal to Christ, his Church and Rome. While Nazism's excesses were condemned, the Pope did not denounce the totalitarian nature of the regime. Instead he left open the possibility of reconciliation. Hitler's first reaction was one of fury. But after time for reflection, he decided on tactics which were devastatingly successful. They accorded with the conviction that he had confided, soon after coming to power, to Hermann Rauschring, that the best method of ridding Germany of effective Christianity would be to "leave it to rot like a gangrenous limb." He had, however, added "but we can hasten matters. The par-sons will be made to dig their own graves. They will betray their God to us. They will betray anything for the sake of their miserable little jobs and incomes." Hitler decided to treat *Mit brennender Sorge* with contemptuous silence, forcing the Church into the position of having to take the initiative in making, if it had the courage, a complete break with the state. It never did. The Nazi government was faced only with sporadic resistance in the lower ranks of the clergy and dealt with this piecemeal. It was always reluctant to move against the senior members of the hierarchy. When, in 1941, Bishop von Galen of Münster made so strong an attack on the proposed euthenasia program that wide-spread public indignation was aroused, the program was dropped. (No comparable protest was ever made in the case of the Jews.)

The great question that still goes on being asked is why Cardinal

Pacelli, after being crowned Pope Pius XII in 1939, remained silent about Nazi aggression in general and the wholesale murder of Jews in particular. A genuinely full-blooded and shattering act of protest might well have averted the Jewish massacre, though this cannot be proved. Pius's defenders point out, among other things, that the Pope was acutely aware that most German Catholics supported Hitler and that many had been disastrously infected by anti-Semitic propaganda. He was faced with the prospect, which horrified him, of making a protest which might well lose him the allegiance of Germany's Catholics, thus putting at risk the integrity of the entire institutional Church in the whole of occupied Europe. In an ecclesiastical Rome operating as the center of an organization based primarily on Europe and still thinking along quasi-imperial lines, such a possibility was unthinkable to a man like Pius XII.

To preserve the Church as he had always known it was more important to him than hazarding all in the hope of saving the lives of even several million Jews. Pius, moreover, did not want to sabotage the German crusade against Russia. For while he detested National Socialism, he detested and feared communism even more. His decision was not a cold-blooded or callous one. Nor was it made at any one ascertainable moment. He faced the situation in its growing tragedy and complexity as each day came and went. He worked with almost superhuman effort to limit hostilities and bring about the peace from which all would benefit. He had faith in the strictest methods of diplomacy and felt that these would be compromised by any stand that could not be seen to be strictly "neutral" as between the warring parties. The prestige of the Vatican might yet stun the world with a glittering triumph of international mediation. The man who had inherited the greatest crown on earth, the triple tiara of world leadership according to the classic papal concept, must surely, in this dark hour, be a man to be reckoned with. The earthly monarch of all Christendom commanded spiritual battalions in every part of the earth. To these, and all other men besides, Pius threw out his arms in dramatic appeal. His passionate pleas fell on deaf ears. He was the last of the "imperial" Popes.

NOTE TO CHAPTER 3: The horrific effects of Nazism have inevitably produced assessments of such men as Pius XII that still remain doubtful and controversial. After the war, for example, important evidence came out that in 1940, though the Pope had granted a friendly audience to the German Foreign Minister, Joachim von Ribbentrop, he was also in touch with anti-Nazi elements in Germany. But he was, at all times, so painfully circumspect that vital opportunities for dramatic action were lost. It is best to let the official published documents speak for themselves. (See in particular, *The Holy See and the War in Europe*, vol I, translated by this author [London: Herder; Washington, D.C.; Corpus Books, 1968.] *The Silence of Pius XII*, by Carlo Falconi [London: Faber & Faber, 1970], gives a robust view. *While Six Million Died*, by A. D. Morse [London: Secker & Warburg, 1968] points out that Pius XII was not the only offender and makes serious accusations against the governments of Great Britain and the United States. See also, *The Vatican in the Age of the Dictators*, by A. Rhodes [London: Hodder & Stoughton, 1973].)

CHAPTER 4

"The Age of Constantine Is Dead"

Divine Providence is leading us to a new order of human
relations which, by men's own efforts and even beyond their
very expectations, are directed toward the fulfillment of God's
superior and inscrutable designs.

POPE JOHN XXIII (1963)

Let us begin anew.

JOHN F. KENNEDY (1961)

So DRASTIC A SUMMARY as that attempted in the last chapter of pre-
1945 Catholic political involvement is inevitably vulnerable. Apart
from anything else, use of the word "Fascist" often causes difficulty. A
witty British journalist, Patrick O'Donovan, writing in the London
Catholic Herald (October 13, 1978) was defending the (originally
Spanish) Catholic organization of priests and unmarried laymen
known as *Opus Dei*. Apart from many other things, this organization
was once well-known for its staunch support of the Fascist regime in
Spain. But not everyone considers that Franco's state merited the description "Fascist." Herein lies part of the difficulty. In countering any
suggestion that *Opus Dei* was itself "Fascist," O'Donovan observed
that "anyone who uses that adjective without a most meticulous exac-
titude is drunk upon slogans and should be treated kindly but not
seriously and taken home before he hurts himself intellectually." He
was quite right. He might even have gone on to add that the same
principles applies to use of the adjective "Communist." But in this regard an interesting development has occurred in recent years. "Fascist"
is no longer a word that is popular in polite society. "Communist" is
acceptable. This has had a curious result. It is possible, even intellectually acceptable, to call someone a Communist even when he isn't
one. But it is unseemly to call someone a Fascist even when he is. This
presents the greatest difficulty of all in regard to the Church's political
preferences. And it has long inhibited commentators from telling the

whole truth. As a result the Church has suffered. A smoke screen of apologies has had to be kept going for a long time to obscure one part of Church activity, but the smoke has got out of control. The Church's genuine, if overformal, concern for social and human problems has not been fully apparent. It is also true that this concern bore disappointingly little fruit before the Second World War. What was happening was that the Church was thinking with its heart about one set of circumstances and with its head about another. One might imagine that its heart was concerned with human problems and its head with political ones. In fact it was the other way around. Many Popes condemned economic and other tyrannies and espoused the workers, but the concern expressed was all too obviously intellectual in its approach. The Church, on the other hand, put its whole heart into the business of preserving itself in certain key European countries between the wars. Hence the political compromises touched on above. The final demonstration that the Church had little heart in its social pronouncements, eloquent indeed though they were, was that they had such minimal effect. The Church, as already seen, invariably supported those political groups most inimical to individual freedom but in favor of collective "safety," law, order and Catholic power. It is painful to have to say so, for nothing hurts more than the truth.

Pius XII died in 1958. He was succeeded as Pope by a man of almost unimaginably different character, Angelo Roncalli, John XXIII. Millions of words have already been written about "good Pope John." He captured almost all hearts, for his own most notable feature was the largeness of his own heart. If one had to sum up his immense achievements in a few lines one might say that he reversed the thought process which had dominated the Catholic Church for half a century or more. He was basically a "conservative," not a "progressive." But he thought with his heart about human problems and devoted his head to the practical ones. It is amazing, now, to reflect how little this had been done in the official Church until then. Even the enlightened approach of Leo XIII had been primarily intellectual. But the pontificate of this extraordinary man (1878–1903) had been, in its own way, catalytic. He checked, even without being able wholly to reverse, the sense of direction given by his remote predecessors Gregory XVI (1831–46) and Pius IX (1846–78). Neither of these men liked what they saw of the world around them. Between them they condemned every important tenet of the enlightened and progressive ideals that most countries accepted as necessary and inevitable. A particularly vehement condemnation was reserved for religious freedom and the separation of Church and State. The latter was anathema to a papacy long used to the idea of the State being only a junior partner with an ultimately all-powerful Church. (After 1870 Pius would have nothing to do with Cavour's principle of a Free Church in a Free State, wherein the Church's rights would be protected but strictly limited to the free functioning of its purely spiritual activities. To Pius, the new sovereign, Victor Emmanuel, was forever a "sacrilegious despoiler" while he, himself, remained Rome's true and only "Pope-and-King.")

The conclave to elect a new Pope in 1878 consequently met at a moment when the papacy's prestige was at a particularly low ebb. Instead of going, as previously, to the Pope's "summer" home at the Quirinal Palace, the cardinals met in quarters hastily prepared for them at the Vatican. Some had questioned the wisdom of meeting in Rome at all in view of the extreme ill-favor the previous Pope had, in his last years, earned for the Church. The ensuing conclave was a turning point in papal history. It was probably the least bedeviled by political intrigue, bribery and personal rivalry since 1455, when the first member of the Borgia family had descended on the papacy in the person of Calixtus III. (Compared to his sinister nephew, Rodrigo, later Pope Alexander VI, Calixtus was not a bad Pope considering the times in which he lived. His three-year reign is chiefly important as marking the obvious starting point of a long almost uninterrupted series of fiercely contested political struggles for the papal "throne.") The papal election in 1878 was the first occasion on which an entirely different situation presented itself. The loss of the temporal power and the affectation of martyr-like "captivity" assumed by Pius IX had greatly reduced (or, at least, altered the character of) aspirants for the succession: from now on the papacy would clearly be much more of a burden and carry less in the way of material compensations. In these entirely new circumstances, the absence of serious rivalries produced a swift result to the voting. The new Pope, Leo XIII, was a complete opposite to his predecessor, as urbane and erudite as Pius had been shallow and uncultured. But he was also very reserved and his efforts to rebuild the papacy's bridges with the rest of the world were cast along conservative lines. He preached submission and tolerance. By "submission" he meant that people should submit to their legitimate governments even if such governments were not to their liking; this upset the French "legitimists" who hated their Republic, and alienated the Irish nationalists whose campaign for their country's self-determination was then building up in earnest. By "tolerance" he meant that governments should, for their part, "tolerate" such "evils" as false religions if the common good required such toleration. This was an advance on previous papal teaching according to which any "false," i.e. non-Roman Catholic, religion was by nature intolerable. But there was still a long way to go before John XXIII, in his decisive encyclical *Pacem in Terris* (1963), removed the question from the area of mere "tolerance" to insist on every human being's right "to honor God according to the dictates of an upright conscience and therefore the right to worship God privately and publicly."

John was nevertheless treading a path first roughly hewn out by Leo. The latter's most famous pronouncement on social matters was his 1891 encyclical *Rerum Novarum*. It followed precedent and convention by putting stress on the rights of private property. But it broke enough new ground to be considered mildly dangerous in traditional Catholic circles. "Labor," said Leo, "is not a commodity," and the state was as much within its rights in preventing its exploitation as it was in safeguarding property and religion. The words were well meant but did not succeed in deterring more than a handful of employers from acting primarily as capitalists and only secondarily as Catholics. Such an approach by the Pope, being still very timid, failed to impel men into action. (Pius XI's reassessment of the social scene forty years later in *Quadragesimo Anno* had a generally similar lack of practical result.) But *Rerum Novarum* had at least broken down into some sort of concrete detail the underlying spirit of Leo XIII's very first encyclical, *Inscrutabili*, which, in 1878, had asserted the Church's desire to back rather than block progress in human affairs, particularly in the social field. The crust of popular imagination, however, was not broken through until the time of Pope John. When it became obvious that the words he was speaking came truly from a generous heart and not from a well-trained head, the response of the world beyond Roman Catholicism was overwhelming and sensational. His actions, indeed spoke louder than the words that poured out in his name and were instantly quoted all over the globe. And there was no question of passing him off as a crank, a headline-hunter or a mere social do-gooder. If you can fool some of the people, you cannot fool all of the media. His classic *Journal of a Soul* proved boring to spiritual sophisticates. But its message was not lost on connoisseurs of sanctity.

One of the Church's new proclamations at this stage was that all men were free to follow their own consciences and were entitled to full and objective justice. The age-old claim that the Church presided over by the Pope was the sole judge of such matters and that all, whether they knew it or not, were subject to such judgment, had gone forever. From this moment onward the Church started to be listened to in places and ways it had not been listened to before. In various parts of Europe, key areas of Africa, certain countries in Southeast Asia, and, above all, in Latin America, the Catholic Church began to grope toward a new role. Its "political" commitments came henceforth to be conceived in terms not of power and protected status but of "justice and peace." The Church in Latin America, for example, has now come to be heard as the "voice of the voiceless." The new commitment has produced fury in some Catholic circles and many accusations of left-wing and even Communist leanings within the Church. In other, and more numerous, circles it has produced relief that the Church seems at last to care more for people than its own privileges and corporate rights. The euphoria prevalent during the short but decisive reign of Pope John was phenomenal. Could it last? Would it survive the actual implementation of an idea which, when first mooted, took away the breath of even normally imperturbable curial cardinals: Pope John's suggestion that the whole Church should once more meet in general council? The "prophets of doom" were willing to wait and see. Even if the great fortress was to be thrown open they could still take refuge in the dungeons once reserved for the enemy. But for most people the writing on the outer walls was clear. Pope John had not been in office a year before the observant leader of the Italian Communist Party, Palmiro Togliatti, had felt able to say: "The age of Constantine is dead."

On Thursday, October 11, 1962, the Second Vatican Council began. A "new look" at this Council became more imperative than ever when its importance was so heavily stressed by Pope John Paul II in what has been referred to as his "keynote" address—the message he delivered to the world the day after his election.

PART TWO

TRAUMA

CHAPTER 5

The Bewildering Council

Another kind of hope has come to Europe with the election
of a new Pope. The 23rd John is the 262nd Bishop of Rome
and Vicar of Christ—figures eloquent of the durable meaning
of the oldest organization in the West.

(LIFE Magazine, November 10, 1958)

The Vatican II Reform was a reform made from above—a
fairly unusual phenomenon—which was not prepared from
below.

YVES CONGAR

THE COUNCIL—usually called Vatican II—gave few signs in its first
session (ending December 1962) of becoming the "milestone" it is in
the eyes of the present Pope. John XXIII said its object was "to restore the simple and pure lines which the face of Jesus' Church wore
at its birth." If it did actually do this, it would indeed produce a revolution. The future Pope Paul, then Archbishop Montini of Milan, was,
characteristically, more cautious. He said that the Council would
throw light "upon those places and institutions where men are working
for the union of peoples, for the welfare of the poor, for progress, for
justice and for liberty." But would its actual declarations amount to a
morally binding program? Or had the bishops of the Catholic world
come together merely to philosophize? The first session suggested the
latter. No decrees were promulgated and the decision to insert St.
Joseph's name into the canon of the Mass seemed to indicate a rather
superficial approach to reform along lines familiar with many centuries of mere tinkering around with rubrics. The broader issues, concerned with making the Church relevant to the deepest needs of modern humanity looked like being fudged.

In 1963, however, came the Constitution on the Liturgy, a "charter
for the most deliberate and comprehensive remoulding of the Church's
worship that has ever taken place" (Hastings, *A Concise Guide . . . to*

Vatican II, I, p. 107). The end of 1964 saw the documents on the Church and on Ecumenism—both distinctly revolutionary compared to anything previously taught. The final months of 1965 saw a flurry of decrees and declarations, including, among the very last, two crucial pronouncements: the Declaration on Religious Freedom and the Pastoral Constitution on the Church in the Modern World. The Vatican civil service, represented by the Curia, openly opposed change. The many backwoodsmen among the bishops saw few good reasons why any real changes were necessary. Yet something amazing started to happen. Some have dared to call it a "new Pentecost." "It has seemed good to the Holy Spirit and to us . . ." is the phrase that still echoes from those days.

A parenthetical caveat must here be entered against the pretensions of some trendy Catholics—now, fortunately, on the wane—that nothing had been right in the Church for hundreds of years. The earlier chapters of this book have, admittedly, stressed the human rather than the spiritual history of the Church to date, but that was chiefly because that aspect is invariably neglected in overall surveys on "The Catholic Church," "Roman Catholicism," etc. Such surveys tend to treat the Church as a rarefied, sacral-legal body which is "out of this world." In fact, it is very much in it, as Vatican II showed—or rather as Vatican II forced people to realize. The corollary to this, however, is that the Spirit, even though it blows where it will, cannot move men without their active cooperation. It can only, on this earth, produce effects *through* human beings, who may be either channels of, or obstacles to, the work of the Spirit. The "renewal" called for by the Council would not just happen automatically; it had to be *made* to happen. But *what,* in precise terms, had to be made to happen? A short summary of Council aims, devoid of the usual clichés, can, if nothing else, serve as a point of departure for subsequent chapters. Such a summary sees the Council as an attempt to replace "filling-station Christianity" with the Christianity of "saving-the-world-by-serving-it."

"Filling-station Christianity" sees the Church primarily as a clerical establishment which professionally supplies people with instructions, directives and grace. These enable them to live, in spite of the world, in such a way as eventually to escape from it. The customers at this clerically operated filling station are individuals, not members of a community. They are regarded principally as souls to be saved.

"Saving-the-world-by-serving-it" Christianity sees the Church as a body of people called to live such a life of truth, justice and love that they will be better able, as a community and as individual members thereof: to promote truth, justice and love among men; to recognize Jesus as a fully human brother, though one uniquely qualified to transform the world; to be receptive to God's Spirit; to offer their bodies daily as a living sacrifice in accordance with their call to priesthood; to banish all disunity among men by being no more male or female, Jew or Greek, black or white; to seek liberation from the subhuman so as to reach the supernatural; to embrace, as the price of freedom, especially in matters of life and death, a heavier personal responsibility than they have ever known before.

The Council has proposed a hard and narrow road. The road has already become pockmarked with tensions among individuals and encumbered with heavy obstacles. Again by way of summary:

1. Sources of Tension

It is asked:

—Of each individual, that he switch from preoccupation with his own salvation to care for others. ("Disturbing.")

—Of each worshiper, that he be at peace (if necessary by symbolic gesture) with his fellow worshipers. ("I hate the Sign of Peace.")

—Of worshipers, that their prayers be more uninhibited and sometimes even shared and spontaneous. ("Dangerously evangelical.")

—Of each individual, that he interpret himself in terms of community rather than in isolation. ("Encourages busybodies.")

—Of the layman, that he assume an active rather than passive role within the community. ("Too involving.")

—Of the layman, that he face special responsibilities and admit special competences in the world at large. ("Smacks of humanism.")

—Of the layman, that he regard his faith as a permanent challenge rather than as a periodic consolation. ("I'm too old.")

—Of the cleric, that he declericalize his image of the Church, (which has nothing to do with which way his collar faces.)

—Of the cleric, that he see himself as the servant not the master of the Church community. ("What do they think I've been doing all these years?")

—Of "progressives," that they do not bully "Traditionalists." ("I'm only trying to follow the Council.")

—Of clergy and laity, that they undertake coresponsibility. ("They'll be wanting women at the altar next.")

—Of bishops, that they work with their clergy as a team. ("Might be bad for discipline.")
—Of all Catholics, that they pray and collaborate with non-Catholics and non-Christians. ("It used to be condemned as indifferentism.")
(The imaginary objections are not facetious afterthoughts. Something like them is heard every day.)

2. *Principal Obstacles*

Most of the above demands run counter to the image of the Church that has developed over the last four hundred years. The Reformation caused a defensive closing of doors and battening down of hatches. The Council called for an opening of windows. But the Counter-Reformation Catholic Church had left many time bombs for those treading the post-conciliar path of potentially revolutionary renewal. Just as important, humanly speaking, is that many of the features of Counter-Reformation Catholicism have a strong appeal to man's natural makeup. For example, in the case of lay people:

—preoccupation with personal salvation appeals to self-love;
—a clericalized Church makes life easier in three ways (among others) : it reduces the minimum range of obligations; it shifts the burden for decision-making to someone else; it makes for greater security. (For clerics themselves, it is a prop to vanity, special status and the sense of power that lurks even among the most humble.)
—Otherworldliness (though involving self-denial) can oversimplify moral outlooks, producing a black-and-white view with no room for greys. (Most moral areas, nevertheless, are largely grey.)

Pastors and other priests often report, moreover, that authoritarianism does not seem to be invariably regarded as a usurpation; it often presupposes a correlative abdication on the part of the subject, an abdication willingly paid as the price for security. (Subconsciously, some people even confuse such security with salvation itself.) At the same time, pastors, missionaries, and the like, do not always stress sufficiently the sensitivity shown by John XXIII toward those whose makeups are resistant to change. Nothing can be more hurtful than the action of the intolerant reformer. The fact remains that, with all its imaginative proposals, and all the resultant goodwill, the Council has been followed by an exodus of many priests from their ministry and many ordinary Catholics from regular attendance at Church.

Some blame it on the Council and its "unsettling" effect. Others blame it on the Pope's "ban" on contraception after the matter had been left in the air for so long and presumed to be "doubtful." For the most part, such people tend to forget that the world and society at large have during the same years changed far more than the Catholic Church. All religions have suffered an "exodus." All authority has come under question. It is the obvious moment to make an entirely fresh start.

Catholics now in their teens were not even born when the Council was in preparation. They have been as much influenced by the disillusionment (or unwillingness to adapt?) of their elders as by any personal rebellion. But, often unknown to conventional churchgoers, there has been evidence of heightened spirituality among the young—and not so young—in groups, "basic communities," schools, factories even; and city churches, once empty because of early Masses only, are now full of worshipers of every age, at all times of the day, midweek and Sundays. One must not exaggerate and to generalize is notoriously hazardous. But there is one concrete example which is not without irony. The Council has tended to misfire just where, outwardly, it has seemed to have been most scrupulously followed. What has happened at certain levels is that instead of revolutionary renewal there has been only institutional reform—the mere substitution of one set of structures for another. Clericalism, in other words, has, instinctively, so penetrated the new framework that no truly new life has flowed out to the community. New clerical bodies have mushroomed but "lay" ones have been given scant encouragement. "Commissions" sit in many countries with "expert" lay people making suggestions for the consideration at the next full session of the bishops' conference. But what happens to these suggestions? For the most part no one is ever told. Is it all just an episcopal ploy to make the "laity" think they have a say? In practice, the whole operation is often an expensive charade.

Meanwhile there has been a proliferation of such purely clerical bodies as synods of bishops; national hierarchical assemblies; national conferences of priests; priests' councils; deanery conferences; and others besides—not to mention the souped-up gatherings now organized by most religious orders, nationally and internationally. What is talked about? Clerical matters. Professional problems. Shop. What items recur most often on a typical agenda at a priests' council? Salary and allowances; conditions of retirement; pastor assistant-priest relationship; money and expenses (on which absolute secrecy must be preserved as far as the laity is concerned.) If the "laity" are referred to at all, it is usually because a need has arisen to protect them from such dangers as "modern catechetics" or "advanced" views on the need for more pastoral care of people who are homosexual, divorced, remarried, etc.

Clericalism is not the only hangover from before the Council. Another is juridicism, and its powers of survival have severely weakened conciliar effectiveness. Its most extreme form is to be found among opponents of Vatican II who protest that the Council was pastoral rather than dogmatic. Their world was (and is) the world where the priest lays down the law, the bishop disciplines those who do not obey, and the Pope excommunicates those who persist in their disobedience. Even "moderates" point out that the system, harsh though it sounds, *did* work. The active-authoritarian-clergy/passive-obedient-laity antithesis—it is claimed—at least produced higher attendances at Mass, attention to Easter duties, full baptismal and "church wedding" registers, and (going back far enough) enforcement of such practices as Friday abstinence. (The "filling-stations" in other words, were always fairly busy.) It has also produced such beliefs as that:

—fulfillment of the law=goodness,
—absence of legal formula=absence of any obligation,
—you can change people by legislation.

The survival of juridicist views and attitudes into the post-Vatican II era has had all sorts of strange effects:

—Often, if conciliar ideas have not been reduced to legal enactments (papal or episcopal), people have felt no obligation to do anything about them.
—Where legal status has been given to conciliar desires, it has usually been considered sufficient to set up the outward forms demanded by the law.

In the first of these situations, you get a very uneven development, since it usually boils down to whether or not the local pastor is interested in or enthusiastic about or understands the Council. A diocese begins to look like a mosaic or a crazy paving of conciliar and non-conciliar parishes. There is frequent friction between the two varieties.

In the second, you can get "on-paper" dioceses where all the structures exist. But what about the spirit that should animate them? It sometimes seems almost wholly absent.

A disastrous example of the formal fulfillment of post-conciliar legislation is the way so many pastors have taken the "new" form of Eucharist and handled it in the way they handled the old: a gabbled or monotonously recited vernacular Mass is even less devotional than hastily mumbled Latin in the pre-1969 form.

Surprisingly recent has been the realization that implementation of the Council is not (and cannot be) a matter of merely legislating into existence new legal forms and institutions. Needed now are not new forms, but renewed men. And such renewal can only come from within. The Council has truly mapped out a hard road. Many have dreaded embarking upon it.

Examples given up to now may seem petty compared with the "great issues" raised by Vatican II. But such "great issues" rarely figure on deanery conference agendas.

Perhaps the depth of the changes required by the Council can be illustrated best of all by the reforms which have been introduced into the administration of the sacraments of Baptism and Penance.

(a.) *Baptism*

In accordance with the overall aim toward a revitalized anatomy for the Church, there has been (as with the Eucharist) a real attempt in the case of baptism, to restore its community nature. Its new location (a literal entry into the Church as the assembly hall of the community) and the preference to associate it with the Mass are important steps toward that end.

There may be something else which is even more significant. It is worth studying the role of the parents in the rite. The priest is now supposed to introduce them to the vital significance of their role. There is a definite attempt to bring to an end the "magical" view of baptism, in which the very pouring of the water and the saying of the words does the trick, once and for all. Parents nowadays are to be brought to realize that without a positive contribution on their part to the Catholic upbringing of the child, the rite is meaningless. It is not so much a question of the priest refusing to baptize the offspring of those who do not "practice," as of bringing them to realize that it is pointless having the child baptized unless he has a chance of growing up in an atmosphere of specifically Christian love.

It is here that in countless cases the priest encounters the amazing strength of the idea of Limbo.* It has survived years of non-propagation among ordinary Catholics as a seemingly quasi-superstitious but deeply held fear inherited from childhood or even a remoter past. It brings people who have never gone to church and people who have been married outside the Church to ask for baptism for their children. They have (in most cases) no intention of resuming practice themselves and often no idea of sending the child to a Catholic school or of having him or her catechized. All they want is the rite, or (they fear) the child will not get to heaven. That there is more to being a Catholic than that has never occurred to them, and on entering hospital they will declare themselves "R.C."

(b.) *Penance*

Here again, as with all the liturgical reforms, the main objective has been to restore the community aspect to the sacrament. Amazing success has attached itself to reconciliation services (and also to general absolution, where bishops have had the courage to make use of it). Periodical confession has lost much of its former similarity to the once famous weekly bath. Of all the sacraments, this one touches the individual at the most personal level. The effect of the new explanation of penance and the use of "face-to-face" confession has been to bring people to reconsider what sin really is and to move away from the consideration of theoretical or automatically presumed sins and categorized faults to a serious assessment of themselves and their relationship with God in their actual life-situation. More than any other single factor, this shift is thought likely, in pastoral circles, eventually to move people away from "looking at their own navel" (the result of the old style examination of conscience) toward living and responsible membership in the community of the Church and the community of people in the world. Such an ideal perhaps epitomizes the whole spirit of the

---

* A formerly held view of some Catholic theologians (never explicitly defined) was that since unbaptized children could not get to heaven but did not merit hell, they went to a place, of probably "natural happiness," in the next world called "Limbo."

Many priests have providentially used the new approach as a means of bringing such people, for the first time, to a realization that there is more to religion than magical rites. Pastors frequently report casual applicants coming to a living faith within the Christian community as a result.

Second Vatican Council and its implicit aim to spiritualize an existing world impetus toward the radical transformation of mankind.

The Council obviously still has a long way to go before becoming a dynamic enough force in the life of the Church to make the latter a dynamic force in the world. The Council still belongs to the Church's past rather than its future, not having been put into full effect "by the implementation which has taken place in these so-called post-conciliar years." Some Catholics feel, however, that too much has already been done in the name and in the supposed spirit of the Council. Others feel that the surface has barely been scratched. The former are often spoken of as taking the "conservative" view, the latter the "liberal" one. This has given rise to endless and usually inconclusive discussion in the classification of post-conciliar Catholics as traditional, conservative, progressive, liberal, radical and other descriptions. Naturally such categories have never been officially defined. But Pope Paul VI clarified the position in practice once and for all in September 1965 just before the Council ended. On the twenty-fifth of that month he spoke privately to the Italian journalist Alberto Cavallari. The text of what the Pope said was authorized by the Vatican for publication. The Pope spoke of the two "sides" which had emerged during the Council and he was making his remarks in the context of the Council as a whole. It is obvious that such a gathering had not been called to take the Church backward in history or to ensure that it stood determinedly still. Progress was, by definition, the object of Vatican II. The Pope took this—rather than conservatism, traditionalism, etc.—as his norm. And he referred to the two camps by the most simple but most complete classification made up until then or since. They were, he said, "progressives and non-progressives." One side was positive, the other negative. But this division, Paul went on to stress, "never raises the problem of fidelity. They are all discussing for the good of the Church" (Cavallari, *The Changing Vatican,* p. 42). A traditional view may, in practice, be either progressive or non-progressive, according to the manner in which it is interpreted and presented. But a final word must be said about a very special category which has come to be known as "traditionalist." This has entirely its own meaning and the quotation marks are unfortunately necessary every time it is mentioned. For "traditionalist" organizations have sprung up here and there and much confusion has arisen through misunderstanding of their aims. The "traditionalist" view stems not from the most ancient traditions of the Church but, almost entirely, from the Middle Ages;

an alternative description for "traditionalists" could be "medievalists."
In practice "traditionalism" refuses to accept the Church's modern,
and official, stand on religious freedom, progress in general and a host
of other matters. It objects in particular to the reforms made by Pope
Paul in the liturgy. In this, as will be seen, its medievalism is seen at its
strongest.

The liturgy, as it happens, was the subject of the Council's first
promulgated decree. For John Paul II, on the other hand, the prior
question on the morrow of his election was "What is the Church?"

CHAPTER 6

The Church Redefined

The necessary and salutary reflection of the Church about itself in Vatican II will not be the final stage of theology. Another even more important one will come, for which this Council will be seen to have been simply the forerunner and indirect preparation.

KARL RAHNER

Christ the Lord, high priest taken from among men (cf. Heb. 5,1–5) made the new people "a kingdom of priests to God, his Father" (Revel. 1,6: cf. 5,9–10). The baptized, by regeneration and the anointing of the Holy Spirit, are consecrated to be a spiritual house and a holy priesthood.

VATICAN II—*Constitution on the Church*

IF THE COUNCIL was a program for quiet revolution, its first fruit has been a new concept of "the Church"—that Church which people once believed could and would never change. The revolution would, of course, be far from quiet if God's Kingdom were suddenly to be realized on earth. Jesus, it is true, came to establish such a kingdom. But, in the famous phrase of Alfred Loisy, "what emerged was the Church." His remark was not meant to be sardonic. It was a statement of historic fact. For the Church was and is only a means, a vehicle, toward the establishing of the Kingdom. Its establishment can only come about by protracted and permanent revolution against the forces of selfishness.

It was St. Augustine who, in the fifth century, first made it clear that where you have the Church you do not necessarily have the Kingdom, and where you have the Kingdom you do not necessarily have the Church. The Vatican Council has now gone much further. It has confirmed it as Catholic belief (*Constitution on the Church*, paragraphs no. 8 and 15.) that non-Roman Catholic churches are also part of the Body of Christ. A many centuries-old tradition was thus over-

turned. The seeds of revolution were here sown. But they have so far
strayed onto stony ground. Members of the Church were told that they
were not to think of themselves as subjects of a hierarchy but as the
"people of God." This, however, instead of being exhilarating, proved
highly unsettling to not a few Catholics. In many countries, particularly in Europe and North America, they have shown little evidence of
knowing what to do with their rediscovered "peoplehood." Despite the
shock of the papal ban on contraception (1968) and the disap-
pointment to many of a "new Mass" (1969), churchgoers who survived have been largely content to jog along much as before. The
"man in the pew" has tended to regard progressivism, where he has
consciously adverted to it, as an intellectual and minority hobby. Some
revolution!

All this is a superficially good argument for "traditionalism." People
are happier to leave things to "the Church." It avoids the necessity for
the type of inner awareness to the Divine Spirit that can be searing in
its intensity. It is much simpler—and is often socially more acceptable
—to fulfill obligations with undemonstrative dignity; to pray quietly at
Mass without having to contribute (except with the conventional
money offer); to remain aloof. "In the old days," as it is put, "we
knew where we stood." The *cri de coeur* has been heard repeatedly
during the last decade or so. Parochial and selfish it may be. But natural. And it is likely to persist for a good few years yet in the "first
world" Church of the capitalist West. It is not nearly so prevalent in
the Third World which, by the turn of the century, will have swept so
far ahead as to leave the old Church of the European-North American
axis isolated and probably in decay. Hence the urgency for the un-
wanted revolution.

The traditional West, however, is clinging on at the moment with
tremendous tenacity to the levers of power in the Church. Its nominees
are still at or near the top of the pyramid which, in terms of power,
the Church still resembles. The base of this pyramid is the jagged
archipelago of its 700 million members—the current global estimate of
nominal Catholics. They thus constitute just under 20 per cent of the
world's population.

At the top of the pyramid is the Pope who theoretically wields immense, almost unlimited power. A practical limitation to such power
comes in the need to delegate functions and an effective isolation if
matters are not brought to his attention as they should be. The body
which is both his outlet to the world but also, quite often, his buffer
against it is the central government machinery of the Church, the

Roman Curia. A vast web of bureaucracy, many of its important deliberations are kept secret from the "people of God." Its power is enormous. It is made up of administrative departments headed by the two super departments of the Secretariat of State—a virtual Curia within the Curia—and the Sacred Council for the Public Affairs of the Church. These two, and the congregations, secretariats and tribunals—backed up by further commissions and offices lower down—are all headed by cardinals. Such "Curial" cardinals are analogous to the Ministers (or Secretaries of State) at the head of government departments in such countries as the United States and Great Britain.

Cardinals are strange, hybrid ecclesiastical personages with, of course, no scriptural warrant for their existence. Inevitably, however, they are, in most cases, men of great power and influence. They are styled "Princes" of the Church even now that the Church has supposedly relinquished its former claims to be a supranational world monarchy. It was only after 1918 that there was an absolute obligation in canon law for men to be priests before they could be cardinals. The Pope, Pius IX, who fought so hard to retain his temporal power in the 1860s was served by a layman as Secretary of State. He was Cardinal Giacomo Antonelli. "Cardinal" comes from a Latin word meaning "hinge" because the original cardinals were "hinge" or "key" clerics in Rome. They were, in other words, glorified pastors, or parish priests, of the diocese of Rome whose bishop came eventually to be styled "Pope." To this day each of the world's (some 125) cardinals has a "titular" Roman Church of which he is the nominal, but usually absent, pastor. Only the Pope can appoint cardinals and only cardinals can elect the Pope. Most cardinals are archbishops of the world's most important Catholic administrative centers. About thirty are Curial Cardinals heading the Church-government departments already mentioned. Nowadays (since John XXIII) all cardinals must be not only priests but bishops. "Below" them, however, in the pyramid, are the 2,750 other bishops (and archbishops) who "rule" local areas. Next come the (270,000) "diocesan" priests who mostly look after the parishes of the world while another (150,000) "religious" priests—those belonging to monastic or other "orders"—are mostly engaged in missionary, teaching or other specialized work.* At the bottom of the

---

* There are also no fewer than a million "women religious" or "nuns" in the world. Such women do immense and invaluable work to which justice could only be done by a whole book on its own. In the male-dominated Church however, nuns have no "hierarchical" status.

pile come the laity who are the "subjects" of their clerical superiors. Or are they? The position is not wholly clear even after the Vatican Council which, though it saw the Church primarily as "the people," left intact its hierarchical structure. Such a structure is, *de facto,* extremely powerful. How does it justify its power?

It does so by equating power with "authority." But to whom does such authority ultimately belong? Some think that Christ handed over his authority to Peter and the apostles, from whom it passed on to their successors, the "Pope" and the "bishops." But in fact Jesus never handed over his authority to anyone. He commissioned others to exercise authority in his name, but it is he who remains forever the one and only "head of the Church." This commission opens with the phrase "all authority is given to me in heaven and on earth . . ." (Matt. 28:18). The older translation had "all *power* is given to me in heaven and in earth. Going, therefore, teach ye all nations." The phrase, in this form, was urgently relied on during the sixteenth-century Catholic reaction to Protestantism known as the Counter-Reformation. The translation in question was from the Latin Vulgate and published by the English College at Rheims in 1572. To the phrase in Matthew 28:18 was appended—in this binding and "official" version of the New Testament—a footnote: "See here the warrant and commission of the apostles and the successors, the bishops and pastors of Christ's Church. . . . How then could the Catholic Church ever go astray?"

"Christ's Church," in other words, had long been equated with the "Catholic Church," which in turn was equated with the Kingdom of God on earth. Hence the resentment felt at the cryptic remark of Loisy's already quoted. For the Church at the turn of the present century was very jealous of its power-pyramid which directed all eyes toward Rome. This pyramid was coextensive with the "Church." Eventually Loisy went too far in his views as far as the official Church was concerned. The enemies of his fellow "Modernists" also, in their turn, went too far. Hence the vigorous heresy-hunting which reached its height in the papal reign of Pius X (1903–14) who, according to Cardinal Gasparri, "encouraged a secret espionage association outside and above the hierarchy which spied on the members of the hierarchy itself, even on their Eminences, the Cardinals" (Gasparri, *Triumph of the Holy See,* p. 278). The witch-hunting which ensued halted all Catholic scholarly efforts to keep pace with modern learning particularly in the realm of scriptural interpretation. So relentless was the silencing of "modernists" that the innocent suffered with the "guilty."

When a new dawn finally arrived, Catholic scholars had to work with almost frenzied speed to make up for the wasted years. The full fruits of such scholarship are beginning to emerge only now. But the apparent "newness" of the resultant theological findings has shocked many Catholics cocooned all their lives in another world. The hothouse "faith" of this other world turned out to be pathetically fragile when exposed to stress and intellectual probing. For inside the safety of the hothouse, the Roman Church had had, as Catholics then believed, nothing to learn from any other church (or "society") or any new age. The Church alone was the rightful teacher of every society, the mistress of every age. God, it was held, had promised her nothing less. "Modernism"—an attempt to meet rather than merely condemn the contemporary intellectual challenges to traditional religious thought—was duly (in 1907) condemned. But the witch-hunting went on unabated until the papacy of Benedict XV (1914–22).

On becoming Pope this mild and liberal-minded man found that his own name was on the list of suspected Modernists. This was some indication of the success, by complicated espionage methods, of the militant anti-Modernist group known as "integralists." The Pope suppressed the main weapon of this modern inquisition, the *Sodalitium Pianum*. But a sinister spy network had already inflicted crippling damage to a Church which was still, at this time, top-heavy in terms of "Establishment" influence and power. "With their connections in high ecclesiastical circles, the integralists attempted to safeguard Catholics by enclosing them in a ghetto inaccessible to the outside world, where a few would make all the decisions and the mass of the faithful would do no more than comply with them. Organized integralism disappeared, possibly not completely with the dissolution of the *Sodalitium*, but the integralist mentality still exists" (*New Catholic Encyclopedia*, VII, 55.3). The "ignorant masses" were, as in the political world, to be governed by the few who knew. Such an atmosphere was inauspicious for any attempt to tackle the neglected question of what "the Church" as a concept was meant to signify for Catholics. In 1921 an analysis of sorts was attempted. It was made by the French theologian, Cardinal Billot already mentioned, but he was tilling hard and barren soil. There had been no treatises on the theology of the Church ("ecclesiology" as it is technically called) since the late medieval compilations of the canon lawyers. Subsequent development was conditioned by history and the need to strengthen the "imperial" concept of Catholicism in the face of the Protestant concept of the church as an "invisible" society. No such concept was permissible according to such pillars of the "Counter-Reformation" as the Jesuit Cardinal, St. Robert Bellarmine. The Roman Church must be shown, uncompromisingly, to be the only true and perfect one; and to demonstrate this, the idea of the Catholic Church as a "perfect society" was developed. It was there for all to see—"as visible as the kingdom of France" said Bellarmine. Since this concept dominated the subsequent three centuries Billot inherited the image of a Church which thought of itself almost exclusively in the secular terms of its governmental makeup and monarchical character.

Against this background Billot produced his monumental, 870-page treatise *De Ecclesia Christi,* whose first long section "proved" that the Roman Catholic Church was true and that all sects separated from her were false. (This, of course, has until recently been universally believed by Roman Catholics; but Billot was responding to a presumed need to "prove" so stupendous a claim.) All baptized persons, said Billot, were members of this Church except those cut off by heresy or schism. (No Orthodox, Anglican or Protestant Christian was therefore a member of "the Church.") More than half the treatise is devoted to the Church's internal constitution, with no fewer than two hundred pages on the monarchical character of the Church and on the Roman Pontiff. Emphasized is the superiority of the Church over the State as the senior partner in the traditional two-power system of maintaining moral order in the world. The errors of liberalism, democracy and Modernism are restated along with the Church's immunity from interference by secular powers. Billot, furthermore, had little hope for the salvation of infidels maintaining that many adults remain forever "children" from a moral point of view and on death go to "Limbo."† (This view was rejected by most theologians even at that time.) All in all it was a spectacular apologia for the still imperial Church which stood triumphantly aloof from all well-meaning but "invalid" religious organizations. No one of the latter, in those days, even merited the name "church." They had long been referred to only as "societies."

Billot both influenced and reflected the Catholic thought of his own time and his theme was in no way startling or scandalous to the average member of the "one true Church." In such a climate, only so recently changed, there was never any question of a Catholic being

† See above, p. 58.

present at a Protestant—which included an Anglican—service. The great sin against the "perfect society" continued to be heresy, even if it was no longer, as in the Middle Ages, a crime punishable with death. Catholics enjoyed a private conviction of effortless superiority in the presence of Protestants, for whom they were sorry and for whose enlightenment they prayed. To talk of "reunion" on anything but a basis of total conversion to Rome was so unrealistic as to be misleading and therefore even "uncharitable." Anglican orders, for one thing, were "null and void." The Pope himself had (in 1896) declared this to be the case, and his decision was final. If Protestant friends became, in conversation, too probing on the subject, a favorite Catholic quip was "Don't let it worry you, old boy. You go on worshiping God in *your* way and we'll go on worshiping him in *his*."

The "old ecclesiology," taken up and redefined by Billot, held the field until after the Second World War. It brought about a view of the Church that was so juridical as to be inexpressible except in secular terms. This, in turn, inevitably produced a quasi-patriotic veneration for Roman and pontifical institutions. Billot thus takes no account of the people of God or even—as did Pope Pius XII—the Body of Christ as models of the Church. He makes no reference to the sacraments other than baptism. He shows no concern with the "laity"—or even with priests—except as the "subjects" under authority. Authority is all in all and it depends on the plenitude of *power* as centrally wielded, that is by the Pope. The key to Billot's theory, in fact, is reverence for "the Church's monarchy as instituted in St. Peter." (Though there is a mention of a "college of bishops" its powers are not defined.)

It is at this point that the present Bishop of Rome must be allowed to make a dramatic entry onto the scene. Pope John Paul II holds certain very definite views on what "the Church" is, and what it should mean, for Catholics. Would he, for holding such views, have been considered a heretic by Billot? Well, the latter was not the man to have lightly ascribed heresy to so exalted a person as a Pope. But had John Paul II, in the person of some totally obscure theologian, expounded, in Billot's day, the views of the Church which he now holds as Pope, it is hard to see how he would have escaped a charge of heterodoxy from the French Cardinal of sixty years ago. What has happened, of course, in the meantime, is that the Second Vatican Council has applied to "the Church" certain titles that were almost shockingly "new" to many Catholics. The key title here is "People of God," which is not only not new, but the oldest, indeed the *original* title of Christ's Church.

The third speech made at the Vatican Council by the present Pope, as the newly appointed Auxiliary Bishop of Krakow, was on the nature of the Church. It occurred on October 21, 1963. Bishop Wojtyla's subject was none other than "the People of God." He showed the paramountcy of such a concept in connection with the Church in urging that it must be dealt with prior to any consideration of the hierarchy. Was Billot to be overturned at a stroke? It was beginning to look like it. The young Polish bishop, still only forty-two, pointed out that the people came before the bishops as did the whole before the part. He was, moreover, consistent throughout the Council in the openness of his attitude in such areas. When the time came to debate the place of the Church in the modern world he said that it was not the Church's function to teach unbelievers. "Let us," he pleaded, "avoid any spirit of monopolizing and moralizing. One of the faults of this 'schema' (on the Church in the Modern World) is that the Church appears authoritarian in it." He felt, instead, that the Church "must seek in common with the world." Before discussion on this particular decree was brought to a final conclusion at the Council, Bishop Wojtyla insisted that the decree ("constitution" as it was technically called) should be described as "pastoral" and that the reason for using this adjective should be made clear. "It is much more concerned," he said, "with life than with doctrine." It is thus due largely to him that this important emendation was made. So, one by one, from the lips of a future Pope, the pillars of the old ecclesiology—the Church as guardian of doctrine rather than life, monopolist of truth, bastion of authority, uniquely qualified teacher of the world, exclusive arbiter of moral law—were crashing to the ground. And yet Bishop Wojtyla was merely putting his own gloss on what was already the majority opinion of the Council Fathers. On becoming Pope, however he went much further. In his "keynote" address his plea was that what in the Council had been "implicit" should now be made explicit. This represented an almost revolutionary advance on any statement previously made about the Council at such a level in the Church. What does it mean in terms of the Church as the People of God, the concept which this Pope originally made, and has subsequently remade, so much his own?

The Church as the People of God is analyzed in chapter 2 of the Second Vatican Council's key document: its Constitution on the

Church. This document was entitled *Lumen Gentium,* since Christ's earthly kingdom was meant to be a light not merely, as once, to the Gentiles as well as the Jews, but to all people. They became "people" in a special way by the very fact of hearing the Good News, that is the "gospel" of Jesus. So Peter could say "Once you were no people but now you are God's people; once you had not received mercy but now you have received mercy" (I Pet. 2:10). This is the clearest statement of its kind in the New Testament. It even appears to reject the ancient Israel now that the "Church" is the true Israel of God (Gal. 6:16; Rom. 9:6) the true circumcision (Phil. 3:3), the true seed of Abraham (Gal. 3:29; Rom. 9:7*f*), the true temple (I Cor. 3:16). But all such titles or images, including the well-known expression "body of Christ," are secondary to the oldest and most fundamental concept whereby the "Church" interprets and understands itself: if it is not the People of God, it is nothing.

The concept, moreover, is anything but theoretical, particularly as compared to such recently revived notions as seeing the Church, with Pius XII, as the "mystical Body of Christ." (Pope Pius developed this theme in his 1943 encyclical *Mystici Corporis.* In making the claim that "the mystical Body of Christ and the Catholic Church in communion with Rome are one and the same thing . . ." he made submission to Rome a condition for membership of "the Church." This position has now, of course, been abandoned.) The "People of God" image, then, has intensely practical implications the most important of which is that *all* members of the Church, the "faithful" (that is those "filled with faith"), belong to the People of God. This makes "clericalization" inappropriate since, strictly speaking, no distinction should ever have been made between "clergy" and "laity." The New Testament constantly uses the word λαός to describe "the people" (of God), but it never uses the word λαϊκός ("layman"). The key word λαός permits no distinction, within the church-community, between priests and people. Such a distinction was a later innovation and gathered momentum only after the third century. (It had, of course, become a dominant preoccupation by medieval times.) This is not to say that the New Testament People of God did not differentiate among themselves in many obvious and practical ways. There was clearly and by design a variety of services, tasks, functions and, above all, gifts (charisms). For the Church is a pentecostal organization. Though the "Body" of Christ, it is the creation of the Spirit. This Spirit permeates the whole Body each of whose members performs a special function according to his or her own particular charisma and in response to his one and only head—that is Jesus, who is Lord.

Such ways of looking at Jesus and his church-community—or community that became a "church"—are still strange to many Catholics. The words and phrases employed are often alien to the "tradition" in which they have been brought up. This is, or was, the tradition, among other things, of papal absolutism—even over the rights of conscience— a priestly caste, an obedient laity, immutability of dogma, indispensability of Latin, infallibility of papal dicta, detachment in the face of social evil, eternal fire as the punishment for mortal sin— such as any sexual irregularity, however slight, or missing Mass on Sunday—the "invincible ignorance" of Protestants and other non-Catholics, and the impossibility of salvation outside the one and only true (Roman Catholic) Church. In every respect, however, such a tradition, far from being as ancient as the Church itself, is more recent than the ideas to which these "new" words and phrases apply. The fresh wave of thought produced by the Vatican Council has gone back to the beginnings, though it has to do so in general, sometimes even ambiguous, terms, with the work of particularization and closer definition still to come. (Hence the papal plea to make explicit what was only implicit before.) The great going-back, moreover, has been accomplished with weapons not hitherto available, namely the latest discoveries of a Catholic scholarship no longer paralyzed by espionage and censorship and enriched by priceless "finds" in the realms of history—both natural and human—science, psychology, anthropology, archaeology and other fields. The Catholic "tradition" prevailing until very recently has been the tradition not of history but of those "traditionalists" already mentioned. It is a tradition in other words, which owes its origin not to the early Church but to the powerful quasi-political ecclesiastical structure of the Europe of the Middle Ages.

The countertradition which, on the other hand, has been emerging since the Council is both the oldest and newest in the Church. It seems that the resulting paradox has not yet been adequately explained by the bishops of the world, or, if it has, it has not yet been fully absorbed by Catholics at large. The present Pope has shown signs of being acutely aware of this disconcerting lacuna. His keynote address pointed not only to the desired end of making the Council's implicit wishes more explicit but also to the prime means whereby this might be achieved. This concerns the area surveyed by *Lumen Gentium* when after giving its all important definition of the *whole* Church, it went on to discuss a constituent part of this whole, namely the episcopacy or "college" of bishops.

The word "college" conveys the concept of the bishops working together, through a representative body, for the good of the entire Church rather than as individuals having no responsibility beyond their own local dioceses. The representative body in question is the Synod of Bishops set up by Pope Paul VI even before the Council was over. This Synod has met in Rome, in full session, every two years since then. The nearest equivalent in civil terms is a parliament. "Collegiality" is the name for the coresponsibility for major decision affecting the Church as arrived at jointly by the Pope and his College of Bishops. Collegiality, if genuinely adopted, means that the Pope can never again act as virtual "sole executive" of the Church's destiny.

The present Pope in his keynote statement singled out collegiality as vital for the future of the Church. He made an unambiguous plea for the full development of the idea which, up until then, had been more theoretical than practical in its application. It had not, for example, been invoked in Paul VI's fateful—and solitary—decision to declare contraception illicit. Had it been, the decision would almost certainly have been different. John Paul II even went as far as to describe *Lumen Gentium* as the "Magna Carta" of the Council. The original Magna Carta, as historians know, was not, in the distant year of 1215, a step toward democracy in England. But it was the first step away from despotism and the rule of a whole people by one man. This, it seems, is the development now desired for the Church by the Pope himself. When and if full collegiality becomes the normal rather than the ideal state of affairs, a revolution will have occurred in the government of the Catholic Church.

On the morrow of the greatest Council in history, however, the people of God were in no way ready for any such revolution. They were too bewildered. In some cases, stunned. A revolution in the Church blueprinted by the bishops themselves? No such thing had ever been heard of before. It was this very factor that was so inauspicious. The Church was tied, it seemed, by its own past mode of proceeding. There was no way by which the people themselves could initiate reform or, indeed, any body of ideas likely to become official Church policy. Reform seemed to have been "institutionalized" before it could even get underway. Without the chance of working from below, there seemed no place to go. Many of the Council's principles were, to them, abstract, abstruse and often ambiguous. There was nothing near to people's lives, nothing concrete, no way the laity could find their own voice, until . . .

Three things happened. Two crises of conscience and a widely misunderstood liturgical reform. In other words: Vietnam, *Humanae Vitae*—matters, literally, of life and death—and the "new Mass."

CHAPTER 7

The Life-and-Death Crisis

Our support of the Saigon government, which is, in reality, no
government; our indiscriminate attacks with bombs and
napalm against innocent peasants in the hope of killing a few
Vietcong; our bombing of industry and transportation in a
nation against whom we have no cause for grievance, and
against whom we have not declared war; our testing of
inhumane weapons and the increasing troop commitment to a
combat role; the whole rising tide of savagery and ruin which
we have provoked and which we now sustain—these not only
contradict the Gospel and make fidelity to it a mockery, they
also reject, out of hand, the theory of the Just War. . . .

PHILIP BERRIGAN

The problem—everyone talks about it—is that of so-called
birth control; that is to say of population increase on the one
hand and of family morality on the other. It is an extremely
grave problem. . . . The matter is under study. . . . No one
should, for the time being, take it upon himself to pronounce
himself in terms differing from the norm in force.

POPE PAUL VI (1964)

THEORETICALLY the Catholic Church never changes. That is, it never
admits to having changed its stance on any basic issue. In practice it
has found itself at the mercy of history. Changes of belief are recorded
as "developments" or "clarifications" of positions previously held but
no longer adequately expressed because of altered circumstances.

The early Christians took Jesus at his word when he said he came to
confirm every jot and tittle of the old law, a particularly sacred commandment of which was to avoid willful killing. Christians conscripted
into the Roman army before the days of Constantine opted to be killed
rather than to kill. Pacifism ("blessed are the peacemakers") was the
original Christian ideal.

A different view was taken in the post-Constantinian Church. St. Augustine gave the Western Church its fatal push in the new direction. Millions of men and women perished through Christian history as a result of the new ideas. St. Augustine, the incorrigible pessimist, recalled that men had always fought each other. War therefore, having a normal place in human activity, must be regulated by the moral theology of the Church. According to his formulation, wars could always be waged provided it was at God's command. This gave rise to the theory of the "just" war and the belief that the arbiter in such matters was the ecclesiastical official mind. War against the heathen was not merely "just" but meritorious. Heretics and heathens had, if necessary, to be "compelled to come in." The Christian Church thus became the greatest war-maker in history in terms of the years it spent at this part of its holy task in different centuries. "Conscientious objection" was, necessarily, a contradiction in terms of the Church's principles of a "just war."

War, says the Church, to be morally defensible, has to be waged by a "proper authority," that is, only by a lawful government; it has to have a "just cause," such as the defense of a country's basic rights, and it has to be fought with the "right intention," including legitimate goals and the use of proper means. Such guidelines have, in practice, been interpreted by individuals and nations as they have wished. The Church, rather than face the necessity of issuing unenforceable directives, has had to accept this situation and presume goodwill on the part of the various interpreters. (No such latitude is permitted in the sexual field where the Church, up until now, has always tried to enforce a strict moral code rather than leave such matters to the dictates of individual good faith and love of God.) In the Middle Ages, moreover, the Church was closely involved with war and herself directed elaborate military operations. Such wars, notably the Crusades, were justified because of a "right intention." The abominable cruelties and murders carried out by the Crusaders against the infidels were, in effect, rewarded rather than condemned.

The situation in modern times has become infinitely more complicated. One major response by the Church has been a body to guide and help Catholics and contribute to the cause of banishing the evil of war. This body is the Pontifical Commission for Justice and Peace set up by Paul VI on an experimental basis in 1967 and made permanent as of 1974. Its president is the outstanding churchman from black Africa, Bernardin Cardinal Gantin of Benin. This central commission has local counterparts in many countries including the United States and Great Britain. The bracketing of justice and peace has done much to revolutionize the Catholic view of war. It has been part of the liberating process whereby Catholics have been enabled to respond more freely than in the past in the face of moral choice rather than to follow, sheep-like, the directives of a Church which decided everything for the individual. (The latter practice obviously robbed individual actions of any substantial degree of meritoriousness beyond the doubtful merit of blind conformism.) An extreme example concerns the right of conscientious objection. Where the conditions for a "just war" were deemed to be present, conscientious objection for the Catholic in the late fifties was held to be "morally indefensible" (*New Catholic Encyclopedia*, XIV, 804). Ten years later this ruling had been changed by the Vatican Council's document on The Church in the Modern World. This document's chapter on war and peace was "one of the most important chapters the Council produced anywhere" (*A Concise Guide to Vatican II*, II, p. 61). It called for "an entirely new attitude" to war and urged all governments to recognize the individual citizen's right to be a conscientious objector. (Previously—and very significantly—the Church had begun to look kindly on Catholic conscientious objectors only in non-Catholic countries.)

For American Catholics the Vietnam war has been the main barometer of feelings on the subject of justice-and-peace. Soon after President Johnson's escalation of the war in early 1965 (authorizing round-the-clock bombardment of North Vietnam) a declaration of conscience pledging total non-cooperation with the government was published in the United States. It was the first statement of its kind. Many leading churchmen of different denominations signed it but only two were Catholic priests. These were the famous (to some infamous) Berrigan brothers. "The Berrigans' belligerence" was seen in some quarters as not only a protest against the Vietnam war but "also a defiance of the heavy-handed authoritarianism, the blind nationalism that makes the American Catholic community the most war-mongering segment of the nation. Goaded by the silence of his Church's hierarchy and of its hawkish flocks, the Catholic radical can become a desperado" (Grey, *Divine Disobedience*, p. 90). In the following year (1966) Cardinal Spellman of New York visited Saigon. A reporter asked what he thought of American policy in Vietnam. The cardinal replied "Right or wrong, my country." But Catholic lay opinion was already swinging in another direction, and the Pope himself had begun to speak out against the war. As early as 1967 American Catholics were becoming less "hawkish" and by 1970 were high on the "dove" lists of statistical tables. In general, by that time, they outnumbered Protestants in favoring American withdrawal from Vietnam within eighteen months (Greeley, *The American Catholic,* pp. 99–100). The Catholic Peace Fellowship gained ground rapidly, but the "establishment" was not yet ready to cave in. "The lines were drawn: the pleading Pope versus the timid, property-loving American bishops: the lonely young curates radicalised by ghetto work versus their cautious, Bingo-mad pastors; the Catholic intellectuals versus the warmongering law-and-order Catholic masses . . ." (Grey, *Divine Disobedience,* p. 95). As a comment, of course, over emotive. But the Vietnam war was an emotive event, and not just for America. It was one of the most emotive occurrences in modern history.

English speaking Catholics the other side of the Atlantic were soon to experience, in Northern Ireland, a bitter conflict which was minor compared to Vietnam but major in relation to the outwardly peaceful relations within the British home communities for more than fifty years. Catholics in the six counties of Northern Ireland had been deprived of certain fundamental civil rights ever since the 1921 partitioning of Ireland. This expedient had been adopted to placate the curiously named "Loyalists" of Ulster who had threatened treasonable military action against the Crown rather than accept the Irish Home Rule Bill that had passed both Houses of Parliament in 1914. Because of the armed threat from the north, the Home Rule Bill was deemed to be suspended by the outbreak of World War I. What began as demonstrations for civil rights in Northern Ireland (in 1969) deteriorated into a full-scale attempt by the "Provisional" IRA (Irish Republican Army) to terrorize the authorities into negotiating for the reuniting of all thirty-two counties of Ireland. This in turn degenerated into a vicious brawl between Protestants and Catholics. A tragically small number of people in England, including those Catholics of predominantly English rather than Irish ancestry, know or understand the historical and social background to this conflict, whose roots are very deep and go a very long way back. A tragically large number of people in Ireland, because of their extraordinary island history—and the fact of a British "occupation" that never really took complete root even after seven hundred years—dwell disproportionately on the injustices arising from their political plight. The Irish Catholic clergy meanwhile have maintained a control over their own people that is so tight as to be largely counterproductive. As soon as

Catholics leave their native shores, a very high proportion of them, free of the hothouse, quite quickly "lapse." Though Irish politics and religion are often impossible to disentangle from one another, the Catholic hierarchy in the north has protested against Catholic violence more strenuously than is often supposed in England.* It is arguable however that had the Irish bishops used their undoubted authority even more unambiguously, the horrible bombings and other IRA murders would by now have stopped altogether. Was it another case of fearing the unenforceability of a moral stand in face of political sentiments? Whatever be the truth here, it is a humbling fact for the Catholic and Protestant establishments that their influence for justice and peace has been proportionately less than that achieved by the small band of Quakers who have been working unobtrusively for some years in such disaster areas as Londonderry (Derry to the Irish.) What, people again ask, would happen if the Catholic Church too were a truly pacifist organization as the New Testament seems to command?

In Ireland—but by no means only in Ireland—it is the Catholic condemnations of sins of the flesh that always seem to be more vehement than condemnations of such sins as sectarian murders, cowardly ambushes, assassinations and deadly booby traps. Not only the sins of the flesh but the various possible moral attitudes which might be thought to minimize the guilt thereof are seen by many to incur greater ecclesiastical wrath than the horrors of war.

In this connection a mischievous observer posed, some years ago, a bizarre hypothetical situation which was discussed with varying degrees of seriousness for some time afterward. One was asked to suppose that a powerful nation, instead of saturating a foreign territory with napalm or some other deadly weapon, had instead, saturated it with contraceptives and multilingual instructions as to their proper use. The Church, on its past record, would have protested eloquently but ineffectively, in the former case. But it is not difficult to imagine the volcanic uproar that would have greeted the second operation. And yet the Church is really not obsessed with birth control as such. It

---

* A quaint sentence crops up in *Violence in Ireland* (p. 119). Though the intended meaning is clear, the phraseology comes near to being "stage Irish": "Since the outbreak of the recent troubles in the North the hierarchy has persistently condemned violence, especially as represented by Cardinal Conway, and by the Bishops of Down and Connor and Ardagh and Clonmacnois."

is rather the ecclesiastical preoccupation with sex in general through the ages that has been the cause for the greatest embarrassment to Catholics in modern times. The 1968 pronouncement against contraception was really only another repetition of the long line of condemnations of sex as an expression of love, but divorced from its biological context. If the biological objectives of procreation were being pursued, mortal sin was always held to be avoidable. But some of the "stars" among the early Church writers, or "Fathers," could not help thinking that any sexual act even in marriage must be at least "venially" sinful. To avoid sin, or at least serious sin, an intentionally procreative intention was required in every act of intercourse. The view was that of the "early Church," not of Jesus. He himself took a much more lenient view of "carnal" than of other sins. For him poverty was more important than celibacy and love more important than a negatively virtuous attitude toward sex. The early Church however, relied heavily on the Stoics. Men like Clement of Alexandria took an exaggeratedly narrow view of sexual morality even to the extent of objecting to the supposed erotic elements in religious dances, pictures and statues which, in another age, would have appeared wholly innocent. His puritanical attitude, however, was arguably justifiable in the pagan (second century) atmosphere of a collapsing civilization. Unfortunately his ideas were not abandoned when the times changed but were taken up and treated as more or less normative by such later theological heavyweights as Origen, St. Ambrose, St. Jerome and, above all, St. Augustine. All were, in one degree or another, anti-sex and anti-woman in their outlook; and their unnaturally severe views became deeply embedded in Western thought for many centuries to come. Only in the seventeenth century did Catholic theologians break with the Augustinian insistence that all sexual acts must in some way be tied to the procreative purpose. It was not however until the time of the Second Vatican Council that conjugal love was put on a par with procreation as a worthy end in itself for Christian marriage. Such an entirely new climate inevitably begat lively speculation as to a revised ruling on contraception, which up until that time, had been considered by the Church to be gravely sinful. Expectation that such teaching would be changed led to widespread unofficial debate.

Such debate became as it were, "official" in 1963 when John XXIII took the matter out of the hands of the Council and set up a six-member commission to study the question and report back. "Good Pope John," however, died in June of that year, with the commission's formidable task only in its infancy. Paul VI, the new Pope, enlarged the commission first to eighteen, then to sixty and finally to sixty-four members including doctors, sociologists, population experts and other laymen from many countries as well as some of the world's leading theologians.

At first the members of the commission were fairly equally divided into three groups. One group held that periodic continence—the so-called "rhythm" system—was (as already officially taught by the Church) the only acceptable form of birth regulation. The second group thought that the "pill" might be used with discrimination; and the third considered that if the "pill" was approved there could be no objections to other forms of contraception.

After a series of meetings the commission became deeply divided in two opposite directions. One section, by far the larger, believed that the traditional ruling on this vital subject was due for revision. The other, and much smaller, section favored no change in existing teaching. According to Dr. John Marshall, an English medical expert who had been on the Commission from the beginning, "the point of crisis was probably reached for many around April 23, 1966, when the four theologians of the minority group acknowledged they could not demonstrate the intrinsic evil of contraception on the basis of natural law and so rested their case on authority and the fear of possible consequences of change both to authority and to sexual morality" (Harris, *On Human Life,* p. 14).

The Pope, at this stage, set up an important "inner cabinet" of sixteen cardinals and bishops to guide the experts' work. As its president he appointed Cardinal Ottaviani, then head (or to be technically precise, "pro-prefect") of the Vatican department known as the Sacred Congregation for the Doctrine of the Faith. The cardinal also happened to be one of the most conservative members of the Roman Curia. The vice-presidents appointed to this inner cabinet were Cardinals Heenan of Westminster (England) and Doepfner of Munich. One of the other members was the present Pope.

Despite strenuous efforts the disagreement proved too deep to be bridged. In June 1966, the progressive majority and the conservative minority on the commission thus submitted to the Pope separate and conflicting reports on their respective findings. The Pope had meanwhile been subjected to constant lobbying from both progressive and non-progressive elements in the Church at large. What was the general drift of responsible feeling? In 1967 Gregory Baum wrote: "Since

1957 the problem of methods of birth control—of the "pill," first of all, but later on of every other contraceptive method—has fully occupied the attention of moral theologians. This may perhaps have been the question most seriously and widely debated during the last ten years . . . And in ten years the positions assumed by moral theologians have been radically altered, entailing grave, or even dramatic, modifications which no one would ever have dared to imagine when the discussion began." (Valsecchi, *Controversy*, p. vii). The "natural law" argument for so long relied on, failed, under microscopic examination, to satisfy even the most conservative of the theologians of the papal commission. And the absence of any scriptural warrant for such a "law" posed further difficulties in formulating any convincing arguments as to its "divine" origins.

Rumors about what the Pope would actually say began to proliferate as of April 1967, when the American periodical the *National Catholic Reporter* "leaked" the report made to Pope Paul in June 1966 by his commission. This revealed that the commission, as a whole, had recommended, by an overwhelming majority, that the Church should end its ban on contraceptives. For the critical vote, the present Pope, John Paul II, was absent; but it is certain he would have voted with the conservative minority.

On October 18, 1967, at a "moment of historical significance" (Roche, *The Catholic Revolution*, p. 31), three thousand delegates to the World Congress of the Lay Apostolate meeting in Rome made a bold and direct challenge to the Pope. They called, in terms that were measured and yet so unambiguous as to be sensational, for revision of past Church teaching on birth control so that Catholics could in future follow their own consciences in selecting the means whereby they might limit their families. This call was coupled with certain radical pleas for the Church to be more vitally concerned with world development. All in all "it was not a moment of rebellion against the Pope, nor was it an attempt to proclaim new Catholic teaching. But it was a testimony, as the Vatican Council had urged the laity to give, of their own experiences and insights—in this case insights into the realities of married life and their informed Christian sense of right and wrong" (*ibid.*, p. 44).

In June 1968 it was reported that a definitive statement was about to be issued from the Holy See, but it was suppressed at the last moment. Three particular cardinals, Koenig of Vienna, Suenens of Belgium and Doepfner of Munich were very uneasy about the probable

Pope-laity "gap." They pleaded with the Pope not to publish a document reaffirming the Church's traditional opposition to all forms of "artificial" contraception. Nevertheless, at the end of July, the bombshell of *Humanae Vitae* exploded. The document was dated July 25, feast day of St. James the Apostle. The operative words of this most famous of all modern papal "letters" came in its paragraph 11; it stated that "every marriage act (*quilibet matrimonii usus*) must remain open to life." The next paragraph insisted that the "unitive meaning and the procreative meaning" of marriage are inseparable. No artificial means may be allowed to come between these two "meanings." Conception, in other words, could only be lawfully avoided by use of "rhythm," a method unknown to Catholics in underdeveloped areas and elsewhere primarily available to those with enough time and leisure to make it work.

In the ten years between the issuing of this encyclical and the election of Pope John Paul II enough was written about its consequences to last most people a lifetime. The glib satisfaction of many "conservatives" was only slightly more distasteful than the snide opposition of many "progressives." More sober was the approach of such observers as the man regarded by many as Catholicism's leading moral theologian, Fr. Bernard Häring, who pointed out that no papal teaching had "ever caused such an earthquake in the Church as the encyclical *Humanae Vitae*" (Callahan, ed., *Catholic Case for Contraception,* p. 77). Reactions, he pointed out, were as sharp as those which had greeted the ultimately discredited Syllabus of Errors in which Pius IX had tried to dissociate the Church from the progress and the thought of the world around him. Häring, however, found that it was "harder to reconcile *Humanae Vitae* with the Council's Constitution on The Church in the Modern World than to reconcile the Declaration on Religious Freedom with the Syllabus" (*ibid.,* p. 89). Nevertheless in the decade between 1969 and 1978 a decisive development was the liberation of Catholics not from the need to think but from the false security of not having to think enough. Personal responsibility for each and every moral act replaced grudging and often loveless adherence—from fear of hell—of the letter of the law. Catholics in other words, found themselves, perhaps for the first time ever, expressing out loud and uninhibitedly their own views on their own actions. They spoke not *against* the Church which, with the new self-understanding flowing from the Council—however dimly perceived at that time—would have meant speaking against themselves, the People of God. They spoke as between brothers and sisters. They anxiously shared a family problem. They finally arrived at a *modus vivendi*, or rather a *modus credendi*, though this was not achieved except at a tragically heavy price. Millions left the Church in despair but not necessarily completely or forever. The bishops in the various countries did their pastoral utmost to stop the exodus before it really got under way. Their prompt action saved the situation from being even worse. It was not that they were faced with a rebellion but with widespread bewilderment and disillusionment.

There was a total split in the Church, the greatest in modern times, and probably the most open one ever. (Few remembered the furious squabbles of the past over such matters as efficacious grace in which Dominicans and Jesuits exchanged abusive arguments for several decades, and succeeding Popes contradicted each other in their desperate desire to bring the controversy to an end.) The chasm of differing opinion over contraception was profound and seemingly unbridgeable. There was an interesting difference, however, between those who gave unqualified support to Pope Paul and those who had conscientious misgivings about the encyclical. The latter respected the opinions of those with whom they disagreed. It was indeed basic to their own contention that each one should do and think what he genuinely thought right after scrupulously and prayerfully looking at every possible angle. Such a "solution"—as far as there could be such a thing—was an agreement to differ without anyone's finally closing his mind. The encyclical's supporters, on the other hand, stated that their "opponents" had no right, as loyal Catholics, to hold and state the opinions they did and must henceforth shut up. This attitude—though sadly the main element in making the whole controversy unnecessarily prolonged and bitter—was really the hub of the problem and the heart of the matter. For it symbolizes as perhaps could no other quandary, the picture of the modern Catholic standing at a crucial point in his personal path of spiritual progress. Some would like to insist that such a person has come to an inevitable parting of the ways and must make an irrevocable choice: private conscience or the authority of the Pope as "head of the Church." But is there really a parting of the ways? For it is not as if, in the past, a Catholic was not bound by conscience. It is not as if, *only now,* he or she is thrown back on conscience as the core of Church judgment. Conscience was always, according to Catholic teaching, the ultimate criterion of truth in the moral order. In *The Difficulties of Anglicans* Cardinal Newman concludes his section on conscience with a famous passage: "If I am obliged to bring religion into after-dinner toasts (which indeed does not seem quite the thing) I shall drink—to the Pope, if you please—but still to Conscience first and to the Pope afterwards."

What has happened in the Catholic Church is that until recently, though conscience was always paramount, the Church's various "teachers" acted as if *they* were the consciences of their pupils or subjects. "Being the conscience of others may seem to be an easier task than helping them to develop mature consciences of their own. But for such antics we pay a frightful price. This exteriorising of conscience does great harm to the Christian community. It keeps people perpetually adolescent in their moral response. It effectively stifles any moral initiative on their part" (McGinn, *Doctrines Do Grow*, p. 73). Thus the Catholic has come of age and found the process painful and puzzling. For conscience—"the experience of responsibility in the exercise of freedom"—means that individual faith must be deeper, love stronger and moral fiber tougher than ever before.

The great question is: what happens now, in the age of Pope John Paul II? Until his advent discussion of birth control always ended up somehow with a reference to or at least an association with Pope Paul VI, one of whose close lieutenants once said to this author "he is a great man. But even great men must be allowed one mistake. His was *Humanae Vitae*."

Entirely different conditions now prevail, but there is no indication that John Paul II, already in office for over a year as of Christmas 1979, intends to make any official change in the Pauline ruling on contraception. No such change is probable. But past mistakes are unlikely to be repeated. The sense of direction, as far as contraception as such is concerned, depends on post-encyclical factors; and North America is, to some extent, the key to the situation.

As early as 1972 a very revealing survey was made of opinion among United States priests on the contraception issue. "Underlying the mass of percentages, coefficients, and hypotheses concerning assumptive systems that have gone into this study has been the basic fact presented in the very first pages—*over half of the priests of the United States no longer agree with their Church's official teaching on contraception*" (Moore, *Death of a Dogma*, p. 111). The study as a whole helps to elucidate how so startling a situation could have come about in a Church which has had a highly centralized, hierarchically structured teaching and juridical authority, one which has previously withstood all attempts from within to question its legitimacy as a moral teacher.

It was just about this time, as already seen, that a significant swing in Catholic opinion on war, particularly the war in Vietnam, had come about in America. The bishops were inevitably more conservative than the majority of pastors and other priests. But this was because they have the less enviable job of administering the Church regardless of swings in the theological pendulum; and they have to steer a cautious passage. They were taken unawares, moreover, by *Humanae Vitae*, having expected the advice of the papal commission to be followed. The decision, however, when it came was taken by the Pope alone. There had been no consultation with his "college" of bishops, though such "collegiality" was a feature of Catholic life which Vatican II had commended for the future. John Paul II (keynote address) made collegiality the basis of his whole platform. The time had come, he said, for "a deeper reflection on the implications of collegiality, so that our minds might be better informed and that we might undertake our responsibilities more conscientiously. The hand of collegiality closely links the bishops to the successor of Peter and to each other. Thus they carry out their function of bringing the light of the Gospel to the world, of sanctifying it by the instruments of Grace and of guiding with pastoral care the whole people of God."

Though the bishops of the Church did not give their views on contraception *before* the Pope made his lonely decision, they did so very clearly afterward. And they did so then in face of hard facts and reactions staring them in the face. The bishops in almost every country took the unprecedented step of issuing full statements clarifying the encyclical's message for the particular needs of their respective flocks. (See: Horgan, ed. *Humanae Vitae and the Bishops.*)

There was an amazing variety among the statements of the world's bishops. Some of them constituted remarkable qualifications of the papal letter, allowing for dissent and showing respect for conscience and a more personalist ethics. What happened as an overall result was that the most important papal letter of modern times, perhaps *ever*, in the sense that it so directly affects the most intimate part of the lives of millions of human beings, can now be read in the context of all these hierarchical statements from around the world. It can be described as a sort of "collegiality post factum," arguably the best possible way for solving what has been for so many a hideous and agonizing conundrum.

The statement of the American bishops was, in the first instance, very short. Priests and people were asked to "receive with sincerity what the Pope has taught, to study it carefully, and to form their consciences in its light." A second statement followed three months later. It turned out to be a massive document of 11,000 words, drafted largely by a commission under the late Cardinal (then Bishop) Wright. The document went much further than the immediate issues raised by *Humanae Vitae*. It brought about notable advances concerning matters quite literally of life and death. It called upon Americans to evaluate war with that "entirely new attitude" for which the Council had appealed. The war in Vietnam was, by implication, condemned, the right of conscientious objection upheld. Life in fact was held to be sacred as never before. Just before the end of the assembly was called to vote on the document, the bishops decided to set up a non-profit foundation costing a million dollars to encourage scientific research on human fertility and reproduction as a practical contribution to the proposals in *Humanae Vitae* for further medical research.

The papal attempt to close discussion on contraception had not only had the opposite effect. It had opened out new horizons to very much more candid discussion of sex, the "new morality," the effective nature of church authority, birth, marriage, death and the "justness" of mass killing. It had caused the American hierarchy to move forward further in certain areas in three months than it had for thirty years. Instead of just speaking, the bishops, this time, had listened first.

Only time can tell how far such progress has been interrupted by the Pope's hard line on contraception and other matters during his controversial visit to the United States in the fall of 1979.

CHAPTER 8

The Restored Liturgy

We have learned with great sorrow that in the kingdom of
France certain sons of perdition, itching with novelties
detrimental to souls, and despising the laws and practice of
the Church, have lately come to such madness as to dare to
translate the Roman Missal and to hand it over to persons of
every rank and sex.

POPE ALEXANDER VII (1661)

The faithful join in the Eucharist by virtue of their royal
priesthood.

CONSTITUTION ON THE CHURCH
(*Vatican II*)

VATICAN II's 1963 Constitution on the Sacred Liturgy "was the
clearest initial indication that the earlier progressive rumblings at the
opening session the previous year had some substance behind
them. . . . But many Catholics were to miss the real point of liturgical
renewal" (McBrien, *The Remaking of the Church*, pp. 35–36). The
very idea of "tampering with" the Mass appalled many Catholics. Did
they lack the courage of Cardinal Newman who cried "to live is to
change."? Or did they think that the so-called "old Mass" that
emerged (posthumously) from the sixteenth-century Council of Trent
(hence "Tridentine") was in fact very ancient? Would they be
shocked to find out that, relatively speaking, it was quite a "new
Mass" and that the Mass authorized for public worship since the big
"change" of 1970, is, in essence, extremely old?

Whatever be the answers to such questions, the fact remains that the
"Mass" is central to Catholic devotional life and, in one form or an-
other, always has been, even though it was not always called the
"Mass." The accepted criterion of whether or not a person is a "good"
Catholic is still whether or not he attends Mass at least on all Sundays
and "holy days of obligation." This is the mandatory minimum. Inten-

tionally, and without adequate reason, to miss Mass on one of these days is a "mortal sin," meriting eternal damnation unless the sinner repents before death. Forgiveness for any such serious sin must be sought through the sacrament of penance, that is confession to a priest, since otherwise the Church can guarantee no forgiveness apart from the special emergency of imminent death when a private act of contrition is held to be sufficient.

These have long been—and still are—the rules of the Church. For the devout as opposed to the technically "good" Catholic, however, little or nothing can be more important and precious than going to Mass. No other spiritual banquet is in any way comparable to it. He will try, if possible, to go to Mass each day or, at least, several times a week and not just on Sundays. Logically indeed, a Catholic can hardly go to Mass too often. Though there is no question of any repetition of the once-for-all sacrifice of Jesus on Calvary, the Mass makes available, as Catholics believe, a unique form of drawing forever on the merits of the Cross in the reenactment of the Last Supper whose full significance depended on the next day's sacrifice at Calvary. The ultimate theological interpretation of the Mass has remained constant through the centuries, even though certain ages have emphasized one element of its character at the expense of some other. The outward form of the Catholic Eucharist, on the other hand, has undergone radical alterations at various periods. More importantly the whole spirit in which it has been celebrated, and the circumstances surrounding such celebration, have altered even more. In this sense, the old or original Mass, as it had evolved from its primitive state, had been replaced by an entirely new sort of Mass by the time the Middle Ages had arrived. This medieval Mass was modified but substantially preserved—and made uniform—by Pope Pius V in 1570 as part of the "Tridentine reform." As of 1970, what is sometimes, incorrectly, referred to as the "new Mass" has become standard because of the reforms of Pope Paul VI. By these reforms the *pre-medieval* Mass has been substantially restored and adapted to the community requirements for which it was originally intended.

Few people argue more forcefully—at popular level—against changes in the liturgy than authors like Professor James Hitchcock in such books as *The Recovery of the Sacred*. His main thesis is that a possibly irreversible movement has set in, away from liturgy seen in terms of sacred rites which symbolize hidden, divine realities, in the direction of devotions, or "celebrations," that are essentially human.

Joseph Jungmann, on the other hand, argues, particularly in his classic work, *The Mass of the Roman Rite,* that an essentially human element had captured the Mass of the Middle Ages and that what was subsequently needed was a recovery of the largely missing spiritual element. By "human element," above, is meant the medieval social scene wherein monasteries had become alarmingly numerous and often worldly, and served chiefly as places for the saying of as many Masses as possible. The system had been building up over a long period as the medieval Christian, living in constant fear of eternal damnation, was willing, if he could afford it, to pay or bequeath huge sums for the saying of Masses for his soul. "So there arose during the last centuries of the Middle Ages an unnatural multiplication of Masses, and, along with it, an unnatural increase in clergy of whom a part, at least, derived their entire income from Masses either through endowments (foundations or chantries) or by way of Mass stipends. For the most part they celebrated Votive Masses or Masses for the Dead, since these the people wanted most" (*Mass of the Roman Rite,* p. 98).

Jungmann, in the course of his monumental and definitive work, which Hitchcock points to as the basic text leading to the Pauline reforms, traces the Catholic Eucharist from its earliest days until the beginnings of reform after World War II. It is not, however, true to say that what has happened since these reforms were taken up has entirely followed the temperate and scholarly lines foreshadowed by Jungmann. And it is important to recognize the vital service performed by such writers as Hitchcock—he happens to argue particularly intelligently—who provide timely warnings against the dangers of excessive zeal in the cause of "reform." What is unfortunate is the extent to which "traditionalist" writers rely on the untypical examples of progressive extremists, such as exaggeratedly informal celebrations of Mass, to bolster their case. This is unfair and misleading. Jungmann, on the other hand, moreover "demonstrated painstakingly the numerous accretions which had built up in the liturgy over the centuries and, more important, the numerous misunderstandings which had attached themselves to various parts of public worships, to the point where the original meanings were all but lost" (*Recovery of the Sacred,* p. 5).

The historical factors which produced the changes in the Mass during the first millennium are, naturally, too numerous and complicated to be summarized without distortion. The key to the arrival of what Jungmann calls "a new basic type" for the Mass is largely due to the

Romano-Frankish formula evolving in the Carolingian empire at a time, in the tenth century, when, as already seen, the papacy was at its nadir. The overall effect of such changes was the "attitude around and after A.D. 1000 which considered the Mass as a sort of clerical preserve, and there was, therefore, not much lay interest in what has come to be 'participation' in the Mass" (*Liturgical Renewal,* p. 12). The Mass came to be seen not as an offering by the people of God with the celebrant as "president" of their praying assembly—the situation as described by Justin Martyr in the second century—but as offered *by* the clergy *for* the people ("laity"). The celebrant ceased to be with or even near his fellow worshipers (that is facing them as at the supper table), but much farther away. The altar was removed to the back of the sanctuary. The priest faced the far wall and the altar became more like a throne whose tabernacle contained the Blessed Sacrament. The priest now "led" his silent subjects in prayer and spoke for them with the help of a choir. The choir occupying an area between people and minister, accentuated the separation. Ordinary people received Holy Communion less and less frequently. They did so very occasionally, as at Easter, as a matter of "duty" after a long period of penance in Lent; but on such occasions Communion was outside of the Mass-liturgy so as not to disturb the "priest's Mass." The segregation of the people from the action of worship was further underlined by the physical separation of "sanctuary" from nave in the great churches and cathedrals that soared to magnificent grandeur in the Gothic period. The clergy alone occupied the sanctuary. Those in the nave could hardly even see what was happening as they were cut off by a wall-like rood screen. It is not too much to say, as has one author, that "the whole religious atmosphere of the late Middle Ages suggests uncontrolled and undisciplined development, a gradual but constant drift from the spirit of the early church, a widening of the rift between theology and liturgy. The flamboyance of Gothic art is reflected in worship. The Mass as a rite became *de facto* a 'spectacle' which the faithful were privileged to witness, rather than a religious act in which they had both a right and an obligation to share" (McNally, *The Unreformed Church,* p. 119). This was something that had to be reformed. It was not just a question of abuses and the scandalous multiplication of Masses for money. Orthodoxy was somehow preserved but the new practices gave rise to a new theology which the Reformers attacked strenuously. This theology was neither systematic nor particularly positive. It tended merely to try and justify what was already happening. It produced an erroneous emphasis rather than erroneous doctrine. The Protestant emphasis was in an entirely different direction. There were mutual misunderstandings of the gravest kind in the absence of civilized and meaningful intercommunication between Catholics and Reformers. The numberless "Masses" said for money made such "Masses" seem to Anglicans "blasphemous fables." (The unravelings of this particular tangle, and the vexed question of Anglican Orders in Roman Catholic eyes, come more within the realm of ecumenism.*)

To what extent was the medieval liturgy actually "reformed" by Pope Pius V? The answer to this important question is given in the 1970 General Instruction of the Roman Missal (Introduction): "Saint Pius V was especially concerned to preserve the *recent tradition*† of the Church then under attack, and only very slight changes were introduced into the sacred rites. In fact the Missal of 1570 differs very little from the first printed edition of 1474, which in turn faithfully follows the missal used at the time of Pope Innocent III (1198–1216). Manuscripts in the Vatican Library provided some verbal emendations, but did not permit research into the 'ancient and approved authors' beyond some liturgical commentators of the Middle Ages." Today, on the other hand, as the Introduction went on to point out, countless writings of scholars had clarified the "usage of the holy Fathers" followed by the revisers of the missal under Pius V. "Traditions dating back to the first centuries, before the development of the Eastern and Western rites, are also better known today because so many liturgical documents have been discovered. Progress has been made, moreover, in studying the actual works of the holy Fathers. The teachings of such outstanding saints as Irenaeus, Ambrose, Cyril of Jerusalem, and John Chrysostom have shed light on the theology of the eucharistic mystery in Christian antiquity."

In reality, the 1970 Roman Missal is both very old and very new. It has revived many long forgotten or recently rediscovered usages, but it has restored them in a modern setting and in accordance with prevailing conditions and contemporary pastoral needs. Such restoration and adaptation is not perfect and probably never will be. Many mistakes have been made. Some of the discarded "Tridentine" usages may well be restored in future revisions of the Mass. In a pluralist age there could even be room for two types of "Latin" rite celebrations, though

* See below, Chapter 17.
† Italics added.

Rome has so far looked with disfavor on any such idea. But some such proposal could well form the eventual compromise "package" with such a person as Archbishop Lefebvre.‡ And his dropping of total opposition to the Council, moreover, could well be just what is wanted by most genuine adherents of the medieval Mass, especially as such people have been accorded scant consideration in some quarters so far.

It is nevertheless historically true that the medieval Mass, with minor adjustments and a strict limiting of alternative forms, passed on to the next generations as the Mass of the Counter-Reformation. During this period, Catholic attitudes hardened solidly against anything "Protestant" and such attitudes went on for two centuries after the Council of Trent.

The non-community type of Mass, in fact, not only survived the Middle Ages but was made apparently sacrosanct by the decrees of Pius V which was expressly to be of perpetual validity. Many Popes used such a formulary at the end of their most solemn pronouncements, owing to the speed with which the pronouncements of one Pope were in any event overturned by successors. The Pope who suppressed the Jesuits, for example (Clement XIV in 1773), declared that the suppression was to be perpetual. The adding of the "perpetuity" clause was, after all, no more than common form, however solemn and forbidding it sounded. No one, taking the long view, was unduly perturbed. It was all political anyway. Pius VII, as soon as he got released from the captivity of Napoleon, had no difficulty in decreeing (in 1814) a full restoration of the Society of Jesus.

Apart from anything else, an important matter of principle is here involved. Each Pope has an absolute right to make his own decisions in such matters. No Pope can bind his successor nor is any Pope bound by a predecessor. The conservative and scrupulously traditional Pius XII, in his encyclical *Mediator Dei* (1947), restated the principle by affirming that the Sovereign Pontiff not only had "the right to permit or establish any liturgical practice" but also "to introduce or approve new rites, or to make any changes in them he considers necessary." Pius V's declaration on the Mass was not only not immutable but quite soon—and quite frequently—changed. His missal was revised by Clement VIII in 1604 and again by Urban VIII in 1634. Substantial changes were introduced into the missal in 1911, while Pius XII, in 1955, authorized a radical revision of all the rites and ceremonies in

‡ See below, p. 100 ff.

the Holy Week liturgy. "He sanctioned a return to more ancient customs and revived almost-forgotten symbolism to restore the worship at that most sacred time to its original freshness and force" (Leonard, *Light on Archbishop Lefebvre,* p. 5).

Nevertheless the revision carried out by Pope Paul VI caused particular umbrage in some quarters. Most Catholic authors have hesitated to admit the brutally basic reason for this despite the thousands of words written in commentary on the whole affair. The 1570 Mass, a culmination of the work of the Council of Trent at the personal hand of Pius V, represented the high water mark of Catholic anti-Protestant expression. Far from being a thoroughgoing "reform" of the Mass, far from removing the bulk of the medieval superstructure that had collected on the earlier form of the eucharistic service, this Mass was a defiant way of saying to the Reformers: "we are right and you are wrong." Today's "Tridentinists" among Catholics look upon their "separated brethren" and still say—under their breaths if not out loud —"we are right and you are wrong."

In what main ways is the 1970 Mass so different? It is, first of all, an expression of the Council's liturgical theology. "The three main features of this theology are that it is firmly anchored in what the Lord said and did at the Last Supper, that it speaks a language that goes back beyond the Council of Trent and belongs to the Fathers and liturgies of the early Christian centuries, and that it is set in a community context" (Crichton, *Christian Celebration: The Mass,* p. 51). The Pope's document authorizing the reformed Roman Missal consolidated or presupposed such interim or tentative changes that had already been made since the Council and now made these and/or others official and universally binding on Catholics. The prayers at the foot of the altar and the "last Gospel," formerly tacked on at the beginning and end of the Mass, had gone. These had never been designed as part of the actual Mass but had become attached through custom in the period before the Reformation. They were originally meant to be prayers or devotions for the celebrant's purely private use and were only added, very late in the day, to the public part of the Mass. Their mandatory inclusion as a measure of supposed "reform" by Pius V is difficult to account for. The 1970 Mass begins as of old, with the Entrance prayer immediately after which the celebrant, as chairman or "president" of the worshiping group, enters into dialogue with those present. *Together* they prepare to celebrate worthily the "sacred mysteries" that are to follow by confessing their (mentally recalled) sins to

God and to each other. Almost immediately the readings follow.
Members of the congregation other than the celebrant, both men and
women, often read the passages of scripture prescribed for that day.
Here is to be found one of the most far-reaching of all changes from
the former framework of the Mass. For centuries the scriptural content
in the Sunday (and Holiday of Obligation) readings at a Catholic
Mass was negligible. The Old Testament was almost entirely ignored.
The readings prescribed were from the same cycle of Epistles and Gospels year in, year out. For the vast majority of Mass-going Catholics
these sixty or so Epistles and Gospels represented the sum total of their
scriptural knowledge. The new readings cover an enormously wide
range from both Old and New Testaments, the chief difficulty being
the inability of older priests, in most cases, to give an adequate "homily" on the day's readings. Seminaries raised such men on a heavy diet
of "traditional" dogmatic and moral theology, served on a solid base
of medieval philosophy and occasionally washed down with the dry
wine of Canon Law, which meant their basic studies in this direction
were conventional and extremely limited. Still less had they been able,
as have the "new theologians," to explore the hitherto obscure meanings of certain Bible texts now that revolutionary discoveries in "exe-
gesis" were being made. So they preached sermons and not homilies.
Such sermons were and often still are, apart from being long and boring, wholly unrelated to the day's scriptural readings. It is comparatively unusual even now, to find an inspired or effective preacher
among Catholic priests. There had never been any proper training on
the subject at seminary. The light is dawning in many areas, but very
slowly. The "homily," to replace the sermon, is designed to help in
this direction by being integral to the "instruction" part of the Mass
(the Liturgy of the Word). It is surprising to think that the homily
was formerly regarded as an intrusion into the "priest's Mass." He
even took off such items of his vestments as the "maniple"—now discarded altogether—and sometimes his chasuble as well, before leaving
the altar to come down and preach to the people. Nowadays the content of the homily is primarily the scripture theme of the day but seen
in the context of the whole history of salvation.

There then follows the Liturgy of the Eucharist in which the centerpiece of the "Tridentine" Mass is preserved totally and intact, in that
the traditional "Roman Canon" reappears as "Eucharistic Prayer No.
1." There are, however, three other and alternative Eucharistic
prayers, the one being used most frequently at weekday Mass being the

second and most ancient (more ancient even than the Roman Canon itself.) The priest, facing the people, celebrates *with* and not *for* them. There is, here, no theological innovation. But the arrangement of the Mass makes far more obvious what was always implied by the prayer to unite all present in preparing for the most solemn part of the Mass. At this point the priest asks all to join with him and to pray "that *our* sacrifice [or: *my sacrifice and yours*] may be acceptable to God the Almighty Father." The inference was less obvious in the Latin days. "Communion" is now what the word connotes in its fullest sense and is usually preceded by the (very ancient) exchanging of a sign of peace or brotherhood as between one member of the assembly and another. Those present then communicate themselves, if they so wish, in accordance with primitive custom. (They may, alternatively, receive the Host on the tongue straight from the hand of the priest). And communion is normally received in "procession" to denote its community nature, as of all partaking together and not as isolated individuals. Many do not like the "new" customs, but such customs have got good reasons, based on sound historical precedents, and have been carefully worked out over many years by various scholars and experts. When they were embodied in Paul VI's Apostolic Constitution of 1970, *Missale Romanum,* it was clear that this was "no formal piece of writing. It breathes the air of personal conviction and concern, and if those who had objected to the new Order had read it, they would have found many of their objections answered. The suggestion heard for instance, in certain quarters that Paul VI had no right to undo what Pius V had done or, more bizarrely, that he had sold the church out to the Protestants, would never have been made" (Crichton, *Christian Celebration: The Mass,* p. 28).

CHAPTER 9

Polarization

The forces of Reform have largely lost their joy and courage.
The Church is becoming polarised.

CONCILIUM, March 1972

If more than one hundred young people in the seminary of
Ecône had not had the courage to testify to their faith in the
eternal Church, and to stand up under the fulminations of the
Vatican, the unrest of a great many Catholics would never
have surfaced. The bishops continue to deny that there is
uneasiness.

ARCHBISHOP LEFEBVRE (1976)

DESPITE EVERYTHING that has been said about the new/old, old/new
Mass, the "Tridentinists" when their arguments are kept free of politics still have a case. They can claim not without reason that the 1970
changeover was mishandled, somewhat in the same manner as had
been the publication of *Humanae Vitae* a year or so earlier. The circumstances were dissimilar but the procedure, in essence, was not.
Rome decided, in each case, to *impose* its will without forewarning itself in advance of the general sense of the faithful, that vital *sensus
fidelium* without which the Church cannot truly act as one body.
Rome's antennae in this regard are notoriously insensitive. The blindly
institutional approach tends to prevail when any major step has to be
taken. Total obedience is presumed. And it is no answer to "traditionalists" to say: "you're always going on about loyalty to the Pope,
and now you object to the form of the Mass he has decreed."

The fact is that the Church, in the past, has always relied on being
able to dictate its will by way of pronouncement from Rome. Even its
recent reforms have thus been executed. The institutional Church is a
prisoner of its own past in this respect. Division and opposition have
resulted both as of 1968 and 1970. To impose without due consultation beforehand and without sufficient explanation and pastoral zeal

afterward, is to invite extremists to take the law into their own hands. The temper of ordinary people had caught up with the Church, but the same had not happened the other way around. Though things had come to a boil inside the Church, the attempt was being made to keep the lid on as far as the outside world was concerned. There was, instead, a sideways gush in all directions. Polarization set in and rapidly built up in intensity and extent. In trying to assess this phenomenon you enter a maze. If you turn "left" you bump into the Swiss theological professor, Fr. Hans Küng. Küng represents either the most responsible or the most "dangerous" voice in the progressive Catholic camp —according to your viewpoint. He was one of the first writers to herald a very different future for the Church—even before the Council. "Renewal and reform of the Church" he had said, "are permanently necessary because the Church consists, first, of human beings, and secondly, of sinful human beings" (*The Council: Reform and Reunion*, p. 14). "It is difficult indeed to exaggerate the influence which that one book exercised throughout the Catholic Church in the early 1960s. Küng articulated openly what many Catholics had evidently believed but had been unable or reluctant to express so directly and unambiguously" (*Remaking of the Church*, p. 41). The author of this comment is Fr. Richard P. McBrien, former President of the Catholic Theological Society of America. He regards polarization as the most serious current symptom of deep-seated unrest in the Church and the failure—so far—of any genuine and abiding reform as a result of Vatican II. As he puts it, the "leadership of the Church has already committed two fundamental mistakes in judgement. First it thought it could maintain the unity of the Church more effectively by suppressing free discussion of theological and pastoral issues in the years preceding Vatican II, and, second, once it belatedly recognised the need for some institutional change, the leadership thought that it could introduce that change under entirely controlled circumstances, by imposing the conciliar reforms from above, without adequate preparation of those whom the changes would most immediately effect" (*Remaking of the Church*, p. 68). Meanwhile Küng was beginning to exert enormous influence. It is now so great that many of his ideas are no longer individually traceable directly to him. They have become common currency among the younger clergy and large sections of the laity—much to the dismay of the bishops. He sums up the findings of his most massive treatise to date, *On Being a Christian*, in a subsequent slim volume, *Signposts for the Future*. Such a summary is contained in twenty succinct theses. "(13) The emergence of the Church," says Küng, "can be explained only in the light of faith in Jesus raised to life: the Church of Jesus Christ as the community of those who have committed themselves to the cause of Jesus Christ and bear witness to it as hope for all men. (14) The essential distinction between 'Catholic' and 'Protestant' today no longer lies in particular doctrinal differences but in the diversity of basic attitudes which have developed since the Reformation but which can be overcome in their one-sidedness and integrated into a true ecumenicity. (15) The ecumenical basis of all Christian churches is the biblical profession of faith in Jesus as the Christ, as the criterion for man's relations with God and with his fellow men. This profession of faith must be translated for each new age" (*Signposts for the Future,* p. 3).

The official Church has found it hard to know how to deal with Hans Küng, though it has had comparatively little trouble in muffling the more timid and temperate voices that have been rising in protest against its pre-conciliar and even repressive attitudes. It is an ironical situation. Soon the prophets of conciliar Catholicism in action may catch on to the secret and realize that their views will only be heard if they are boldly expressed. The official efforts from Rome to silence Küng have generally, so far, proved stillborn. It was left to the German hierarchy to take some action in an area where they had strong feelings.

In early 1978 they denounced Küng in what was described by Andrew Greeley in his syndicated column as "the nadir of post-conciliar reaction" (April 8, 1978). This reaction had germinated from the Roman Synod of the previous fall at which Fr. Greeley had noticed that "a Christological witchhunt was brewing. . . ." Rome was seen to be hitting out indiscriminately at all "new theologians," and there was now a "danger that old adversaries, envious of Küng's continued popularity and influence, will use the Christological review as one more occasion to attempt to do him in, and in the process hurt their own and the Church's credibility far more than they ever can hurt Küng's effectivess." Greeley pointed out the fatal flaw in the German bishops' argument in that, unable to pin Küng down on "heresy," they presumed that he did not believe something merely because he did not specifically say that he did. Such dishonest argumentation is familiar enough from the old days. It even affects the "official" Vatican newspaper *Osservatore Romano* which Paul VI, before he became Pope, once said reported not what had actually happened but what it felt *ought* to have happened. Whatever else he is, Küng is an honest and forthright controversialist. It is almost always possible to tell exactly where he stands. An examination of his works shows that this is in a very advanced position. And yet the Church has not been able to move against him except through (unsuccessful) oblique and often underhand methods. No doubt it is still being hoped that one day he will overreach himself and lose favor with the more moderate reformers in the Church. It is true that he tries the patience of many, even of his would-be supporters, by his supreme confidence, if not cheek. Despite the undoubted backlash now operating against genuine reform in the Catholic Church, time is still on Küng's side. He is young enough to be campaigning for many years yet and at the rate of change, where change has been daringly attempted, there is reason to believe that the backlash will ultimately be defeated.

The fact remains, however, that the changes envisaged by the Council are *not* being daringly attempted. The Church in the United States, for example, though far more advanced than the Church, say, in Britain, has settled back into a comfortable jog trot of cosmetically applied reform. The wrappings are novel. How different is the product within? The visitor is struck by the unspoken collusion between the conservative churchgoers and line-holding bishops, with (in between) plenty of very busy administrative whizz kids talking reform from their spacious offices. The genuine, inspired and inspiring pastors or lay people—and there are many—are making such running as they can. But they mostly have to operate as individuals, or even individualists.

Where then, in the Church as a whole, has reform been *daringly* attempted and what has happened in such cases? The obvious answer is the Netherlands, which, a decade ago, was causing a furor in conventional Catholic circles for actually implementing at parish level the suggestions and principles of the Council. The liturgy was not just changed in a dry and formal way after the "new Mass" had been decreed. It was allowed to live. The result was startling, and, inevitably, some of the experimentation was excessive, as has also happened here and there in America. But instead of losing their nerve and calling a halt to everything they could lay their hands on, the Dutch bishops decided to watch, listen and take part where possible, rather than retreat into their houses and issue warnings and proclamations. Yes, there was certainly polarization of the Church in Holland in the late sixties and early seventies—possibly on a more intense scale than anywhere else in the European-North American Catholic Church. It has turned out, however, that the wide experimentation, particularly in the course of efforts to make parishes true communities, no longer suspect, is now accepted almost everywhere in the country. Polarization was a stage only. The Dutch Church, though far from being without problems has at least grasped the main nettle and killed the sting of novelty. The "heresy-hunters" have slunk away with empty hands though there have been woundings and casualties on all sides. But the speed with which Dutch Catholics showed understanding of what Vatican II was all about was the decisive point. Almost as soon as the Council was over the pattern for the future was beginning to emerge. It was recognized that "for every Catholic the successor of Peter is more than merely the head of a local Church so that he also has a function to fulfill with regard to all other local Churches. But it is equally obvious that this centralisation of the world church has, in its empirical form throughout the centuries, created a tension with the necessary individuality of the local Churches . . . the question we must answer is this, granted the recognition of the distinctive character of the local Churches, what must be preserved in order to remain true to the Christ-willed unity of the whole?" (Van Der Plas, *Those Dutch Catholics*, p. 149).

Holland, a small country used to assimilating foreign ideas without losing its individuality, has been working out this problem ever since. It has not been afraid of tension as a necessary element in the whole process. Most other countries have gone to excessive lengths to avoid the outward tension, but have created much more unhappiness among individual Catholics as a result. Tension, moreover, does not imply continued polarization. Rather is it its best antidote in a necessarily pluralist Church. The failure to admit the fact of pluralism is, on the other hand, a main contributor to the presence of polarization. In the United States for example, there is little real tension in the Church, barring particularly difficult outcroppings of ethnic problems. But these are usually as much sociological as religious. There *is*, however, considerable polarization, much as its presence is denied at official levels. For at such levels an agreed limit of institutional reform has been reached and this is, where necessary, imposed with as much rigor as any of the restrictive practices of the pre-Council days. The American Church, in this way, has changed surprisingly little in the last twenty years. It has merely kept pace and rendered many improvements innocuous by allowing them to become respectable. Native American genius, nevertheless, has at least broken through that inhibited

characteristic which has checked even this amount of reform from taking root in Great Britain. To "enjoy" going to Church there because it
is a gathering of God's people and not a dreary duty is still looked
upon as something daring and even shocking. This, at least on the surface, is the most notable difference between the two countries. Nevertheless, in the United States the reforming party, enjoying a decep-
tively comfortable majority, has so slowed up the pace of any radical
happenings, that ultra-progressives are beginning to feel people don't
want to be bothered any more. Soon they may give up themselves. Not
so the ultra-conservatives, or "traditionalists." Here one is dealing with
a very different sort of character.

In global terms, the chief representative of "traditionalism" is the
now fairly well known Archbishop Lefebvre who operates from Ecône
in Switzerland. The "leader" of America's "traditionalists" is, according to himself, Fr. Gommar de Pauw of Westbury, Long Island, New
York. Though both are fanatics, the two men are, in most other ways,
quite different. Lefebvre is transparently holy, a cultured man and a
persuasive orator. He is no crude propagandist and Rome takes him
very seriously. Many people meeting Lefebvre find themselves, whatever their convictions, drawn to him as a man. His main drawback (as
with de Pauw) is an almost total lack of sense of humor or irony,
though the latter happens to be the very element which gives his case
its tragicomic features. Of Pope Paul he said, "He took us further
away from the Faith. He cancelled the liturgy of the Mass." He says, of
himself, however, that he is "not a rebel" against the papacy or the
Church.

The Vatican Council ended on December 8, 1965. On that same
day, so the story goes, the "loyal" Archbishop Lefebvre sat with some
friends in a café near St. Peter's. He made it clear then and there that
he would not accept the findings of the Council at which he had been
a participant. (He was at that time Archbishop of Tulle in France.)
His reasoning was interesting. The Council, he argued was "pastoral"
rather than "dogmatic" and did not declare that disobedience to it
would carry the condemnation of "anathema." Gommar de Pauw
relies on the same argument: that unless the Church threatens you
with excommunication you are not bound to obey it. This is the language of papal absolutism and unconditional submission on the part of
all subjects. Purely "pastoral" concern doesn't count. This is really the
hub of polarization. On one side, in the final analysis, stand those who
want to go back to the old, dictatorial and anathematizing Church

outside of which there was no salvation: on the other, stand those who labor, often suffer, and feel the need to be refreshed. It is regimentation versus the free response of love. It is the anti-Protestant fortress against the "danger" of a house with many "mansions" but without bars on the windows. The "danger" (in the eyes of "traditionalists") is that the inmates may respond to faith through love rather than fear. This is actually what it boils down to though many flinch from stating it so boldly. The Lefebvre school believe that the Church has the right and duty to "make" people believe. The impossible contradiction involved is ignored.

Historical precedent, however, is largely on the side of the Archbishop. The Church had long felt that it could not risk allowing Catholics to think for themselves beyond a certain point. Duties, obligations and prohibitions had to be spelled out exactly and promulgated as laws. This was indeed the tradition of the Church as crystallized after the Reformation and still championed by "traditionalists." Lefebvre spotted straightaway that the Vatican Council had, on paper, changed this tradition and that the change could permeate almost every part of Church practice. He thus did not hesitate to say that the Council had erred and been infected by "neo-Modernism and neo-Protestantism." Protestantism remained the principal enemy: Let there be no going back on the cherished axiom "We're right and you're wrong"!

Lefebvre, however, did not move into active and militant opposition to the post-conciliar Church until after the issuing of the revised text for the Mass. The Pope, for his part, was anxious to be conciliatory and the French Archbishop was granted permission to set up his own institute and seminary at Ecône in Switzerland (1974). By 1976 he had become well known and showered with gifts by rich supporters. He soon owned several châteaux in France and wrote a book *J'Accuse le Concile*. The political aspect of his movement was readily detectable and his supporters, especially in France, were largely from the extreme right. Such survivors as there were of the *Action Française* philosophy flocked to his banners. In June Lefebvre was suspended by Pope Paul from his priestly duties for ordaining his own priests. The Pope's main fear—it became almost an obsession—was open schism. Both Lefebvre and Rome would rather do anything than risk this. It is a significant indication that underneath all the squabbles the desire for an outwardly united Church (almost at any cost) is a strong underlying desire on both sides.

Who, it may irreverently be asked, is kidding whom? Catholics at large are weary of such ducks and drakes. Is it, they ask, just part of the boring "institutional" game? Even Fr. Yves Congar, who wrote an important booklet on the whole topic, asks "Ecône and Mgr. Lefebvre again? Aren't the burning questions the Church is facing throughout the world far more important?" (*Challenge to the Church*, p. 11).

The suspension of Lefebvre by Rome was taken seriously by him and he stopped short of ordaining his own bishops—whereby a possibly schismatic church could have been perpetuated in the strictly legalistic sense so beloved of both Lefebvre and, indeed, the Vatican itself. Nevertheless, the Archbishop, though he hesitated in view of the suspension, decided to go through with a plan to make a personal appearance at Lille (August 29, 1976) and preach during Mass. He was afterward interviewed about the occasion, and other matters. The results were published in an amusing book which consists largely of long apologias for the Lefebvre position couched as "questions" to which the Archbishop gives, usually quite short, answers taking full advantage of the carefully worded "questions." Regarding Lille, the Archbishop admitted mentioning Argentina in the course of his sermon explaining that "I just simply wanted to cite the example of a Catholic country which had again taken up Christian principles, the principles of the social Kingdom of Our Lord Jesus Christ." He did not specify how military dictatorship accompanied by particularly flagrant and widespread use of torture, imprisonment without trial and judicial murder accorded with the "social Kingdom of Our Lord Jesus Christ." He merely said (artlessly?) that he "had been told that the situation there had improved and that the leaders were Catholic" (Hanu, *Vatican Encounter*, p. 69). (The *Action Française* supporters present at Lille had naturally been delighted.) The book, as a whole, is worth reading. Much of what the Archbishop says is quite true about the moral laxity of the modern world. He and Pope Paul were once more in agreement. The Archbishop cites (usually the most glaring) cases of prelates who do not do enough to fight such laxity. His deadly serious tone does not even vary when he gives his reasons for not wanting priests to discard the traditional cassock. He himself, he said, had once done this while traveling in Africa but had been told that he should stick to his cassock or the "wild tribes would otherwise take you for a Protestant minister and would be scandalized" (Hanu, *Vatican Encounter*, p. 124). The thought of the "scandal" of possibly being taken for a Protestant minister brought the Archbishop to his senses. "Since then," he records, "I have always traveled in my cassock."

On September 11, 1976, Paul VI and Mgr. Lefebvre met at the Pope's summer residence at Castel Gandolfo. The meeting was cordial but inconclusive and the archbishop continued to ordain priests in defiance of his suspension. Though his movement is far from massive it has enough supporters, particularly in France, to discomfort the Vatican. Supporters in England are estimated at only twenty-five hundred (Leonard, *Light on Archbishop Lefebvre,* p. 22), and their once militant leader, Fr. Peter Morgan, resigned from the movement in 1978. What chiefly upsets Catholics who, for theological reasons of their own, would like to see the "Tridentine" Mass once more permitted is the constant intrusion of European extreme right-wing politics into the sermons and arguments of so many of the priest-protagonists. Partly for such reasons, Fr. Gommar de Pauw, of Westbury, Long Island, will have nothing to do with Lefebvre who, he says, is "outside the Church." (There are about half a dozen Lefebvre enclaves in the United States.) De Pauw claims to be working from within the Church and to be loyal to its "true" teachings. His claim to be, in effect, "leader" of America's "traditionalists," is, however, not accepted by the other groups which are scattered here and there and are mostly divided among themselves. De Pauw's Sunday Mass at Westbury is so self-consciously "Tridentine" that it is almost a caricature. So are the legalistic arguments he puts forward in his leaflets for the invalidity of Masses other than those properly following the "traditionalist" formula. In a sermon preached on Sunday, September 17, 1978, he managed not to mention spirituality or love at all but launched a spirited attack on "the New Mass" which, he said was "a meaningless concoction of part Jewish, part Protestant and part Masonic elements." The lurid front cover of one of his propaganda booklets (*Truth and Tradition,* Spring 1975) displays a skull and crossbones over a "Warning" about "the New 'Mass'—Sacrilegious at its best. . . . Invalid at its worst. . . ." (Not surprisingly Fr. De Pauw's publication relies on long extracts from *The Wanderer,* the U.S. periodical.) Unlike Lefebvre, de Pauw sadly lacks personal magnetism or warmth. His approach is aggressive and relies on attack as the best means of defense. His autocratic stance does, on the other hand, appeal to certain people. In a favorite photograph of his, he is to be seen grimly posing outside his church like the chief warden of a prison. His services exhibit the same characteristics of regimentation common to all ultra-"Traditionalist" liturgical functions. His tortuous arguments as to why he is not "outside the Church" but why everyone in it is really "out" without knowing it (including the Pope), are almost incomprehensibly technical and not only unconvincing but ludicrous to the open-minded inquirer. His one and only tame "bishop" is dead so there is no way that he can perpetuate his movement.

Archbishop Lefebvre has, meanwhile, not yet dared to ordain any bishops. What then is the future of "Traditionalism"? De Pauw's one-man band has little relevance to the mainstream situation but Arch-bishop Lefebvre's organization could have a lot, as became evident soon after John Paul II had been elected. On November 18, 1978, Archbishop Lefebvre had an audience with the Pope reputedly lasting nearly two hours. The meeting was meant to be secret but like most "secrets" in the Vatican it was soon found out. What became known was largely what "was said to have" happened, notably that the Pope received the Archbishop with "paternal solicitude" and that the Frenchman went to the audience "in a state of humility." The reputed length of the meeting constitutes something of a record and was thought unlikely to be the last meeting between the two men. The Rome correspondent of the London paper *The Universe* (November 24, 1978) reported a series of monosyllabic answers by the Archbishop to the questions put to him;

"Are you satisfied with your meeting?"

"Oui."

"Was there accord?"

"Oui."

"Will you see the Pope again?"

"Oui."

"Can we say dialogue began?"

"Oui."

Hope thus began to flicker for the return, in an alternative and no doubt modified form, of the pre-1970 Mass. Non-extremist "Triden-tinists" may have cause for gratification, for the 1970 reform of the Mass was undeniably put through in bureaucratic and mechanical fashion often with the obvious reluctance of the bishops who did little to promote its success within a community setting. This approach was patronizing to enthusiasts and provocative to conservatives. From the ranks of the latter, without going to the lengths of "Lefebvreism," there emerged such phenomena as the "Latin Mass Society" type of organization. Yet such a title is a misnomer and has caused endless, stupid misunderstanding and has naturally misled the secular media. If not due to ignorance in the organizers it suggests disingenuousness.

For the Latin language itself was never a central issue of controversy in the liturgical changes. The "new Mass" was promulgated in Latin. This is still the official language of the Mass of the Roman Rite though the Mass is usually said in the vernacular for parochial purposes. It is the revised *structure* of the Mass which has come under fire from a wide cross section of Catholics ranging from those who mildly miss the medieval form to those who consider the revised structure to be a sellout to Protestantism. Such representatives of the latter school as Fr. de Pauw are self-contained fanatics. They live in a fantasy world of their own and are happily immune to any rational argument.

For moderate-minded "old-fashioned" Catholics, life is not so cheerful. They go, from a sense of duty, to the only form of Mass that is normally available. And it's probably true to say that if the pastors of most parishes had been consulted beforehand they would have said "no" to the "new Mass," knowing how intensely conservative their flocks are and how complicated the changes would make life for them (the pastors). Younger priests usually feel differently, as do young people. So there is, apart from anything else, a generation gap, as with so many changing mores of today's world. At the same time, most people after nearly ten years, are getting used (or reconciled) to the Mass as it now is. But this is hardly an exciting situation. In fact it is mostly very dreary and it becomes more and more obvious every day that the desire of the majority of the clergy is merely to hold things steady.

It is thus not polarization as such that has caused the great overhaul of the anatomy of the Catholic Church to falter within fifteen years of the Vatican Council. It is the retreat to the defensive middle ground which has caused the stagnation. It is felt that to budge in either direction might rock the boat and encourage extremists who, it is fondly hoped, will gradually polarize themselves out of sight.

This will not happen quickly. Men like Lefebvre have enough centers in France, Britain and the United States (twenty or thirty) to exert influence far in excess of the actual numbers of his adherents. When seen up close, however, many of his henchmen are not always likely to endear. When for his November 1978 meeting with the Pope he set out from his center at Albano outside Rome, "there was the usual drama: the green gates with sharp spikes, the only access to the Lefebvre enclave surrounded by unclimbable walls, opened and 'seminarians' who look more like bodyguards than men of prayer flanked him" (*The Universe*, November 14, 1978). The archbishop's personal appearances around Europe are often turned into political occasions by the neo-Fascist supporters present. The Lefebvre movement, in fact, is the nearest thing imaginable to a clerical "Blackshirt" party in today's Church. And yet it is not without impact in surprising quarters. Just like extreme right wing political movements it plays on fears and prejudices and thus receives a response from that hard subsurface of pious, simple conservative Catholics who, in so many places, have been brought up in the "one true Church" to love God and the Pope, and to distrust all Jews, Protestants, Freemasons and never to compromise with "God's enemies." On a smaller scale the same thing happened for a few years in England when a man called Fr. John Flanagan was alive. He operated from a parish in Sussex and was successful largely because of the disastrous timidity and "play safe" attitude of the bishops. His grossest libels went uncorrected while the hierarchy refused to make any move against him for fear of "upsetting the faith of simple Catholics." They knew, of course, that the things people had been previously taught, but had been revised at the Council, were still being clung to by some, and the terrorist tactics of Fr. Flanagan paralyzed the hierarchy into supine inaction. The Catholic Mass Media Commission (which was meant to advise and help the bishops) drew up a list of the worst of the libels being spread by Flanagan and other similar voices, but the episcopal chairman of the commission refused to report its findings to the bishops' conference. He was himself a notable reactionary and his general attitude made a mockery out of such commissions.

The general situation has greatly improved recently but the damage done in the past is irreparable. It has, in fact, helped to pave the way for Lefebvre who was quite right in maintaining that the Council had made a radical break with the past. But the failure of the "establishment" to give full support to the Council's reform enabled Lefebvre, quick to take the initiative, to make a daring "profession of faith" on November 21, 1974: "This reform," he said, "the fruit of liberalism and modernism, is completely and utterly poisoned. . . . It is accordingly impossible for any aware and faithful Catholic to adopt this reform and to submit to it any way whatever. For our salvation, the sole attitude of fidelity to the Church and to Catholic doctrine is the categorical refusal of acceptance of the reform."

No one could say he was not frank. He has, since that time, achieved surprising success in holding the official Church up to ransom. It cannot, as it would like to, simply ignore him. It has, as mentioned, retreated to the apparent safety of the middle ground, but this very retreat inhibits it from taking any decisive action in any of the pressing fields on which the peace of mind of millions of Catholics, not to mention the possible integrity of their souls, now depends. Not everyone admits that the tail is distinctly wagging the dog. The Council's declaration that man, in matters of religion, is totally free, was a major bone of contention. Lefebvre, moreover, bitterly opposes ecumenism which he equates with "Protestantism." Officially, Catholicism supports ecumenism. But what, in practice the Catholic Church seems to offer with one hand it often snatches away with the other. The same applies in different ways to the confused picture concerning Church attitudes to sex, liberation, the new theology, marriage, priesthood, the missions, status of women and even such organizational matters as policy over Church finance. There is some form of uncertainty almost everywhere and stifling frustration just at the point of apparent breakthrough. And yet the breakthrough when it comes, can only be to another stage of transition. It prompts the thought that perspectives are out of joint. The "early Church" is looked upon as some primitive, nebulous point two thousand years ago. But what if the world is still evolving two *hundred* thousand years from now? Christians must believe that their religion will still be there in some form. Impatience therefore is out of place. Is it *we*, perhaps, who are part of the groping, fumbling, "early Church"?

The Church, then, at this junction, has made—in theory—the second of only two great changes of stance in its whole history thus far. Will it have the courage, in the long run, to face up to the practical implications of this change in the midst of a world that is being transformed? To do so will mean sacrificing certain cherished beliefs held for many years—but not necessarily always. If the Church's nerve fails there is a natural danger that future historians will say: "And what were Roman Catholics doing at the end of the twentieth century? They were mostly squabbling among themselves. The world around them was changing at unprecedented and breakneck speed. An entirely new world was being born. But they didn't seem to notice." The main factor in this unprecedented change is the immensely powerful Godless religion which, under the umbrella of Marxism in its various forms, has captured the minds and hearts of hundreds of millions of people. In terms of numbers Christianity pales by comparison. What can tame and temper this gigantic force as once Christianity tamed the northern barbarians and received undreamed of strength from them in return? What can bring this new religion into double harness with the old? For the medieval ideal that only man's soul mattered is dead. Christ came to save man's body as well. What then will balance the Godless religion if not a religionless God? By this is meant a God approached through a faith which, by definition, must be free—rather than through the man-made structures which history has shown to be so imperfect. What, then, happens next?

*　*　*

John Paul II has lived more than half his life in one of the world's most Catholic countries. During that time, it has been politically dominated by this Godless religion. On October 16, 1978, he was elected Pope, the first non-Italian in the papal line for over four centuries. Many saw this as the opening of a new era for the Catholic Church.

PART THREE

READJUSTMENT

CHAPTER 10

The Papacy

The Knight (Sir Roger de Coverley) in the triumph of his
heart made several reflections on the greatness of the British
nation; as, that one Englishman could beat three Frenchmen;
that we could never be in any danger of Popery so long as we
took care of our fleet . . .

JOSEPH ADDISON

Beyond the time of Pepin the august dynasty (the Papacy)
extends, until it is lost in the twilight of fable.

THOMAS BABINGTON MACAULAY

---

1. The Pope in History

THE POPE WIELDS his theoretically immense power with the utmost
restraint and his "temporal power" is now confined to the 107 acres of
the Vatican City State. His sovereignty thereof was conceded by
Mussolini in the Lateran Treaty of 1929. It provides the last of his several titles which, in full, are as follows: "Bishop of Rome, Vicar of
Jesus Christ, Successor of the Chief of the Apostles, Supreme Pontiff of
the Universal Church, Patriarch of the West, Primate of Italy, Archbishop and Metropolitan of the Roman Province, Sovereign of the
State of Vatican City." In terms of the theology of the Church
("ecclesiology") the most important of these titles is the third, Successor of the Chief of the Apostles. But a strictly defined theology on the
subject emerged only very late in the history of the Church, namely at
the First Vatican Council of 1870. Pius IX was Pope at the time. He
may be considered to have been the last in that long line of Roman
pontiffs which began, in shadowy fashion, with Gregory the Great and
reached its climax with Pope Innocent III. This Pope was the real
founder of the Papal States, the central object of his policy having
been to ensure the papacy's independence forever by establishing a
substantial territorial state in central Italy under the Pope's direct rule.
Pius IX was the last Pope to preside over such a state. He did so as a

secular king in all but name, ruling in great majesty from the palaces
of the Vatican and the Quirinal. (Catholics themselves are no longer
at home with this worldly image of their "Holy Father.") In 1860 all
papal territory except the city of Rome itself had been lost to the Piedmontese troops of King Victor Emmanuel II. But in 1864 an agreement was reached whereby Piedmont agreed to annex no further
papal territory. In the same year the once liberally inclined Pope issued his famous—or infamous—Syllabus of Errors condemning naturalism, indifferentism, communism, socialism, liberalism and freema-
sonry. This astonishing papal directive, after making every possible
allowance for historical circumstance, turned the face of the Roman
Church for the next century firmly toward the past rather than even
the present, let alone the future. But by 1870 Italy's progress toward
unification was unstoppable despite papal intransigence. Piedmontese
troops reached Rome while the First Vatican Council was still in session. It was forced to adjourn indefinitely with important business left
unfinished, notably a decision as to the status of the Church's bishops
in relation to the Pope.

This unfinished business was tackled at the Second Vatican Council
under the head of "collegiality." By the new expression for an old
theory, the Pope was seen to be the ruler of the Church as head of a
"college" of bishops in which all were equal. The unique position of
the Pope is preserved but a former exaggeration of papal powers is
curbed. The Pope, above all, can exercise no authority in his sole
name. It is not even correct, strictly speaking, to call him without
qualification, "head of the Church." This fact is not always fully appreciated, even by many Catholics. The position, however, is set out
fairly unambiguously in scripture. Matthew holds the key. His gospel
(though not, as already mentioned, those of Mark or Luke) contains
the passage with which most Catholics are probably more familiar
than almost any other. It tells of the rock (Simon, henceforth called
Peter) on which Christ's "Church" was to be built. The passage is
emblazoned on the inner base of the great dome of St. Peter's in the
Vatican. Without it the whole history of the Roman Church would
have been different, notwithstanding the other scriptural passages
singling out Peter for a special place among Jesus' first followers. Having called Peter the "rock" and having given him "the keys of the
kingdom of heaven" Jesus, according to Matthew, then said "whatever
you bind on earth shall be bound in heaven, and whatever you loose
on earth shall be loosed in heaven" (Matt. 16:19). The authority of

the Pope is based on these words. The average Catholic has, for countless generations, been encouraged to look no further for assurance of
his membership of a body uniquely competent to preach the word of
God. "On this rock I will build my church." It was as if, from that
very moment, a structured institution had come into instant existence
with a head already called the "Pope."

Matthew alone reports Jesus as having used the word "church" for
what elsewhere in the gospels was described by a term such as "community" or some similar expression. And even Mark, who probably
wrote first and had been Peter's own companion and listener, surprisingly omitted, or thought unimportant, the reference to the "rock" and
to the singling out of Peter for special office.

Nevertheless the passage in Matthew is generally taken in Catholic
tradition to be the principal and most striking evidence of Peter's "primacy," as it eventually came to be called. The fact that the same
powers (of "binding" and "loosing") were conferred, as all three
synoptic writers agree, on the body of apostles as a whole, means, for
Catholics, that the apostles were to share such powers with Peter as
their *leader*, the implication being that Peter could not make important decisions arbitrarily or on his own.

Did Peter hand such powers of leadership on to a successor? If so
how, and who was the successor? To take the last point first, Peter's
immediate successors have long been taken to have been Linus and
Cletus (or Anacletus) though practically nothing is known for certain
of their lives. Anacletus, moreover, appears in the *Liber pontificalis*
and the Roman martyrology—the two most important early sources—
as not one but two Popes, both martyrs and each with a separate feast
day. Some light dawns with the "pontificate" of Clement I (88–96)
though even his life is obscure. Attested for certain, however, is a bitter
dispute in about the year 96, among members of the Church in
Corinth. Clement sent them a letter which has become one of the most
important documents of the early Christian community. Indeed, it was
Clement who first turned this community into something more than a
loosely knit group. If the Christian communities were to survive within
the Roman empire, they would have to adhere to an organization
which could be traced to apostolic institution. But does his letter to the
Christians of Corinth prove a supreme power of jurisdiction inherited
from Peter? It goes a long way toward doing so, at least by implication. Clement himself was alive in apostolic times. He speaks of the
martyrdom of Peter and Paul as being of "our generation." He traces

the ministry of the Church back to the inspired institution of the
apostles themselves. It was they who had not only appointed the first
"bishops and deacons" but had also made provision for the sake of the
Church's future that such offices should continue. St. Irenaeus (c.
125–c. 203) says that "this man (Clement), as he had seen the blessed
Apostles (Peter and Paul), and had been conversant with them, might
be said to have the preaching of the Apostles still echoing in his ears
and their traditions before his eyes. Clement's letter is worthy of the
Roman Church, and the influence of the imperial atmosphere is not
wanting in it. The writer clearly looks upon the discipline of the
Christian society as divinely ordered and its ministry as appointed
from above" (Whitham, *The History of the Christian Church*, p. 56).

Clement, speaking with obvious authority, emphasized the necessity
for men to follow Christian teaching, the need for a hierarchy, and,
above all for present purposes, the preeminence of the Bishop of
Rome. It is the occupation of this particular See that constitutes, in
Catholic tradition, a guarantee of inherited jurisdiction from Peter
"the first Pope." The final test, therefore, will be whether or not Peter
was himself Bishop of Rome. This cannot be proved beyond all possible doubt. Arguments for Peter's presence in Rome appear only much
later, in the writings of bishops, theologians and Church doctors. Even
the *New Catholic Encyclopedia* is cautious: "All that can be said with
certainty is that he (Peter) went to Rome and was martyred there."
This "certainty" depends on the assumption that the first of the two
epistles ascribed to Peter was definitely written by him. For this letter
was written from "Babylon," thought to be a code word for Rome.
The same Irenaeus quoted above was clearly well acquainted with the
Church of his day, and he is quite explicit about Peter's activity in
Rome. He is the first of the scholars to establish the tradition of the
Petrine episcopal ministry in Rome. Later writers are more emphatic
as the centuries proceed, but by their time the political factors
strengthening the Roman primacy had come into play with increasing
influence, climaxed by the stupendous growth through the Middle
Ages of the papacy as a political and military power.

It remains true that scripture itself furnishes, for Catholics, the best
indications that the powers conferred on Peter were not meant to die
with him. Jesus promised to be with his flock until the end of time.
Apart from the almost "done-to-death" quotation from Matthew 16,
there are several other sayings of Jesus which show that Peter was
singled out for a special and leading role. After Christ's resurrection-

ascension, Peter clearly exercised his leadership on several notable occasions. And although the Vatican Council has tried to bring the
Church back to a lost "collegiality" (so that the Pope cannot count on
universal obedience if he is observably speaking in isolation) the same
Council has nevertheless reasserted a plenitude of papal power as such.
The key phrase comes in the Council's Constitution on the Church
Lumen Gentium (art. 22): "The Pope's power of primacy over all,
both pastors and faithful, remains whole and intact. In virtue of his
office, that is, as Vicar of Christ and pastor of the whole Church, the
Roman Pontiff has full, supreme, and universal power over the
Church. And he is always free to exercise this power." This passage,
taken by itself, seemed to indicate that, despite the much vaunted
"openness" of the Second Vatican Council, there was to be no change
in emphasis whatever at the very top of the Roman Church. Hence,
such expressions, still being used, as: "the Pope is supreme head of the
Church." Such statements, however, are inaccurate, if an inevitable
carryover from a centuries' old habit of viewing the Church in purely
jurisdictional terms. Prior, sometimes exclusive, attention having been
given to Matthew 16:19, not only is Matthew 18:18 put at a discount
but Matthew 23:8–11 is easily forgotten. In the latter passage Jesus set
—or tried to set—his own disciples a different direction from the
scribes and Pharisees who loaded their spiritual leadership with a
desire for power and a fondness for certain titles. "You, however," he
said, "must not allow yourselves to be called Rabbi, since you have
only one Master, and you are all brothers. You must call no one on
earth your father, since you have only one Father, and he is in heaven.
Nor must you allow yourselves to be called teachers, for you have only
one teacher, the Christ. The greatest among you must be your servant."

The highest authority in the Church can thus never be anything but
authority among brothers. One in particular of such brothers represents the voice of the Father without having any authority of his own.
The only real authority in the Church is always the authority of
Christ, its head. Only he is master and teacher. All members of the
Church, from Pope to postulant, are brothers and sisters. Their frater-
nal unity is infinitely greater than is possible in any purely natural
community. For, apart from other bonds, they are united, whether men
or women, in a common priesthood. We have this on the authority of
St. Peter. He is of course taken to be the first "Pope," even though he
knew nothing of the title "vicar of Christ." This came to be applied to

the Bishop of Rome after the time of Gregory VII (eleventh century) but has given rise—along with the Vatican I description of the Pope as visible head of the whole Church—to a fundamental misunderstanding about the nature of the papal office. The role of *every* Christian is to be, in some way, the representative of Christ among his fellow believers. The Pope is such a representative in a supreme way when he acts as the head of the whole community of brothers; "but his representation is not qualitatively different from any other in the Church" (Müller, *The New Church,* p. 43). As for the expression "vicar of Christ" it is, in one sense, very old but, in another, comparatively new. Each of the apostles was Christ's ambassador to the rest of the brethren. He was a *vicarius* in the term, borrowed from Roman civil usage, later assumed by bishops. Later still, after Constantine's time, the Bishop of Rome would refer to himself as the *vicarius* (or successor) of Peter. Only in the early Middle Ages did the title "vicar of Christ" come to adhere to a single person, and by then that person was (as of Charlemagne's era) not the Pope, but the Emperor. Even Gregory VII did not claim it for himself as, however, did Innocent III, consolidator of the world empire-church. It may, ironically, have been the ascetic yet militant monastic theologian, St. Bernard of Clairvaux, who induced Innocent to take over the imperial medieval title of "vicar of Christ" which the Pope bears to this day.

It is a marked feature of Catholic history that when once a title, custom or jurisdictional claim has been thrown up by a certain historical situation, and comes to be an important prop of centralized Church power, it becomes, after a few centuries, sacrosanct. The Middle Ages were the most fruitful period for throwing up such phenomena.

2. *Infallibility*

When, in 1870, Italy was finally united, the Pope became a self-imposed "prisoner" in the Vatican. He refused to recognize the new state, forbade Catholics to vote at its elections and refused the generous offers made for accommodation and financial compensation. (It is difficult to resist asking, parenthetically, if the new occupant of the Quirinal Palace, King Victor Emmanuel II, was a more wicked man than Adolf Hitler. The former was and remained a devout Catholic but his political stance in depriving the Pope of his temporal power earned him excommunication which was never lifted. Hitler, born and brought up a Catholic, never formally left the Church and was never excommunicated.)

Before it had broken up in face of the approaching Italian troops, the First Vatican Council had made the most important pronouncement of all history regarding the official character of the papacy. From now on the Pope was to be considered as "infallible" when speaking in certain strictly defined circumstances. "It is a dogma divinely revealed," the Council had said, "that the Roman Pontiff when he speaks *ex cathedra,* that is when acting in the office of shepherd and teacher of all Christians, he defines, by virtue of his supreme apostolic authority, doctrine concerning faith and morals to be held by the universal Church, possesses through the divine assistance promised to him in the person of St. Peter, the infallibility with which the divine Redeemer willed his Church to be endowed in defining doctrine concerning faith and morals: and that such definitions are therefore irreformable of themselves, and not from the consent of the Church."

The passage deserves minute study in every nuance. It will be noticed that the Pope is assumed to be the teacher of *all* Christians. At the same time the infallibility with which he is invested accrues to him by virtue of its belonging to the whole Church. Most Catholics favored some such definition if only to clarify confusions and to curb exaggerated views of papal prerogatives. No one worked harder for it than the Pope himself. But there was considerable opposition, chiefly on the ground that so solemn and fateful a declaration would be "inopportune." In the first test of opinion among the Council fathers the "infallibilists" outnumbered their opponents by 500 to 136. In the United States particularly, papal infallibility had not been generally taught as revealed doctrine. Among its bishops, John England (of Charleston), John Hughes (of New York), John Purcell (of Cincinnati), and Michael Domenec (of Pittsburgh), had publicly declared that it need not be believed. And Archbishop Spalding of Peoria, Ill., warned the Prefect of the Propaganda Congregation that we would view any such definition as inopportune. The final count, however, after sixty-two Council fathers had left Rome rather than oppose the Pope to his face, contained only two votes against official acceptance of the Constitution, *Pastor Aeternus,* in which the definition was incorporated. One of these was Bishop Edward Fitzgerald of Little Rock, Arkansas.

The Secretary of the Council, the Austrian Bishop Fessler, wrote an important book on the true meaning of the infallibility decree. Pius IX himself read and approved of the work (*The True and False Infallibility of the Popes*) and had it translated into Italian. The Pope, said Fessler, had "the gift of infallibility, according to the manifest sense of the words of the definition, only as supreme teacher of truths necessary for salvation revealed by God." This put severe limits on the practical implications of papal infallibility and the Austrian bishop's interpretation was confirmed at Vatican II (*Lumen Gentium* art. 25). Nevertheless, "the crucial defect of the Constitution *Pastor Aeternus* was that it failed to explain exactly what is the nature of the Church's infallibility which the Pope is said to share. . . . Vatican II also has failed to give this vital point the full examination and clarification that it needs. Even now the doctrine of infallibility is far from being a fully defined article of Church teaching; it is still wide open to examination and clarification" (Sewell, *The Vatican Oracle*, p. 72).

At the time, however, the triumph of papalism after its long struggle so enhanced the enormous mystique of the papacy that it somehow propelled the actual holder of the office onto an unreachably high plane of supremacy over ordinary mortals. It was a victory for what has sometimes been called "triumphalist-populism." It was welcomed not only by the power-jealous curialists in Rome and the militant papalists abroad, but also—with due prompting from the parish clergy —the Catholic masses. To some of these the Pope became an almost folkloristic symbol as they voyaged, otherwise rudderless, through the world's stormy waters. The moral force of the Pope's authority, moreover, was in the end greatly strengthened by the loss of temporal power.

The 1870 view of Church and papacy was, interestingly enough, inconsistent with Catholic history as a whole. An excessively authoritarian interpretation was a novel one, and there was no attempt to back it by an unchanging tradition from times of antiquity. Perhaps most significantly of all, there was no "Tridentine" base for the Vatican I position. The Council of Trent had attempted no definition either of the Church or of papal primacy as it was impossible to reconcile the conflicting conceptions of Church and papacy that were then still operative. As mentioned above, the matter has not even now been finally clarified. Hence the view taken by the "new" Pope who, in his first public address, spoke of the need for further examination of the true nature of the "Petrine ministry."

3. Papa Wojtyla

The election to the papacy on October 16, 1978, of Poland's Cardinal Karol Wojtyla was naturally hailed as a "new era" for the people of God. Such euphoria is usual at the beginning of each fresh papacy. Various predictions were made but, even after three or four months, Pope John Paul II remained something of a mystery to Vatican-watchers. He was known to be a naturally cautious and philosophic man and his hard years in strife-torn Poland had not been such as to impel him into impetuous action. But within days of settling into the Vatican he seemed as if he had been born to the job. And "job" it is for him. His strength was soon apparent to all and was enhanced by the unhurried deliberation of his first weeks to which his approach was workmanlike. Like his predecessor, John Paul I, he had not been "crowned." The idea of the papacy as a monarchy, already dead, was now decently buried. A modern Pope has to be, like St. Paul, and in the best sense, all things to all men. There were many kinds of men waiting to catch the Polish papal eye.

There was the audience granted to Archbishop Lefebvre already mentioned. Journalists could do little more than note that whereas Pope Paul had always refused to meet the rebel Archbishop without at least one top aide present, John Paul had seen him alone. Some ob-servers went on to try to speculate on the future of the "traditionalist" movement. But they had barely had time to file their copy before the Pope, the very next day, had had another startling private meeting. This time it was with Bishop Sergio Mendez Arceo of Cuernavaca, Mexico, often accused of Marxist tendencies by other Mexican bish-ops. Then, toward the end of 1978, there was a meeting at the Vati-can of a kind which would, a few years earlier, have caused an uproar. The Pope received, once more privately, a group consisting of five members of southern African liberation movements who were prom-ised by John Paul that he would use his moral authority against racial discrimination in their countries. The men were: Oliver Tambo of the African National Congress; George Silundika and Kumbirai Kangai of the Zimbabwe Patriotic Front; and Sam Nujoma and Shapua Kaukunga of the South West African People's Organization.

According to Mr. Kaukunga, the Pope (speaking in English) "ex-pressed his deep concern about the system of apartheid and about the suppression of human rights in southern Africa. He obviously knows what is going on there and he spoke in particular about Bishop Donal Lamont who was deported from Rhodesia." One of the questions thought to have been discussed was the likely position of the Church in the now independent Zimbabwe. (*Catholic Herald* [London], December 8, 1978).

What was the Pope up to? It was not only the outside Vatican-watchers who were in the dark. Those inside the Vatican, accustomed to being in the know, were now being kept guessing as well. To some there was something ominous in the quiet power of this man who had the makings of a "loner" as far as major decisions were concerned, even if, so far, he was only building up his position by taking everyone's measure with such almost tantalizing care. The silence of the "official" Vatican was beginning to look as significant as the famous fact noted by Sherlock Holmes of the dog who did not bark in the night. The papal audience for the African "guerrilla" leaders thus had a curious result. The Vatican's various news services declined either to confirm or deny that any such meeting has taken place! What did the new Pope think of the Vatican's traditional style of reporting—or not reporting—what was going on? It so happened that, within a few days of the papal meeting with the Africans, it became clear that there was to be a major, in fact sensational, shake-up in the hitherto impervious and apparently impregnable offices of the deadpan *Osservatore Romano,* often referred to as *"The Times* of the Vatican." Certain editors of the paper were told by the Pope that their days were numbered. These men, inward-looking and ultra-conservative, had long had great power. Like governesses, they had always felt that they knew what was best for those whom they looked after. John Paul felt that the Church deserved something better of its leading newspaper than one of the dullest and least enterprising publications in the world. The Pope, on discovering accidentally about the Curial attempt to rid the *Osservatore* of one of its forward-looking directors, reacted swiftly. The paper's senior director, Valerio Volpini, emerged crestfallen from a papal audience after finding that it was he, rather than his progressive colleague, who would be looking for another job. It was then learned that the *Osservatore* would shortly be "reconstructed."

Nevertheless, there was still no question of facile "labeling" in the case of John Paul. The main tests would come during 1979, even if it had become clear early on that, at least in everyday matters, the Holy Father was very much his own master. He quickly showed his desire to walk about freely among people and firmly shook off the restraining

influence of his household and the police. They wanted him to keep a
low profile in accordance with established practice. But this has en-
tailed the Pope's still being a virtual prisoner in the Vatican. It is true
that Paul VI broke new ground in becoming a "pilgrim Pope." He
made notable trips to such places as New York, Bogotá, Jerusalem and
Bombay. But what was sensational—and unprecedented—was not that
he traveled a lot but that he traveled at all. And all his trips were for-
midably stage-managed and stiffly formal. When a Pope's visit to a certain place no longer constitutes headline-news, he will then be on his
way to being a Pope for all Christians. This is the great ecumenical
dream. There are signs that John Paul would like to make such a
thing possible, even if the actual role falls only to a successor. For there
will have to have been some profound changes in "Romanism" before
this can happen.

John Paul's first steps in loosening conventions were characteristically cautious. But, though small, they were not insignificant.
Within five weeks of taking office he had left the Vatican six times.
His tastes and ambitions gradually became known by their impromptu
and informal character. He approached people as their Pastor and
never as "Pontiff." He wished to be known by the former rather than
the latter description. He saw the bishopric of *Rome* as a real job and
not as his traditionally nominal entitlement, as if by little more than
legal fiction, to universal pastorate. He wanted to acquire personal
knowledge of the people of whom he is spiritual "overseer" as the term
"bishop" originally meant. He planned to visit at least one Roman parish every other Sunday, and was able to look back, at the beginning
of 1980, on visits to Puebla (Mexico) for CELAM III in January–
February 1979; Poland a few months later; Ireland and the United
States. In days gone by, people went to see their supreme Pastor; now
the Pastor is going to mix freely with his people all over the world.

Such activity may well seem to imply far greater delegation than
anything hitherto normal in papal circles. But this is not necessarily
the case. Such is "the System" in Roman Catholicism that delegation
and subdelegation have long been the order of the day as regards matters that have to be "referred to Rome." And, despite the theoretically
vast decentralization that has been going on since Vatican II, the apparent power of "the Pope" is still immense. What does it really mean,
however, when it is said that "the Pope has confirmed . . ." "the Pope
has decided . . ." "the Pope has refused . . . ," "the Pope has af-

firmed . . . ," etc. It usually means that the relevant Vatican government (or "Curial") department, has "in the Pope's name," acted in
the manner described. These departments are mostly called "Congregations" and deal on a worldwide scale with such matters as the
appointment of bishops; conduct of priests; ecumenism; liturgical regulations; education; evangelization; orthodox teaching, etc. The 1967
"reform" of the Curia was largely a mere change of names. The
department supervising orthodox teaching, the Congregation for the
Doctrine of the Faith, was, for example, formerly called the Holy
Office, and is the modern successor of the Inquisition.

Each congregation is headed by a cardinal but the day-to-day work
is attended to by the ecclesiastical "civil servants." The cardinals who
head the departments also serve on other congregations. The result is
an interlocking directorate of extremely powerful men. It is they who
run the Church with the Pope as "president." Each diocese reproduces
this pattern in microcosm. This is the System, and local clergy "play"
it for all it is worth as politicians, trade unionists, industrialists, etc.,
"play the system" in Western, capitalist countries. But "the System," in
each case, can only last as long as the world's spiritual hunger, on the
one hand, and physical hunger, on the other, do not actively and dramatically demand something more satisfying for their respective needs.

Let us assume, as is indeed probable, that the Church does no more
for the moment than pursue a course of moderate reform. It has, of
course, no representative legislative arm; but increased collegiality
which this Pope wishes to promote, will considerably augment the representative nature of Church government. One instrument for such increase will be the giving of greater weight to a more frequently meeting synod of the world's bishops. All of this could and, eventually,
perhaps will, free the Pope to exercise more effective "charismatic"
and inspirational power. As a pastoral and pilgrim figurehead he could
well wield considerably more influence in the world than as a mere
chief executive, however efficient. In the course of 1979 the signs
began to emerge that John Paul II has the kind of personality to fill
the prophetic rather than the pontifical role. If, at first, he seemed to
do little more than promise to carry forward the major reforms and
policy directions of the post-conciliar Church, he made the vital and
specific pledge to try and make explicit what had been left only implicit by Vatican II. It is in this regard that history will probably see
the main difference between Paul VI and John Paul II. The former
implemented the Council decrees in theory; the latter claims to desire

their implementation in practice. If he succeeds, it will mean that the Catholic Church no longer intends to operate in lofty isolation from the world revolution, if and when this phenomenon becomes an inescapable reality. It would also mean that the Church was beginning to think in terms of a world in total, almost apocalyptic, transformation. But that moment is not yet. Reform in the Church is still essentially "churchy." The "System" remains intact. It is bound to be as long as priests are confined to one sex and set aside as a professional caste. The Church, in such circumstances, is prevented from becoming a movement; it remains an organization. Many say this is essential, even if the Church as a more freewheeling movement, traveling where the Spirit directed it, might initially have a greater impact on a world obviously craving "something" in the way of a missing ingredient. But would the impact last after the novelty and early enthusiasm had begun to fade? If not, it might then be too late for the Church to reconstitute itself as a tightly knit and highly disciplined body. This is the heart of the dilemma.

It is a dilemma, however, which does not unduly depress John Paul, the philosopher pastor. While Pope Paul put great store by the integral humanism and essential goodness of man, John Paul adds the dimension of his own instinctive sense of balance. He sees a corresponding need for balance in the norms that are set up to regulate moral behavior, and shown himself to be far less rigorous than Pope Paul. He has, for example, heavily stressed the importance of individual conscience on the question of contraception. But this does not portend (or, in the Pope's eyes, make necessary) any actual repeal of *Humanae Vitae*. The Pope's views on the matter had been clarified in a paper he read to a congress held at Milan in June 1978, under the auspices of the International Center for Family Study. It was one of three congresses called to commemorate the tenth anniversary of *Humanae Vitae*. The paper was published in December 1978 under the title of "Fruitful and Responsible Love." He quoted extensively from the Vatican Council's document on the Church in the Modern World (*Gaudium et Spes*) which was pastoral and descriptive in tone and avoided the synthetical approach of *Humanae Vitae*. He explained that responsible parenthood, which implies responsibility for life, is rooted in responsibility for love. He took the meaning of love in marriage as his very starting point: "It is necessary to throw into still greater relief the basic dimension of the responsibility which husband and wife take upon themselves, the responsibility for their love itself." Parenthood, he said, belonged to this love: "conjugal love is fulfilled by parent-hood." Remarking—almost as an aside—that contraception was essen-tially opposed to love and parenthood, his main stress was put much more strongly on conscience than it had been in *Humanae Vitae*. Con-science, he declared, was the whole pivot of the matter. Conscience alone, in the privacy of marital intimacy, was the judge. Conscience alone drew out and balanced the whole delicate variety of duties im-plied in the life-acts of spouses. But the cardinal did not, in so many words, gainsay the official ruling of Paul VI. The latter's standards, however idealistic, remain the norm to be constantly striven for.

Among others addressing the June congress in Milan had been Dr. Jack Dominian, the consultant psychiatrist and Catholic writer on marriage quoted below in Chapter 15, and Fr. Arthur McCormack, the Vatican expert on population. The former remarked that there was very little in Cardinal Wojtyla's speech about birth control and contraception, but a great deal about love, person and the respon-sibility of love between people. "I feel," he said, "that this is precisely the order of priority in the tasks facing the Church today." Such tasks clearly involve people en masse as well as individuals. Yet another mo-tive for revolution is the injustice brought about by the constant threat of population explosion, in which the poor will become poorer while the rich can take steps to avoid or mitigate any hardship to themselves. Shortly before the publication of the Pope's words on "Fruitful and Responsible Love," Fr. McCormack was in London for a conference on trends and developments in world population. Within this context, Fr. McCormack said that Catholics were split into five main groups over the birth control ruling.

There were those, he said, who believed there had to be strict ob-servance using only natural methods of birth control. Secondly, there were those—particularly clergy, including bishops—who accepted the law but allowed exceptions in hard cases where it seemed morally im-possible for couples to observe it. Thirdly, there were those who stayed in the Church but ignored the ban. Fourthly, there were those who left the Church because they felt they could not reconcile the use of con-traceptives with their religion. Lastly, there were the intellectuals and theologians who stayed in the Church but argued against the en-cyclical *Humanae Vitae*. They now felt freer than before to express their views. Fr. McCormack said that although there was an official Vatican policy on birth control, many bishops, cardinals and clergy in developing countries tried to enable people not to be unduly harassed by the teachings of *Humanae Vitae* when they are in a very difficult situation. He said this pastoral approach was now quite widely accepted. He quoted the case of a man in an area of high unemployment in the Philippines, who had to go to work in a factory in Manila and who got home to see his wife and family only once or twice a month. If his wife says it is the wrong time to make love the marriage won't survive. Some would say in this context that the use of contraceptives is the lesser of two evils—its use to prevent the evil of a breakup of the marriage. "I disagree," he said. "It is choosing the greater good, the harmony of married life. In certain circumstances people should not have any more children and they would not be wrong to use a contraceptive."

He summed up his own position by saying: "No married couple who have serious reasons to limit their family and cannot do so through natural methods should be inhibited from limiting their family by contraception. If the couple cannot keep to the teaching because of concrete circumstances, then it cannot be wrong for them to use an effective means."

Such opinions, however, no matter how cogently and eloquently expressed, do not solve the problems of those millions of Catholics brought up to believe that when the Pope has spoken authoritatively on a matter of "faith or morals," for them there is no more to be said. Such Catholics feel they must obey.* Will this dilemma ever be solved? Can "collegiality" help? If a representative section of responsible churchmen give a definite lead, will the "new Pope" feel impelled to make, *as Pope,* an unequivocal and definitive statement on the whole subject? The test could come in 1980 when representative bishops from all over the world will meet in Rome for their sixth meeting as a synod to advise their supreme Pastor on behalf of the flocks whom they represent. And the theme of the synod will be "the duties of the Christian family in the contemporary world."

Many think, meanwhile, that before the end of the century, the Pope will convene another ecumenical council. It could become Vatican III, or it could even be held elsewhere than in Rome. Its discus-

---

* Objectively speaking, a distinction must be made as to the kind of obedience expected in face of "ex cathedra" (infallible) pronouncements, as opposed to encyclicals. It was quite clearly indicated that *Humanae Vitae* was not a definitive pronouncement, but it did carry the seal of the Church's ordinary *magisterium* or teaching office.

sions will inevitably go beyond the question of Renewal as it affects individuals and the Church. The theme of the twenty-second ecumenical
Council of the Universal Church could well be concerned with renew-
ing the whole face of the earth. It was this task that the Spirit-filled
Church was originally called upon to perform.

*   *   *

The fact remains that "Papa Wojtyla"—as he has become widely
called—is basically very conservative, though this fact, in itself, pro-
duces a paradox. The fresh air—and not just produced because the
Pope himself is a fresh air fiend—that started blowing through the
Vatican was inevitable with the arrival of a comparatively young man.
He has brought almost boyish enthusiasm to his task and is known to
sing at his desk if work is going well. But just as one or other section in
the Church began to think they had got him "taped" away his image
escaped again. Sometimes it was the Pope himself who was on a faulty
wave length. He told (early 1979) a group of women religious that
they must remain identifiable as nuns. This was probably meant to be
a suggestion that they should no longer shed their habits even when
more appropriate dress seemed desirable. To effect this, as one American nun put it, would be trying to get the toothpaste back into the
tube. But will John Paul II accept that even Popes cannot do that?

Changes at the top in the Curia, moreover, do not necessarily mean
drastic changes of policy. Theologically the Pope is likely to make few
important new initiatives. Despite his views on the importance of conscience there will, as mentioned, be no change of official ruling on
Humanae Vitae. Nor will there be on abortion, marriage and its
indissolubility or confession and absolution. Women will not be admitted to the priestly ministry: John Paul has only spoken of the need of
more "men" for this role.

At the same time, the Pope, in most ways, belies the archetypal conservative image. His vitality is apparent in his brisk daily routine. It is
not a crushing sixteen-hour day spent mostly at his desk as has often
been the papal habit. It is a sensible twelve-hour working day, with
one hour for exercise and two for prayer and meditation. He has
changed such habits little if at all since coming from Poland. He
brought with him his Polish secretary and skiing companion Don
Stanislau Dziwisz and his Polish nuns to look after him. They know he
likes fried ham and sausages for breakfast. Such things matter at the
beginning of a hard, driving day. Then there is Polish *bortsch* to look

forward to at lunch time; but no guests in the middle of the day, or rarely so. Guests come, if at all, for dinner. On such occasions Papa Wojtyla sits alone on one side of an eight-foot table. His two secretaries—the second is the same Irishman, Fr. John Magee, who was secretary to Popes Paul VI and John Paul I—sit at either end while the two or three guests sit opposite the Pope. If there are more, the secretaries dine elsewhere. No one ever sits next to the Pope at the dinner table.

To begin with, the new Pope has begun to stand out as something of a giant among men. But to adapt the gospel passage about "him to whom much has been given," it may be said that of John Paul almost too much will be expected. The Church and the world have no right to expect too much of any one man.

Rather has it become clear that the People of God, however much inspired by their broad-shouldered Supreme Pastor, must look more than ever to themselves as they look toward the future. For *they*—"the Church"—are no longer meant to be the supine subjects of arbitrary authority, the passive spectators of an unshared liturgy, or the impotent victims of social injustice with no hope for betterment until the afterlife. They, the People of God, have a responsible part to play in understanding and influencing theology, morality, ecumenism, Church administrative policy, and many other matters.

CHAPTER 11

The New Theology

The best way to hide the meaning of what anyone is saying is
to wrap it up in verbose and technical language. Most books
of theology are written in technical language. Some are
verbose as well.

HUBERT RICHARDS

Christ himself, innocent though he was, had died once for
sins, died for the guilty, to lead us to God. In the *body* he
was put to death, in the *spirit* he was raised to life, and in
the spirit he went to preach to the spirits in prison.

I PETER 3:18–19

EVERY ANATOMY is made up of mind as well as body. The mind of the
Catholic Church is its theology. Such theology has, since the Council,
come to be subdivided into "old" and "new." The old theology started
"from above" with a largely abstract theory of God which was duly
applied to men. But it has become of recent years less and less successful in its application. It has increasingly failed to reach man in his actual state and spiritual condition today. The new theology comes to
complement more than to correct the old theology. It does not attempt
to drag the old and usually more abstract, impersonal theories down
closer to man—and in so doing disfigure them. It makes a new beginning by starting "from below" with man's existential needs viewed in a
spiritual but personalist light. Though it helps to make traditional theology more comprehensible to modern man it has nothing in common
with "traditionalism." Exponents of the latter usually condemn the
"new theologians" as heretics who "deny" the incarnation, the divinity
of Christ, the resurrection, and many other sacrosanct dogmas. Unfortunately many conservative and conventional Catholics heed such accusations in the belief that to do so is more "safe." But they pay heavily
for such "safety." They are often, especially the older generation,
thereby blinded to the religious motivations of their own children and

grandchildren. The new theology, rightly understood, represents a safety net, a bridge between the traditional and the modern, even though, like all schools of theology, it is prone to error and sometimes exaggeration. New theology is a vast subject whose importance can only, here, be hinted at by the offering of two or three examples of its operation.

It is first of all "new" because, as already mentioned, it begins its explorations within the same spectrum as the "old" but starts from the opposite end. The two thrusts of inquiry are directed toward an area of mystery the inner core of which belongs to God alone and into which no school of theology has ever claimed to take the finite mind beyond a certain point. Both directions of thrust, however, "from above" and "from below" are vital if the human mind is to be enabled to approach the mystery in question with any kind of balance. And obviously there always has been, and has always had to be, a theology which was "new" in relation to its own time, since man's intellect was always making new discoveries and finding fresh ways to tackle old problems. What happened after the Council of Trent was, if anything, far more disturbing to contemporaries than the discussions of today. Man's will, Trent asserted, was wholly free. But it was also essential Catholic doctrine that man can only be led to salvation by God's merciful promptings within him—amounting to a form of predestination. Herein lay total contradiction. To make man wholly "free" meant that there must be areas which the omnipotent God could not control. The psychological dominion of man's necessarily unprompted action seemed to be in mortal conflict with the inescapable concept of the sovereign efficacy of God's grace. The controversy raged for years. The Dominican-Jesuit conflict was bitter. Both sides could claim to be right since both in logic were. The question has never been solved but the Church has come to tolerate the conflict "since faith is more concerned with revealed realities than theological explanations" (*New Catholic Encyclopedia*, I, 94). This notable precedent is a consoling demonstration that today, as much as ever, faith can be helped rather than hindered by new theological explanations even if they have started from the other end of the trail you yourself have been following for many years. They thus meet you head on. Sometimes, when you are therefore taken unawares, the first impact can be a shock.

How can the bare essence of the old and new theologies be summarized? In starting "from above" the old or traditional kind centers itself on a philosophic notion of God and builds up a picture of the at-

tributes which "necessarily" belong to him, such as omnipotence, om-
niscience and the like. The reality of such a God can even, it is
claimed, be proved since the very existence of matter implies, in the
metaphysical order, a victory over nothingness which can come about
only through the agency of an infinite being. The next step is to insist
on the literal truth of scripture and the intrinsic reasonableness in
God, man's creator, wanting to send a redeemer to save man from the
consequences of his free choice in the direction of evil (which God
could not have created because God is all-good). This redeemer had to
make an infinite act of reparation for a course of human conduct that
was of infinite evil. So this redeemer must himself have been God, who
came on earth in the person of Jesus Christ. There followed a Church
which, being divine in origin, had full authority to lay down the law.
All men had to follow this law in order to be saved. Their response to
the law must be through faith. Such faith can be cultivated by reason
and an open mind but consists, above all, in accepting the authority of
the Church. Once grasped, the tenets of this faith lead the believer
necessarily back to the God first proposed from which all else inevitably follows.

The summary is brutally short but it follows the same pattern as the
leaflets once familiar in Catholic schools and other circles outlining the
steps whereby any "reasonable man" of goodwill could not fail to be
led to the God of Catholicism. Such an approach, going by the general
name of apologetics, fell out of favor with the realization that its
presuppositions were being nullified by the psychological and other advances of man, and above all by man's new awareness of himself.

This awareness has finally worked its way into every department of
Catholic theological thinking, but only after many painful vicissitudes
and the radical "air-clearing" operations of the Vatican Council. Self-
awareness is the looking glass where man sees himself with maximum
clarity. But as what? Not as an essence, a nature, a species, a being,
nor even—at least not at first sight—a creature. He sees himself as a
person. This reflects itself very strongly in the new theology, the initial
approach to which is first and foremost *personal*. "It is not interested
in presenting a systematic elaboration of religious truth, but in bringing home what religion means for man" (O'Connell, *Keeping Your
Balance in the Modern Church*, p. 30). It is not interested in what
God means in a purely abstract sense which, in turn, will determine
what role human beings must play. The latter must be allowed their
natural role and to perceive, through this, what God's significance is.

In other words it stresses the subjective element in recognizing God—primarily as an agent/object of love—rather than the objective element which tends to reduce God to something like a geometrical theorem. It may sometimes realize itself more through the heart than through the head, but it is far from being non-intellectual. It relies heavily on scientific method when examining, for example, the nuances of scripture. It is at the same time *existential* in relating religion to man's everyday experience. It sees the Church not primarily as a law-giving authority which must be blindly obeyed, but as the mysterious vehicle of God's love for his people and his desire to bring them to his kingdom. Each man, according to the new theology, is supremely free and must always give a fully free—and therefore fully responsible—reaction to the demands of duty, faith and, above all, love. He seeks a truly personal relationship with a Jesus whom he desires to know, love and understand—a Jesus who is not obscured by unintelligible titles or attributes that constitute a barrier between himself and other men. For Jesus, also, was a human being, and only as such can he inspire others and help them to overcome their weaknesses. This leads directly on to the most important of all questions for Christians, the question which has often been "answered" in Christian history, but never with finality. Who exactly was Jesus? The particular theological field which attempts to formulate answers to this question is called Christology. It is one of the best—because one of the most testing—examples that can be given of the different approaches of the old and new theologies. And the question asked—"Who is Jesus?"—even if "settled" or academic for elderly Catholics—is unsettled but vital for young ones. If both knew more about the latest arguments, all would gain.

Advance in this field has been extraordinarily rapid over the last ten years. Classic Christology, molded for a millennium and more by the creeds and councils of earlier Christianity, has been overtaken by this advance. If its full reasoning is not followed there are bound to be shocks. The situation is made worse by warnings about "quasi-heretical" writers whose "demythologizing" has undermined the belief of simple Catholics so that even the divinity of Christ is no longer sacrosanct. "Simple Catholics," in turn, have become so conditioned that many will register a predictably unfavorable reaction to names such as Moltmann, Pannenberg, Kásper, Raymond Brown, Schillebeeckx, and even Karl Rahner. Such warnings are dishonest if the arguments of the "new" men remain unmet on their own ground. The

stonewall approach of referring everything back to "authority" begs
the question. This was the approach tried by the Popes toward Luther
and other Reformers—with disastrous consequences.

Who then, for modern man, is Jesus? The question implies an entirely fresh approach, a personal quest for Jesus primarily through the
scriptures. The quest is exciting for it results in the dawning of a new
and very much deeper appreciation of Jesus than anything previously
possible. It approximates, in fact, to the ultimate experience of the
apostles themselves. It was not until after the resurrection that they
began to take in the reality of who Jesus was and what the significance
of his life had been. Ironically, the disciples took the approach of what
we now call the "new" theology since they started "from below"; from
themselves; from the standpoint of man. They could not start from a
settled notion of God since they had so little on which to go. If, which
to this day is doubtful, Jesus had even made an unambiguous claim
to the possession of divinity, the apostles had not understood it. He
was ever the "Son of God," whose Father was greater than he. But
after the resurrection they began to understand more.

Christians, all these years later, can still share their experience. For
"the resurrection reveals to us the true face of God and provides the
starting point for a Christology: it accounts for the dynamism of
Christian existence and therefore constitutes the foundation for a theology of hope and for the mission of the Church" (Geffre, *A New Age
in Theology*, p. 98). The same author goes on to stress the in-
separability of the revelation of God and the revelation of the meaning
of history. This represents a tremendous and—to many—a welcome
and liberating step forward from the static, allegedly changeless,
rigidly objective and necessarily theoretical basis of the old theology.
New theology to repeat oneself, does not cancel or condemn this
school; it adds to it the missing dynamic, flexible, subjective and concrete elements by its determinedly anthropological approach.

Was Jesus, then, God? People naturally want to get to the heart of
the matter and have long been fed up with the arcane jargon of professional and private disputes among theologians. (The latter, aware
of vulnerability, ensure themselves against damage by warning the
faithful against the clumsiness of amateurs and "popularizers.") The
fact remains that Catholics, if they are interested at all, want to penetrate more fully into the "sacred mysteries" that are celebrated daily in
their churches. The new theology here makes perhaps its most positive

contribution. It accepts the divine Sonship of Jesus without trying to explain in human terms the relationship between Jesus and God. For no such explanation is possible. It can only be left in the realm of God's own mystery. (The same applies to the insoluble conundrum posed by free man's supposed "subjection" through grace to the sovereignty of God's total power.) The same even applies to the Eucharist for we must be content to believe that Jesus is really present under the appearances of bread and wine without insisting on a completely satisfactory intellectual explanation of how, in human terms, this can possibly happen. Again, there is none. The new theology, thus, does not trespass into the realm of mystery known only to God. For this reason, the Church's classic definition of Christ's relationship to God no longer provides a coherent explanation for all Catholics. The definition was given by the fifth-century Council of Chalcedon which found that the Nicene formula ("Of one substance with the Father") had not proved conclusive. Jesus Christ, according to Chalcedon, was truly God and truly man. This however, it was explained, did not involve two persons, but rather, two "natures" in one "person." The word "person" was used in the theological sense then prevailing. This meant something entirely abstract compared with the modern interpretation of a "person." It meant an essence or substance, or in Greek (transliterated) a "hypostasis." Hence the catechism phrases, learned (but not necessarily understood) by Catholic children forty years ago: the Mother of Jesus *is* "the Immaculate Conception"; Christ is God because of "the hypostatic union." Today most Christians including Catholics want to encounter a Jesus they can understand enough to love more deeply.

Chalcedon was the Church's last official word on the subject of the Trinity of three "persons" in one God. It is therefore important to see how traditional Catholic theology has interpreted its message. It has done so by stressing that Christ, though he had a human nature, was not really a human person, but a "divine person." Indeed, any other interpretation would have resulted in the necessity of believing that God's "godness" had somehow to be limited, or that Christ's humanness had somehow to be infinite, in order that two incompatible and distinct "persons" should in fact be identical. This would have resulted in a proposition as impossible as imagining a square circle. So Jesus, in the tradition handed down from Chalcedon until recent times, is said to have assumed a human nature without assuming a human personality. New theologians, however, such as Schoonenberg, ask how Christ can be completely human if he is not a human person. And the concerned and involved Catholic of today finds difficulty in devoting his life and adoration to someone as unreal as an "historical" human being who was not a real human person. The recurring note of unreality is frustrating to him. He is willing to allow the full mystery of the God-Jesus relationship to suffuse his faith, but he seeks no less of a personal relationship with the Jesus who really agonized and bled for him than with his own brothers, sisters and friends here and now. The medieval mind was satisfied, even mesmerized, by the notion of a God "out there," unapproachable except through sacral language and symbolic gesture, perceptible if at all only through almost impenetrable veils. For Jesus, the Lord, was in no way a person like ordinary humans. But "modern" thought latches onto self-awareness, freedom and —in a particular way—intersubjectivity as key characteristics of personhood." We become persons in dealing with other persons, sharing a common language and experiencing a common history. Human persons exist only in the plural. We repeat the traditional word ('person') at our peril. It has changed its meaning" (O'Collins, *What Are They Saying about Jesus?* p. 8).

There is another dimension to the new theology—the scriptural one. The scriptural awakening of the last few decades has opened up for Catholic scholars horizons undreamed of in the past. The medieval heritage hung heavy, even right up to and into this century. For the exegetes, or scripture scholars, of the Middle Ages endlessly rehearsed the old theories about passages in the Bible but made a minimum of direct reference to scripture itself. For the most part, they were themselves ignorant of the original languages. They dealt only with the Latin ("Vulgate") text and added their own commentaries (in scholastic Latin). The Vulgate is the official edition for the Latin Church. The Council of Trent (in its scripture decree *Insuper*) declared that "precisely the ancient and widely current (*Vulgata*) edition that has been approved by long use within the Church for so many centuries . . . should be held as authentic." No one, for many years afterward was ever allowed to impugn such authenticity. The scriptures were considered inherently and even literally true. What happened if scholars—particularly in the post-Darwinian age—had serious doubts about the supposed inerrancy of scripture? They had to cultivate "docility" in deferring to the official judgment of the Church. But what if an undoubted and glaring error was discovered?

One particular case history is instructive since it concerns a passage that had had an important bearing on the development of Christology.

It is, if taken at face value, a striking vindication from scripture itself of the Chalcedonian version of the Trinitarian relationships. It occurs in the first Epistle of John in the "Clementine-Vulgate" (i.e. official) version of the Bible for Catholics of the Latin rite. The passage refers (I John 5:7–8) to "the three witnesses in heaven: the Father, the Word and the Spirit, and these three are one." With such a passage in scripture itself how could there ever again be any dispute about the Trinity? The passage did indeed help to hold the line for over a thousand years. But the passage turned out never to have been in scripture at all. It could not be found in any of the earliest (Greek) manuscripts and was not quoted by any of the early Fathers of the East in their Christological writings, though its existence would have been an invaluable boon to their arguments. It is now almost universally agreed to have been a gloss inserted in scripture much later on. It was liberally employed from the fifth century onward (the century of Chalcedon) to confirm the Church's official teaching on the Trinity. What remains disturbing is not just the mistake itself. It would be too technical to mention here were it not for the attitude of the Pontifical Biblical Commission which remained unchanged long after the mistake had become glaringly obvious to scholars. The age-old fear of loss of face was here at work. This commission—the Vatican's official watchdog on scripture—refused even as late as 1897 to admit the inauthenticity of the interpolated phrase—which has come to be known as the "Johannine Comma." It was only in 1927 that the Commission finally relented and eased up on its previously inquisitorial blocking of all scholarly Catholic inquiry into the validity of disputed scriptural texts. (The very fact that the controversy had been such a silly one renders all the more anachronistic the refusal of the Pontifical Commission to give way.)

Finally, in 1964, the commission changed its stance on another vital front. It admitted, in an important "Instruction," that the Gospels were not necessarily accounts of the words of Jesus but were based on the writers' memories of such words and the traditions handed down to them between the time of Jesus himself and the time the Gospels were written. The interval is thought to have been about thirty years in the case of the first Gospel to be compiled (Mark) and about sixty in the case of the last (John).

This encouraged Catholic scholars to explore more adventurously for the truth whereby believers could be made free. Some have overreached themselves and conservatives are rightly skeptical of certain of their findings. Most have undertaken their task with due caution. They realize that the "Johannine Comma" was an exceptional case and that most rereadings of scripture have less sensational results. After patient "form criticism," comparing of manuscripts, stripping down the New Testament "parlimpsest" to the sources nearest to Jesus, and much other laborious work, they often end by producing little more than a different emphasis on accepted positions. But this is enough. Modern scholars, including the new theologians, are not iconoclasts. It will be seen, in fact, in the last example of their work to be given, that "demythologizing" is not an objective. If anything, "remythologizing" would be a more apt word to use. This can be seen most clearly in the "new" findings—revolutionary to some, intensely spiritual, comforting and free of preoccupation with merely physical life to others—about Jesus' resurrection.

The resurrection, as already seen, is the starting point for Christology. We cannot know the most important things about Jesus without as clear an idea as is humanly attainable of what really happened at the resurrection. Again the different schools of theology, old and new, start from different ends of the pole. But adherents of each believe, without doubt, in the resurrection itself. The old theology, however, has, for many people, produced an image of bodily resurrection in which Christ rose of his own power to become a revivified corpse walking round the earth once more as if he had never died at all. (It does not *necessarily* presuppose any such thing, but has unquestionably produced such a belief among those who look no further.) The new theology sees Jesus as being raised by his Father; and raised not to go back to the old, physical and mortal life but to an entirely new life, the same life to which we will all be raised (as Christians believe) on the last day. Resurrection, in other words, means not just the raising of one particular man, though this was the all-important "first fruits." Resurrection betokens the victory over death (the death of sin) for all men. Jesus, then, "was raised by God as an objective echo to the whisper of a hope in the human heart that craves unending and fulfilled existence. Only in the splendour of his unique risen life does his pre-Easter personality draw our attention. The apostle Paul always emphasised the centrality of the resurrection in Christian faith, but the thinking of future centuries lost sight of its importance" (McGinn, *Doctrines Do Grow*, p. 59).

What happened to the original Pauline message? Because of such official interpretations as were given, it tended, in the realm of popular piety, to be accepted as the supposed account of a purely physical event brought about as if by magic. The supernatural element was all but lost on many. People were not conscious of this fact because, for a surprisingly long time, Christians—Catholics especially—did not think of questioning the account handed on to them of an empty tomb (not even mentioned by Paul) as being explainable only by the fact that the man who had been buried in it had, after once more walking about as if nothing had happened, finally ascended into heaven on the "fortieth day." Now, starting "from below," Christians, Catholics included, want to come nearer to the truth than the rather simplistic conclusions that fail to take account of the self-contradictory gospel accounts.

A new sort of "myth" is thus required, bearing in mind that myths are not legends but symbols in which are expressed insights so deep that ordinary narrative or pedestrian words cannot in any way do them justice. It is in this key sense that the new theology can be said to be a "remythologizing" of scripture. And myth is more important in describing the significance of the resurrection than mundane facts that conflict with each other.

In what way are the gospel accounts contradictory as far as pure "reported" fact is concerned? The resurrection appearances occurred, for Luke in Jerusalem, for Matthew in Galilee; it was the once-for-all happening of one day only (Luke) or protracted over several weeks (John). In Matthew there is no ascension. Rather must Jesus be presumed to have remained forever, but invisibly, with the Church. John, without actually describing the ascension, equates it with resurrection, since he sees death, resurrection and ascension as part of a single spiritual movement. In Luke, again, all resurrection happenings, including the ascension, occur, even though in different places far away from each other, all on the same day. It is only in the Acts of the Apostles that an actual description of the ascension is finally given and a definite date (fortieth day) specified.*

"These contradictions make us realise that there is no question of history; all the details of the ascension 'narratives' are symbolic. The ascension is not a fact but a mystery that can be expressed as follows: Christ passed—whole and entire—from the human world to the divine world" (Guerin, *I Believe,* p. 61). But this "passing" was made known by Jesus in a series of apparitions to those who believed in him. Their

---

* If Luke was the author of the Acts, it is difficult to account for the discrepancy with his own earlier account of the sequence of events.

encounter with him as risen from the dead was an encounter of faith. It was through the eyes of faith that they saw him. To those without faith he was invisible. Although the New Testament writers stress the reality of Jesus's body as seen, and even touched, by them in the course of his apparitions, they did not shrink from recording that he passed through walls, materialized as if from nowhere, and (at Emmaus) suddenly disappeared into thin air. Such apparitions were real but yet —and this defies explanation—quite different from the human encounters of everyday life. From the evangelists' accounts of resurrection experience it is clear that "the awe which surrounds the experience, the repeated initial failure to recognise the Lord, and perhaps most clearly of all, John's careful teaching that an affinity in faith and love is the prerequisite of recognising the risen Lord, all these show that the experience of meeting the risen Christ cannot simply be equated with our day-to-day familiar associates" (Wansbrough, *Risen from the Dead,* p. 104).

That author goes on to show how, by his resurrection, Jesus has passed out of history but not out of the consciousness of those intimate friends who, up until then, had not even begun to grasp the full import of his work and his unique manifestation on earth of God himself. Compared to this message, moreover, any factual contradictions in the narratives are "minor." What "the gospel writers are trying to express is precisely this meeting between the historical and the transhistorical, the disciples within history and Jesus already beyond it. This accounts for the stutterings and for the minor contradictions between the narratives; what they try to express is that he remains himself, but is free from all the limitations of our world" (*ibid.,* p. 107).

As a result of such findings and researches—and the attempt to compress countless volumes into a short chapter is extremely hazardous —today's Catholics have been given a wider and more spiritual view of who Jesus was and how he showed the significance of his whole life by means of his resurrection. They have been relieved, at the same time, of the burden of believing in something which has so often been presented as Christ's final and decisive conjuring trick. "Our English translations of the New Testament have misled us here. They have accustomed us to thinking in terms of a 'rising' from the dead, and suggested the image of Jesus reanimating his own corpse. But the word normally used in the original text is not the active verb 'to rise' it is the passive verb 'to be raised.' The New Testament does not state that Jesus rose, but that he was raised. The resurrection is a statement about God, and about how he is related to the Jesus who died" (Richards, *The First Easter,* p. 57). (The error is once more traceable to the Vulgate even though the Latin for "he rose" is a technically possible translation from the original.) It is the actual texts of the New Testament that are decisive, particularly perhaps where Paul says (I Cor. 15:20): "but Christ has in fact been raised from the dead, the first fruits of all who have fallen asleep."

Needless to say, however, no Catholic is obliged to accept the findings of the "new" theology, even though he often felt obliged to accept the findings of the "old" whether he liked it or not. This is an important difference, for the new, unlike the old, is not laid down in doctrinaire fashion. Faith, nowadays, has become a freer, more personalist and more mature response to God's message. The Church remains as the principal guide to this message. But the Church—now more than ever in its history—permits a wide "pluralism" in theological approaches. Apart from anything else, this brings present-day Christians closer to the minds of the apostles and closer to Jesus himself, particularly through the writings of St. Paul.† Thus faith, in our day, is undergoing a major transformation. This is not surprising for faith has gone through many metamorphoses in the past and we live now in an age in which change is apparent everywhere. But a revolutionary situation means that the greatest changes have yet to come. Will Catholics be ready? Only, perhaps, if they realize that since the Counter Reformation, they "have generally looked upon faith as a submission of the mind to the teaching of the Church. Compared with the biblical view of faith . . . This was an impoverishment. In biblical times faith did not mean the acceptance of a collection of dogmatic formulas on the authority of an institutional church, but rather the liberating recognition that the God of love was present and active in the ongoing life of his people. Today men are once again concerned with the movement of history . . ." (Dulles, *The Survival of Dogma,* p. 153).

---

† The "new theologians" are sometimes criticized for giving scant attention to the Empty Tomb when discussing the Resurrection. St. Paul, the first of all writers on the Resurrection, does not mention the Empty Tomb at all.

CHAPTER 12

Sex—Hateful or Holy?

Mary Magdalene is the prototype of the penitent whore, but
she has colleagues in this particular brand of hagiography,
which so neatly condenses Christianity's fear of women, its
identification of physical beauty with temptation, and its
practice of bodily mortification.

MARINA WARNER

It is a subject of humiliation of all the mothers of the
children of Adam to know that while they are with child,
they carry within them an infant . . . who is the enemy of
God, the object of his hatred and malediction, and the shrine
of the demon.

ST. JOHN EUDES (Seventeenth Century)

NEW THEOLOGY deals mainly with dogmatic beliefs but has its counterpart in the moral field. Hence the "new morality." Was such a
thing, it is asked, endorsed by the Vatican Council? The answer is "if
by the 'new morality' one means an emphasis on personal responsibility
rather than the mere observance of laws, then the council did endorse
the 'new morality'" (McBrien, *Who Is a Catholic?* p. 197). In its
decree on the Church in the Modern World the Council stated that
"in fidelity to conscience, Christians are joined with the rest of men in
the search for truth, and for the genuine solution to the numerous
problems which arise in the life of individuals and from social relationships. . . . Only in freedom can man direct himself toward
goodness." Naturally neither the Church nor the Council endorses any
view of the "new morality" which equates it with permissiveness. But
why did Cardinal Hume, on becoming Archbishop of Westminster,
feel that the Church needed "a new theology of sex"? Because he saw,
along with many others, the lack of reality implicit in an older theology on the subject which, in the final analysis, demanded repression
rather than responsibility as the solution to most individual sexual

problems. And it had also happened that when he made this remark, a statement had just been issued by a department of the Vatican on the whole subject of sexual morality for Catholics. This was a *Declaration on Certain Questions Concerning Christian Ethics,* issued by the Sacred Congregation for the Doctrine of the Faith on January 16, 1976.

In reaffirming traditional Catholic teaching the main thrust of the declaration was predictable: the genital expression of sexuality belonged, of its intrinsic nature, to marriage alone; it followed from this that premarital intercourse, masturbation and homosexual acts were grave abuses of the sexual function. The declaration also displayed a tie-up with *Humanae Vitae* (in the year of whose issue its composition had originally been prepared) by continuing the Vatican policy of presenting apparent unanimity in theological circles on the necessary link between married sex and procreation. The statement was originally intended for theologians. It was doctrinal rather than pastoral in tone. It could therefore afford to be coldly clinical in its statement of Catholic dogma in the abstract. What was widely objected to in the Catholic world after the declaration was issued to the public at large was its view of sexual acts in isolation and not as related to individuals and personal relationships; its effective stress on law rather than love; and its lumping together of all sexual irregularities as necessarily and equally evil in the sense of all being "mortally sinful."

What had really appeared, yet again, was another demonstration of a long-standing dilemma for the institutional Church. "Christianity has been afraid that if it drops prohibitions, human beings will go to pieces, and be left to the mercy of hedonism. While the dangers exist, this attitude seriously ignores the innate tendency towards wholeness which human beings have" (*The Church and the Sexual Revolution,* p. 58). A conviction that the Church is doing too little in helping men to achieve such wholeness is the origin of the demand for a "new theology of sex." Many Catholics even become more convinced than ever that in the official mind of the Church, sex was still something hateful as it was to men like Augustine, and not as holy as it was to Jesus himself. Priests concerned primarily with the mission to young people were disturbed chiefly by the Declaration's insistence that the natural state of man was a "moral disorder" in itself. This made the difficult task of pastoral counseling even more difficult. The vast majority of "moral problems" experienced by young Catholics are, after all, concerned in one way or another with sex. Before leaving the subject of the 1976 Vatican Declaration on Sex, an ironical twist must be revealed. It had been given great fanfare as a pronouncement of the Congregation of the Faith and widely referred to as "the Pope's Declaration." In fact it was soon discovered that the declaration was a rehash of the chapter of a recently published book by one of the Vatican's most theologically "non-progressive" cardinals. A leading Roman theologian, the Redemptorist, Fr. Sean O'Riordan pointed out that to attribute the declaration to the Pope in order to put it beyond criticism "would be a mythological rather than a theological exercise."

How then does the average Catholic and the pastoral counselor cope with this dilemma, already conscious as they are of the depressingly large number of Catholics who have long since despaired of their Church's predominantly negative attitude on the question? Part of the answer has proved to be, as with the new theology, to have a fresh point of departure; to start with man and woman and to aspire to get as near as humanly possible to God in every single part of human life. This precludes the mechanical and abstract isolation of any one human function or part thereof (such as the purely genital aspect of sex) and the seeing of sex in general as something isolated from the whole man. It precludes the rigid imposition of an abstract code on every man, woman and child regardless of individual circumstances. (It does not deny the objective validity of such a code, but rebels only against its rigid imposition.) Before examining how this "other-ended" (theological) approach affects human sexuality at its various stages, it might be as well to dispose once and for all of a certain subject which always crops up in such discussions, namely the historic attitude of the Catholic Church toward sex and the fact that it seems to often to have been wrong in the past. It has only seemed "wrong" to us who live in the present. And the only real danger comes from those who still insist on applying the attitudes of third- and fourth-century Christian writers to the quite different conditions of today. Nor is it just that outward conditions have changed. Humankind has reached a state of knowledge which alters not only the conclusions of those past writers but even the very premises on which they relied. It is useless to say that immutable principles were laid down then once and for all. Jesus himself was careful not to do so. No body of teachings could be more vague and less dogmatic than those of Jesus Christ on the subject of sex. He did not even exalt celibacy above marriage even though the Catholic Church came to do so and enshrined its dogmatic adherence to such a proposition in the Council of Trent. For by that time celibacy had become a necessary element in structured Catholicism.

Traditional Catholic teaching on sex derives less from Jesus than from the early Fathers and the medieval schoolmen, with all the limits of the prescientific condition prevailing at that stage in history. "Inadequate knowledge of biology, as well as religious taboos, the tradition of subhuman treatment of women, and a dualistic philosophy of human nature have all left a distinct imprint upon Catholic thinking" (Kosnik, *Human Sexuality,* p. 1). The true Catholic progressive does not despise such past traditions. He lets them fall—or, rather, fall away—into their correct historical perspective. And he does not, as do some gluttons for punishment, try to demonstrate past errors by wallowing in the sex-obsessed fantasies of men like St. Jerome in the course of their thunderous denunciations of the monstrous evils of sex. Psychologists have now explained to us the nature of such unfortunate aberrations. We now accept that the Church has changed its mind on many fundamental matters. St. Augustine, in his extreme anti-sexualism and anti-feminism, may have been "right" according to certain criteria accepted in his time and because of psychological determinants of which he could know nothing; but he was wrong in the light of what has subsequently become clear to the human mind. God's revelation goes on from one century to the next. It is still discernible to those who read the "signs of the times" and are receptive to the promptings of the Spirit. But to do this believers must talk less (even to God) and listen more. This they find hard to do.

The concerned modern Catholic, worried about the sex life, say of his or her sons and daughters growing up, is not helped by a masterly grasp of the past sexual agonizings of Christian theologians. but he *is* concerned about the residual effect such agonizings have had on our own times. He has been told in the past to be docile and to demand of himself and others what is often impossible. The discouragement of repeated, if inevitable, failure has often brought on neurotic fear. A vicious circle is in operation and has been from time immemorial. The key to the vicious circle is fear. Fear entered the religious world with the "revelation" that knowledge of "good and evil" meant ability to distinguish between wearing clothes and being naked. However "holy" sex was proclaimed to be at a later date, the fear had been planted and has never wholly left us. Celibate Catholics tend to be particularly prone to this fear but all religions now face the same difficulty. They have often tried to resolve it with a device that makes sex within the "law" permissible. So, a marriage contract makes holy what the day before would have been hateful. It makes clean what a few hours before would have been filthy. Love, as such, does not come into this particular argument: it would upset the simple solution.

This fear of sex, implanted so long ago, and based on well-known prebiblical fiction, was a constant reality to the celibate, all-male, thought molders of our Catholic and Christian past. We cannot wipe out what they did and said, but we can (and are now being asked as Catholics to do so) deal more intelligently than hitherto with the legacy of their moldings on our lives. There is thus a growing hope that more and more priests will lose their embarrassments over sex as their predecessors gradually lost their embarrassment over people's poverty and began to do something about it beyond uttering meaningless platitudes. Hence the relevance of starting from the untraditional "other end" in order to reach God through love rather than start from the metaphysical conception of God and impose this on men in the form of law.

How does all this apply to the moral implications of man's developing sexuality from his earliest years until the point of marriage—if ever—is reached?

In days gone by—and in a few places even now—Catholic children were brought up not so much to be pure in heart as, more negatively, to avoid all "impurities" of the body. Circumspection however, usually ruled out anything more specific than this. Children were more struck by the embarrassment of their teachers (usually nuns) than the teaching itself and were constantly being reminded at home or at school of the dangers of the "nasty" side of the body. Fear was implanted into children at an early age. They became slightly more clued up when teachers mentioned, sometimes in little more than a whisper, the word "masturbation." Later, if they took what they learned at face value, they naturally concluded that every act, or quasi-act, of masturbation was mortally sinful and, unless confessed to the priest in confession, merited eternal punishment. Any dallying with an "impure" thought, an "unsuitable" picture or publication came to assume in the scrupulous young Catholic mind an aura of depressing evil. Confession had constantly to be resorted to. The period between puberty and marriage often became for the devout Catholic a long and fearsome struggle with this endlessly recurring situation. In such circumstances the Church's official view of marriage as a "remedy for concupiscence" had an ominous logic about it.

Meanwhile, for young men training to be priests matters of sex came under the euphemistic heading of "pastoral theology" and were only studied by the more senior seminarians. Those who manage to look back on these days with candid eyes, remember how the mention of "pastoral theology" was often accompanied by schoolgirlish giggling on the part of supposedly mature male students. Everything came under either the sixth or ninth Commandments. The very word "sex" was a dirty one. The Church's future priests accordingly developed their own slang. The pastoral theology "tract" became the "dirt tract," or, because it was meant to be a theological paraphrase of the sixth and ninth Commandments, the "fighting sixth and ninth." The tract was negatively designed primarily to meet and defeat almost every possible objection to the Church's rules on sex. Elsewhere, these were summarized in the half dozen or so answers which were all that were devoted to sex in the average catechism of the day. In one of the most widely used English language catechisms the key question came just after that which reminded the pupil that the ninth Commandment was "Thou shalt not covet they neighbor's wife." The next question asked: "What does the ninth Commandment forbid?" And the answer was "the ninth Commandment forbids all willful consent to impure thoughts and desires, and all willful pleasure in the irregular motions of the flesh." Such questions had to be learned by heart, whether understood or not. They were naturally mysterious to children of eight.

The whole pastoral atmosphere in this and related fields changed radically, after the Second Vatican Council. One of the Church's leading moral theologians, Bernard Häring wrote a book in 1953 entitled *The Law of Christ*. Twenty-five years later he brought out a new work, *Free and Faithful in Christ*. Each was a comprehensive presentation of Catholic moral theology, but the difference in titles is indicative of the general development in the years between. "I believe," he says in his introduction to the latter work, "that a distinctively Christian moral theology for this new era has to be a theology of responsibility essentially marked by liberty, fidelity and creativity. This new vision lends courage and guidance to the rethinking of a number of doctrines, traditions, teachings and practices and to distinguishing the deposit of faith from ideologies, taboos and other obscuring factors" (*ibid.*, p. 4). Unlike the old-fashioned manuals once used in seminaries, Häring's latest work is far from being a forbidding catalogue of sins with all their possible subdivisions and degrees of gravity. As Häring points out "At a time when absolutist monarchs and Church authorities were extremely concerned with the control of orthodoxy by formulations, and with total submission of the faithful, many moralists asserted that the smallest doubt in matters concerning orthodox formulations, whether in thought or word or in superstitious practices, had to be a mortal sin" (*ibid.*, p. 406). On the other hand "during the last centuries the faithful were particularly troubled by many moralists and by the Roman Inquisition who taught that all sins in thought, desire and deeds against the sixth commandment are *ex toto genere* mortal sins" (*ibid.*, p. 407). This, however, has led to no official relaxation of attitudes. On the contrary the modern successor to the old Inquisition, the Congregation for the Doctrine of the Faith, in the course of its 1976 Declaration mentioned above, "not only confirmed this rigoristic tradition but even added a new dimension by teaching that no parvity of matter can be admitted not only objectively but also that everyone has to presume that subjectively, too, a mortal sin is given unless there are particular signs to the contrary" (*ibid.*, p. 408). Ultraconservative, or "traditionalist," observers—often preoccupied with the sexual sphere—are thus right in maintaining that the Church has not officially modified its view on the seriousness of this type of sin. Häring, though not strictly a "new theologian," tends to take what is in effect a more existentialist view in maintaining that "A constructive approach that leads to serenity and peace of mind is much more conducive to chastity than rigorism excessively inclined to judge as mortal each sin of weakness against chastity" (*ibid.*, p. 410).

Häring was here voicing a view that had become widespread just when the 1976 Declaration was published. Up until then sins of adolescence were being handled by confessors, parents, teachers, counselors, etc., not, indeed, as "non-sins," but as stages in human development which had to be looked on in their total perspective. The exact words of instruction, advice, counsel, etc., given to any individual ideally came to depend on his or her age, circumstances, psychological makeup and even the social and economic factors of each particular case. The constant effort to get to know God better through Jesus and to love him daily more and more was, in practice, the tackling of an age-old problem by working from below. Naturally such an approach has uneven success and demands great patience and hard work. It is easier to make a blanket rule and insist on its being adhered to. This is what was attempted once again in 1976, thus rocking back so many pastorally concerned Catholics on their heels, as had happened after *Humanae Vitae.* The shock having been absorbed, the painful process has started all over again of mitigating the rigors of the declaration's literal demands by sympathetic and imaginative counseling and confessional help. But the whole position is almost irreparably weakened by such a totally paradoxical situation. Realization of this has led to the call for a more "honest" approach to the whole problem, as reflected not just by the strugglings of individual pastors to "get around" the letter of the written law, but a change by the official Church itself. "There is need for a totally new conceptualisation of the morality of masturbation, now seen primarily as an intrinsic component of personal growth during puberty and adolescence, with its own distinctive phase morality, which in no way justifies the anticipation of principles governing sexual activity at any later stage in human development" (Dominian, *Proposals for a New Sexual Ethic*, p. 50).

Throughout the book just quoted, the theme is that the basis of a new sexual morality must be founded on the concepts of person and love. "Masturbation does not involve any other human being whereas the pleasure of sexual intercourse does involve another human being and so entirely different considerations prevail" (*ibid.*, p. 50). The author goes on to argue, on the same principle, that different considerations also prevail, as a matter at least of degree, in every kind of interpersonal sexual relationship, particularly in the troubled area of homosexuality and premarital sex. Here the official Catholic position is straightforward enough: complete prohibition. The fact that there may be much more love in an extramarital (or even homosexual) encounter, isolated or habitual, than in a married one (where love may even be totally absent) is no excuse. The law says that all acts of premarital intercourse are acts of "fornication." So fornication has come to be defined as any act of sexual intercourse without marriage, not, be it noted, any act of sexual intercourse without love. Naturally the Church, as even the most advanced progressive Catholics would recognize, cannot, in view of mere semantic objections, just meekly change its rules. It would no longer be true to its mandate. But there are changes it could very usefully make by examining its sexual code alongside its code with regard to other moral activity. This process reveals a far more lenient attitude toward those who abuse such human instincts or appetites as the desire for food, drink, money and power. Men are, here, asked to make an equally thorough examination of their consciences, but it is realized that any absolute categories of "mortal sin" (as opposed to the less serious "venial sin") would often be impractical. The whole Catholic attitude toward such behavior is far less legalistic than its attitude toward sex. It does not hold out the specter of "automatic mortal sin." It sets up a norm, an ideal, and asks men to try and live by it. If and when they fail—as they do—they must be sorry and constantly determined to improve. They do not normally live in constant fear of hell on account of their transgressions in these fields because the Church in their regard is not conditioned, as with sexual behavior, by its own past neurosis. They are treated as adults by the Church, and expected to make their ultimate criterion of behavior that abiding love which alone unites men with men, men with women, and humans with God—through Jesus their Lord.

To apply this very same approach to the sexual world would revolutionize the whole of Catholic thought on the subject. It would produce, at a stroke, a "new theology of sex." It would integrate sex into the wholeness of human life. It would help rather than, as often happens, bedevil the Christian's daily aim to achieve self-awareness, self-realization, as a person and through relationships with other persons of either and both sexes. It is such self-realization that, with the "new" approach, aims at union with God as far as such communion is possible while still on this earth.

To some Catholics all this sounds much too idealistic, too elusive, illusory even, if not downright "wet." Was Jesus "wet" in refusing to take the "robust" line against the adulterous woman? All wanted to condemn her. He did not condemn. But he did not deny the fact of sin. He showed that not only *she* but the accusers too were all—by their own tacit admission—sinners. And to the woman, he said, "Sin no more." The text can be overdone in the name of "liberation." But it does show that the paramount necessity in Church leaders (who are meant to be other-Christs) is for the most sensitive compassion and imaginative sympathy in such highly delicate fields. This leads to the question of how much the Catholic Church really cares about actual *people* whose lives are led under the cloud of some problem or deprivation that is, in some way, sexual in nature. Homosexuality is one of the most important testing grounds; another is that of the person living in the single state. It has been found that in the modern age the "solution" formerly relied on by the Church—to repress temptation—has failed. And theorizing on the omnipotent power of supernatural grace when properly used has ceased to convince. For this was "filling-station" Christianity. There was seldom a question of saving-by-serving: or of solving-by-sharing. Each man, each woman, was isolated. There was little communion between believers, little soul-to-soul intimacy. Now such things are beginning to be taken for granted—not just in charismatic groups but at almost all levels of Catholic life.

On the purely practical plane, however, there is much that can be done that is barely being attempted at the moment. While it is far from true that all single people have some sort of sexual problem, it is true, if not always admitted, that every single person has a sexual side to his or her life. There may be a deliberate decision to give up marriage for the sake of God in the "religious" life. This opting for celibacy is something special and is taken only by a minority of men and women. Even after the decision has been taken, that person's sexuality does not cease to operate. The sexual factor is at work in every phase of every person's life to some degree or other. There is a constant flow of invisible messages between people of opposite sexes: quite licit, quite natural and potentially beneficial. It occurs even in the carrying out of religious exercises, particularly those that involve genuine contact, including bodily contact, between one person and another. A greeting, a sign of love, a laying on of hands to heal; all these and many others are symbolic of human exchanges of the *whole* of one person with the *whole* of another. And it is only by the spurious reasoning summarized above—which isolates sex from the rest of the human makeup—that can deprive such person-to-person exchanges of their healthily sexual element. Women impart different messages from those imparted by men. Usually they complement each other. Or a woman minister—in such churches as allow such people to exist—can impart something quite different through her ministry from what a man can impart. Sexuality is everywhere. It was, Catholics believe, created by God and is good. If sexuality is everywhere, what happens to it in the case of a single person who has not freely decided to opt for celibacy? There are many reasons why such a person does not marry. When he or she would like to but can't it may be for some reason connected with home responsibilities (such as an ailing or aging parent) or conflict with professional commitments. But the largest specific category of such cases is that of men or women who would like to marry but just don't. Why don't they?

The most frequent reason is, in some way, psychological, and it is precisely here that the Catholic Church is woefully underequipped, or even unwilling, to help. Nevertheless "the specific contribution of Christianity must be to focus attention on an increasing understanding of the reasons that prevent people who wish to marry from doing so, and to help them overcome the obstacles. . . . Such men and women are frequently sensitive, anxious people who find closeness overwhelmingly difficult. Deep in their personality are fears of being overwhelmed and trapped into childlike situations in the hands of others, and frequently they are imbued with a deep sense of mistrust and fear of persons of the opposite sex" (Dominian, *The Church and the Sexual Revolution,* p. 62). This is a very common situation and leads to immense suffering, as hope is aroused only to be dashed repeatedly. While the Western world merely exploits loneliness through sexual stimulation, the state is only concerned about the civic and material aspects. (It is, ironically, the Communist countries which are "puritanical" about pornography but realistic about individual problems arising from sex.)

The Church clearly has a duty to do more than merely forbid transgressions of its law. To prevent sin is better than to condemn it. And to realize, better late than never, that people in such situations deserve much more imaginative help is no unworthy Christian aim. It was not forthcoming in the closed Church of the pre-conciliar days however great that Church's outward unity and strength may have been. Massive—and unnecessary—internal bleeding was too high a price to pay for such "unity" and was bound, one day, to betray its external effects. A more open Church, however, should enable such problems, even apart from expert and specialized help, to become the problems no longer of lonely individuals but problems that are shared. A lonely person remains lonely as a mere member of an institution; he ceases to be lonely as a member of an organic community. "Let religion and psychiatry, therefore, continue to study persons in relation, persons as agents of acceptance and as means of grace . . . realising that in ten generations from now our understanding will be deepened and broadened . . . If there is to be a creative world revolution, it will come as a result of men accepting their role as agents of divine love and living their lives as sacraments of the personal" (Rian, ed., *Christianity and World Revolution,* p. 116).

Perhaps that perceptive Dominican, Donald Goergen, should be allowed the last word. In his excellent book *The Sexual Celibate* he writes (p. 95) : "A too common attitude among Christians is that the sexual is sinful. Despite recognition of the sanctity of marriage, Christian tradition has not conveyed positive attitudes towards sexuality. The other attitude with respect to sexuality in the history of Christianity is that the sexual is primarily procreative. It exists so that the species might continue. Neither of these presuppositions is the basis for my theology of chastity. Neither is biblical nor is either self-evident in the twentieth century."

CHAPTER 13

Marriage

We do not underestimate the heavy cares of every Christian
couple. . . . If they find they cannot shake off sin, let
them not despair, but keep on humbly searching for God's
mercy.

POPE PAUL VI
(Humanae Vitae) 1963

Even Christ defended the rightness of divorce.

TERTULLIAN
(Treatise Against Marcion) c. 207

FEW AREAS of Catholic teaching are in greater need of readjustment
than that which surrounds marriage. One reform has already come in
the rewriting of the sacramental liturgy of matrimony. The old Roman
rite had the effect, or at least the appearance, of downgrading marriage. The view that married Catholics were second-class ones was
never propagated as such but the Council of Trent condemned anyone
who maintained "that it is not better and more blessed to continue in
the state of virginity or celibacy than to enter on the state of matrimony." This notion—which cannot be shown to have been that of
Christ himself—colored all Catholic post-Reformation thought until
modern times.

The sacramental reform in regard to marriage is in conformity with
sacramental reform as a whole. Gone is the former emphasis on the
automatic efficacy of any sacrament (to which no obstacle is inter-
posed) merely because an all-powerful Church confers it. Such sacraments, according to the old theology, gave grace to the recipient *ex
opere operato,* by the very action performed. The impression in the receiving Catholic's mind, was of a mechanical, a penny-in-the-slot operation with a "prize every time," provided the machine was in working
order. It was a function of "filling-station" Christianity. The new sacramental theology starts, as may be expected, with the person receiving
the sacrament and then moves on to contemplate what is being re-

ceived. Stressed in the new rite of marriage are the importance of the human love of those about to be married and then, but only secondarily, the element of covenant. The new view of the latter may eventually mitigate the hitherto rigorous insistence on a highly legalistic, contractual view of Christian marriage. The Church, following the recent Council, is no longer concerned with the contract as such, but rather with the whole institution of marriage and that private "community" —microcosmic of the wider Christian community—of the man and the woman which the contract initiates. The two partners who are in love thus marry each other. They have long been considered to confer on each other the sacrament of matrimony, with the priest as no more than the principal witness. But the central action of the whole liturgical love drama has never been so obvious as in the reformed liturgy. Modern theologians thus tend to see the man-woman *relationship* in its fullest context as the grace-giving sign of the sacrament. The relationship thereby entered into is meant to be permanent. If it irrevocably breaks down, does the sacramental life of marriage become inoperative?

No, says the Church. Marriage—technically at least—is indissoluble. But there *are* loopholes. All, from this point onward, is a tangled jungle of legalism. "A bewildering mass of law has grown up around Roman Catholic marriage which it is impossible even to summarize" (McKenzie, *The Roman Catholic Church,* p. 219). It is particularly bewildering for the non-Catholic who wants to marry a Catholic, though considerably less forbidding since the Council.

Despite the momentum for reform, the Church feels that it cannot abandon its basic position on marriage without possibly precipitating moral chaos. But it is not unaware of the force of the argument of the "liberal" case which, at its best, can be summed up as follows. Leaving aside technical "dissolution" of marriage, and annulment, there is already moral chaos and it is not helped by a too rigorist Catholic Church. Signs, particularly in America, are that the Church will have to give way or face the unenviable alternatives of either losing many of its sons and daughters or condemning them to unbearable unhappiness for the rest of their lives. Why not, then, says the argument, be realistic about marriages that have totally broken down and at least let Catholics who have divorced and "remarried" be received back to the sacraments on certain conditions? The onus must be on the individuals to show good faith and the desire to do the best for their own souls and for their children's moral and general welfare. In the final analysis, after all, only God can know what is in their secret hearts.

A legalistic solution is empty by comparison. (If, for example, people lie to achieve the respectability of an annulment, they are no better off in the eyes of God.) The argument is not based on pure sentiment or on the supposition that Jesus did not mean what he said when he declared marriage to be indissoluble (Mark 10:2-12; Luke 16:18; Matt. 5:31,32). It is true that the passage in Matthew appears to contain a distinct qualification. This qualification—the case of adultery— was a grounds for divorce in the early Church; but such an interpretation is not easily supported by the context as a whole. It is not justifiable to prefer Matthew—although the Church does so in the case of the passage "Thou art Peter" etc. (which is not to be found, as already seen, in Luke or Mark). Our Lord's teaching on marriage in the other two synoptic gospels is unambiguous. But the question still remains: was Jesus holding out an ideal or laying down a command? The practice in the early Church in both East and West—and in the East until today—would suggest the former. (Adultery could, as seen, be a reason for divorce and remarriage.) Christ's words were taken to be a counsel of perfection. They were not, along with many other counsels, taken literally. People did not—and still do not—gouge out their eyes and cut off their hands purely because Christ said they should do so if they have seen or done evil (in Matt. 5:29). Christians have long sworn oaths though this was specifically ruled out by Christ (Matt. 5:34). They offer resistance to injury despite Christ's admonition that they should not do so (Matt. 5:39). They have no hope of ever, on this earth, being perfect as required by the words reported in Matthew 5:48. The early Fathers thus took what we would now call a "liberal" view of Jesus' words on marriage though none doubted that its indissolubility was the ideal to be aimed at. The Council of Trent, however, has laid it down that anyone was anathema who affirmed that the Church erred if it taught that marriage was indissoluble. The decree in question was very carefully and skillfully phrased before being formulated and passed on November 11, 1563. But it did not, and could not, in view of the teaching of the early Fathers, lay it down as Church practice from the very beginning that marriage could not be dissolved because of one partner's adultery. What it could and did do was to establish the Roman Church's adherence to this practice from that moment onward.

The Council of Trent was thus taking a stage further the encroachment of Church practice as "law" into the teaching of a moral ideal. In the premedieval period law and moral ideals were separate if inevi-

tably connected. It was the state, i.e. the Roman Empire, which
legislated on marriage and after the days of Constantine such legislation applied to Christian marriage. Divorce and remarriage were permitted, and remained permitted for several centuries afterward. The
ideal of indissolubility remained, but the opinions of some, even of the
most prominent, of the Church Fathers allowed dissolution to prevail
in practice. The right of a husband, for example, to divorce an adulterous wife was always upheld and he was considered justified in mar-
rying another woman. The practice was approved by such Fathers as
Origen, Lactantius, Basil the Great, Ambrosiaster, Asterius of Amasya,
Epiphanius of Salamis, Victor of Antioch, Avitus of Vienne; and by
such Church Councils as those of Arles (314), Milvis (416), Vannes
(461), and Agde (506). It is even true that "some Fathers felt obliged
to permit innocent wives, maliciously deserted by their husbands, to
remarry. These and other relaxations were granted by the Fathers in
the belief that such mercy or condescension (Origen, Basil the Great)
behoved the Church" (Prospishil, *Divorce and Remarriage*, p. 52).
One of the most regrettable developments of the Middle Ages, however, was the confusion of Canon Law with moral theology. The
Church began to impose as law what it formerly only commended as
right practice to the individual conscience. The *societas perfecta* of the
Church-dominated theocracy—the Roman Catholic empire—was, in
other words, emerging. Bishops became the lawmakers for monarchs
and princes. Such legalism largely prevailed over the pastoral needs of
individuals at the Council of Trent. Even now, in many fields of which
matrimonial practice is a vital one, law-dominated theology still
prevails. This is why, wherever possible, the Church prefers its moral
theological practices to be backed by State enforcement and bitterly
opposes any national constitutions which do not endorse Church law
on such matters as marriage and divorce. When, in December 1978,
Spain voted for a democratic and largely secular constitution, the
Primate (the Cardinal Archbishop of Toledo) was furious. He had
called for a rejection of such separation of Church and State since it
would lead to a situation where the Church could no longer rely on
the secular arm to enforce under penalty what it could not itself bring
about through love and devotion. The medieval idea that people must
be forced by the State-Church/Church-State to be good Christians has
thus, here and there, survived into modern times. The hierarchies of
such predominantly Catholic countries as Ireland and Italy have
fought every inch of the way to ensure that the State should do as

much of their own work for them as possible by legally enforcing moral precepts. Sex is usually at the center of such fights which invariably concentrate on divorce, abortion and contraception. This is very characteristic of the official Roman Catholic moralist-legalist mentality at work.

The Council of Trent, then, appeared to settle the question of marital indissolubility once and for all. It had adopted the medieval churchmen's conception that moral precept, once taken over as law by the secular arm, could then be turned into Church dogma. The modern churchman's view is that moral precept loses its soul if imposed with the cold-blooded rigor of a legal enactment. Surprisingly, however, the indissolubility of marriage is not a *de fide* doctrine of Catholicism. In other words, the relevant decree of Trent was not—at least, not certainly—a doctrinal one. Its careful phraseology showed it to be disciplinary in scope. Is there, then, any chance that the Church, in view of today's pressing needs and numerous heartbreakingly hard cases, will return to the discipline of the first millennium?

Very little, it would seem. Those who availed themselves of the Church's lenient interpretation in the first thousand years or so of Christian history came mostly from the educated and upper classes. Those lower in the social scale rarely even knew, let alone took advantage, of such privileges. In this sense, the "privileges" were limited. Today, no such limitation could hold. The modern world is too different for the Church to reintroduce its earlier experiment without appearing to undermine the whole "system" of seemingly indissoluble marriage. Its dilemma is acute. It is against every one of Rome's instincts—and they are far from being invariably unsound—to open the possible floodgates. The loss of outward discipline might prove permanently damaging to the institutional Church to say nothing of the welfare of families and children yet unborn. At the same time, more and more Catholics, such as the innocent victims of wrecked marriages, are —through no fault of their own—suffering agonies at being cut off from the sacraments and having to attend Church with their children without themselves going to Holy Communion. Estimates of the number of U.S. Catholics who are divorced and remarried vary between three and five million and one recent estimate is that about 250,000 Catholics obtain divorces a year and that 80 per cent of them remarry (*1978 Catholic Almanac,* p. 136). It has been unofficially worked out that at least every other American family is affected directly or indirectly by a matrimonial problem connected with some member of the family. The remedy of annulment of the first marriage applies, if at all, to only a small minority of cases. It has long been hoped that the "internal forum solution" could be more widely applied. By the "internal forum" the Catholic Church means, in effect, a person's private conscience. The chance to make a clean start is here envisaged if the person or persons concerned give every possible sign of being in good faith. But in August 1973, there was a setback to such ideas. The Vatican Congregation for the Doctrine of the Faith advised bishops throughout the world against the solution known as the "good conscience procedure." The procedure, where carried out, involves administration of the sacraments of penance and the Eucharist to divorced and remarried Catholics unable to obtain a decree of nullity for a first marriage and living in a subsequent marriage "in good faith." Thus the procedure in question can have no standing or recognition in Church law. It is nevertheless being advocated by some priests and practiced by remarried Catholics. The worsening situation led to the formation early in 1976 of the North American Conference of Separated and Divorced Catholics (an enlarged version of a preexistent organization) which has roughly two hundred groups in various parts of the United States and Canada. It has developed into a growing and urgent pastorate and its purposes have become shared by other groups and even by official ministries in many U.S. dioceses as well as by other church agencies and a large number of priests. The central problem in this specialized ministry is the degree of sacramental participation open to persons in irregular unions. The increasing number of cases of people being readmitted to the sacraments may force an eventual change of attitude at the top. But it will take a long time and many millions will suffer meanwhile, without any real hope, many for the rest of their lives.

The situation, however, has already changed dramatically over the last decade. Fr. James J. Young, C.S.P., national chaplain of the Conference of Separated and Divorced Catholics, has been long in the field. He estimates that the decrees of nullity issued has risen from about seven hundred in 1967 to fifteen thousand in 1976. But his chief aims are more positive and his methods sometimes startling. He even devised, in 1972, a "liturgy of divorce" at which married couples whose marriages had utterly broken down at least separated in prayerful spirit. They symbolically parted hands and said separately "I declare before all present that our marriage has come to an end. I beg forgiveness for all I have done that has wounded this relationship, and

I promise to love you even though we are no longer man and wife." A blessing followed with the prayer they might both "choose life and love again."

On the credit side of things, many Catholics have profited by the revival since the Council of the Church's long-lost sense of intimate communion as between its members. Whatever the Church authorities once patronizingly said about marriage being a "remedy for concupiscence" and whatever else they did to make married couples feel inferior to virgins and celibates, Catholics knew in their hearts that sex was good and that married human happiness was one of its allowable goals. Enlightened pastors, after all, had long been saying that marriage was a noble vocation. Priests and ordinary folk were discovering that even this was a defensive description of something that was intrinsically good and that sexuality was implanted by God in men and women to be enjoyed and not merely "used" for procreation. But a fully responsible attitude was recognized as being essential. So it was that a certain Fr. Gabriel Calvo was to be found doing some interesting work in Spain in the late fifties in collaboration with a married couple called Diego and Fina Bartolomeo. Other couples joined in for what was to become a special kind of ministry to the married. In 1962, twenty-eight couples held an "encounter" in Barcelona. This meeting was to have historic repercussions and five years later an "encounter" was held—the first in the United States—in conjunction with a convention of the Christian Family Movement at Notre Dame University. It was a phenomenal success and in 1969 "Marriage Encounter," as it came to be called, "went nationwide." It is now worldwide and though almost exclusively Catholic in most countries, in the United States it has ecumenical dimensions. It is designed for ordinary married people with the ordinary thrills, perplexities and problems of marriage which they share at periodical weekends. It is not for troubled couples nor is it, its organizers insist, an exercise in group dynamics. It exists chiefly to make good marriages better by discovering, as in homeopathic medicine, the naturally curative and health-giving elements that the body (in this case of two-in-the-flesh) secretes. It has effects outside individual marriages since it attracts a totally heterogeneous cross section of married couples. Every possible type is represented; black, white, rich, poor, good, bad, even indifferent. It has remarkable side effects in many countries. In Belgium, for example, "the people are split along language lines the way we are by color. After Encounter, French and Flemish couples who lived beside each other for years without speaking now visit each other's homes and are close friends. In Ireland, the class barrier between blue-collar and white-collar workers is very strong. After Encounter, they see each other as persons" (Gallacher, *The Marriage Encounter*, p. 5). Marriage Encounter is reckoned to be the fastest growing contemporary development in the Church apart from the charismatic renewal. (It has an Encounter Resource Community at Valley Stream, New York, and a central office for worldwide activities at Long Beach, California.)

Apart from Marriage Encounter and the growing—but necessarily unofficial—ministry to the Divorced and Remarried, many place hopes on eventual acceptance of the mounting arguments for a radical review of Catholic legislation on marriage. Few if any put the case better or with more succinct scholarship than Mgr. Stephen J. Kelleher in his "milestone" work, *Divorce and Remarriage for Catholics?* One of his other concerns is for revolutionizing the procedure for assessing marriage in the tribunals that now exist to grant annulments where such a possibility exists. He feels that a prior duty exists to examine whether the marriage is in fact dead. If so, this fact should be admitted without the necessity of recourse to the cumbersome procedure of investigating the possibility of a successful nullity suit. His long experience of tribunal work in this field has left him sadder but wiser at the end of it all. He claims that despite the fact that more and more annulments are now granted annually in an effort to allow Catholics to make a fresh start, the process is self-defeating. Some even find it dishonest, the principle of annulment being the necessary establishment of the fact that there never was a valid marriage contract in the first place. There are numerous possible grounds, many highly technical. The one most often invoked nowadays is officially termed "lack of due discretion." In practice it means acceptance that there existed before the marriage a situation wherein either partner was incapable of entering into the contract subsequently concluded in formal fashion. This "lack of due discretion" can take any one of many possible forms. (New ones are being discovered all the time.) It often means, in practice, proving that one partner would have been unable from the very beginning to get on with the other (or that neither would have been able to get on with the other) in proper marital union. The definitions are necessarily loose and there is infinite variety, even in the types of evidence admissible. This frequently relates to some sort of psychological or neurotic blockage, or it could just be immaturity. It may well have existed without being provable. One of the aspects of the Catholic marriage tribunal which many think unfair is that the presumption is always in favor of the matrimonial "bond" regardless of circumstantial evidence. There is an automatic appeal to the Rota in Rome from a local diocesan finding on the part of the "defender of the bond." There are often interminable delays. While more and more annulments are in fact given each year, the number of Catholics resorting to divorce and civil remarriage leaps ahead even faster. Can the Church continue indefinitely to hold the line with only the legalistic remedy, on the one hand, and on the other, such severely limited pastoral care as is officially allowed?

Mgr. Kelleher states bluntly that "the tribunal is dying" and that the Church should not "play games with persons' spiritual and religious lives." To the "tribunal solution" and the "good conscience solution" he offers an alternative. He calls it the "Welcome Home" solution and urges that the Church community may refuse the Eucharist to those wishing to be received again only "in the most unusual and extraordinary cases where a person has clearly shown a blatant disregard for the basic values of marriage."

One obstacle to this, however, is that the Catholic Church has not yet got used to thinking and acting—once again after so many centuries—as a genuine community. Catholics in the wilderness can thus see no "home" in which they might once more be welcome.

CHAPTER 14

Ecumenism

During the first two centuries, the words *hiereus* and *sacerdos* were attributed exclusively to Christ and Christians, never to the bishop or *presbyteros*. These last were considered solely as the holders of an office within an assembly of priests.

MAX DELESPESSE

John said to him, "Master, we saw a man who is not one of us casting out devils in your name; and because he was not one of us we tried to stop him." But Jesus said, "You must not stop him: no one who works a miracle in my name is likely to speak evil of me. Anyone who is not against us is for us."

MARK 9:38–40

FROM THE ROMAN CATHOLIC point of view, ecumenism—the movement to restore Christian unity—is, for the time being, stagnant. So gloomy a statement is not made lightly. The enthusiasm of the late sixties has almost entirely evaporated. It was, at that time, largely accounted for by the very novelty of seeing Roman Catholics talking to other Christian bodies if not as equals, at least as potential equals. Such dialogue was made possible by the Vatican II declaration that although there were "differences that exist in varying degrees between (non-Catholic Christians) and the Catholic Church," nevertheless all those "who believe in Christ and have been properly baptized are brought into a certain, though imperfect, communion with the Catholic Church."

Today's spirit of revolution in the world looks toward the removal of artificial barriers productive of inequality between humans. Christianity, as a faith, is meant to be a supreme equalizer. Christianity, however, as a religion, is in fact divisive in today's world.

For, at the center of ecumenism there is, for Catholics, an apparently insoluble quandary. Can discussions with other Christian bodies have any real meaning if the Catholic Church maintains its traditional claims to be the one and only true Church of Christ? What is needed today is a much more specific commitment than anything hitherto attempted on this issue. For centuries the Catholic Church has taken literally that axiom that has come from Origen and Cyprian right down to Pius XI's encyclical *Mortalium Animos:* Outside the (Catholic) Church, no salvation. Though the problem of the "salvation of unbelievers" was always a troublesome and worrying one, there seemed to be no solution to it without fatal compromise to Catholic claims. It is surprising to think that the pioneer attempts of Henri de Lubac, particularly in his major work *Catholicism,* were thought very daring thirty or forty years ago, in trying to redefine this forbidding-sounding axiom. It did not, he ventured to argue, mean that "outside the Church you are damned" but that "it is only by the Church you will be saved"—even if you do not belong to it. His answers vaguely satisfied theologians of most shades at that time. Now, however, ecumenism has forced men to ask questions that are more logical than theological. If you can be saved outside the "one true Church" is not that very expression really meaningless? If exclusive possession of religious truth is not necessary for salvation, it is therefore a mere academic luxury, if not almost a legal fiction. "No!" say "traditionalist" Catholics. "Heretics, schismatics, apostates, pagans, renegades, etc., are all outside the Church and cannot go to heaven." Such "traditionalists" would feel treacherously let down were the Pope, tomorrow, to make some spectacular statement permitting instant unity and intercommunion between the Roman and some other Christian churches. And such people are very numerous. There is thus from the Catholic point of view no chance of Christian unity within current terms of reference, even though a lot of pious humbug is talked on the subject. The speed of the convoy is that of the slowest and most conservative Catholic travelers. The official Church dare not defy them. It looks therefore as if the Christian churches—in the revolutionary sweep of twenty-first century history—will be left behind bickering among themselves as to the canonical "validity" of this and that while fewer and fewer people, at least in the Western world, go to any Christian church at all. The church of the Third World may well prove more healthy.

Catholicism, at all events, officially declared itself a member of world ecumenical activity when it set up the Vatican Secretariat for Promoting Christian Unity in 1960. (World Protestantism had, of course, been at it since the early part of the century.) In 1964 a Bishops' Committee for Ecumenical and Interreligious Affairs was established by the American hierarchy. In the same year the Vatican Council promulgated its Decree on Ecumenism. This Decree stated, in a vital passage:

> Men who believe in Christ and have been properly baptized are brought into a certain, though imperfect, communion with the Catholic Church. Undoubtedly, the differences that exist in varying degrees between them and the Catholic Church—whether in doctrine and sometimes in discipline, or concerning the structure of the Church—do indeed create many and sometimes serious obstacles to full ecclesiastical communion. These the ecumenical movement is striving to overcome.

The ecumenical field is vast. As elsewhere in this book, a key example must be allowed to replace exhaustive coverage. The example of Catholic relations with Anglicanism (or Episcopalianism) has been chosen. For this represents dialogue as between the Roman Church and a church larger than any other said to be separate from Catholicism by allegedly having no "valid orders" to celebrate the Eucharist. At the same time Anglicanism is nearer to Roman Catholicism than strictly "Protestant" communions. If unity is unattainable with the Anglican Church, there is little hope in any other direction. Despite supposedly absolute separation, attitudes can be seen to be slowly changing if one looks carefully behind the scenes. (Whether they will quickly lead to intercommunion is another matter.)

In 1968, for example, the American Episcopalian priest, John Jay Hughes, became a Roman Catholic priest without having to do more than receive "conditional ordination." His admission in this way into the diocese of Münster (Germany) made history as he was not required to deny the validity of his Episcopalian (or Anglican) orders. He has spent much of his time since then in scholarly research into the whole question of Anglican orders and the view taken of them by Rome. His book *Absolutely Null and Utterly Void,* published in 1968, was the first detailed description of the behind-the-scenes negotiations and intrigues which resulted in the condemnation of Anglican orders (as "absolutely null and utterly void") by Pope Leo XIII in 1896. The papal bull was written by Cardinal Merry del Val and the three representatives of England's Cardinal Vaughan. The latter—a stanch Roman or Catholic—was anxious for Anglican orders to be officially condemned as he felt that such a condemnation would be followed by a rush of Anglican clergy and lay people back to the "one true Church." (He was disappointed.) A difficulty inevitably arose from the fact that Anglicans and Romans—totally cut off from one another since the Reformation—hardly any longer spoke the same theological language. When they spoke of "priesthood" and "validity" they tended to speak of different things. It was as if an American had said that British democracy, because different from the American model, was therefore not "valid." For this reason alone—though there are many other much more complex ones—Leo XIII's bull is not now considered the final word in Roman Catholic circles, though some still maintain that it can never be reversed.

John Jay Hughes, in an important subsequent book *Stewards of the Lord,* shows how the recent renewal in theology has largely failed to touch discredited theories dating from Pope Leo's bull but relying on even older, uncorrected, arguments. Such arguments generally contented themselves with repeating the rejection of the views of the sixteenth-century English Reformers on the priesthood and the Mass, not because they were unbiblical or illogical but because they were novel. As such they threatened the inner establishment of the Roman Catholic empire. The Protestant views were themselves open to objection but the two sides could not engage in anything like civilized debate. The atmosphere was purely polemical and remained such for nearly four centuries.

The Protestant reformers were faced not with an established eucharistic theology that had produced a certain type of eucharistic service, but with a eucharistic service, the medieval Mass, that had produced its supporting theology. This service was part of an elaborate "mass-system" something of which was glimpsed earlier in Chapter 8. This system had permitted the garden of pious souls to become overgrown with the weeds of abuse. Such abuse has remained unknown to Catholics at the popular level. Very few, even now, are fully aware of its historical implications. But awareness has begun, and with it an initial glimmering of why the reformers were so successful and why so many priests and bishops so quickly embraced the reformed liturgy. In the polemical past, Catholics have been protected by a virtually impenetrable armor. The post-imperial Catholic fortress was well sealed against Protestant propaganda and no differentiation was made in favor of Anglicans although their tradition is considerably different from that of general Protestantism. Anglicans, for their part, are be-

ginning to get a much clearer and overall view of Catholicism. Thus
the way is being prepared for these two communions to reunite and
the Catholic position is no longer a solid one demanding "return" to
the one true Roman faith as the only path to unity. For one thing
unity does not mean the same thing as union. But progress is painfully
slow.

One reason for such slowness is that the whole process is in the
hands of specialists. "Until the rank-and-file membership perceives the
importance and relevance of ecumenism to their own Christian lives, it
will tend to remain stalled in its own tracks" (McBrien, *The Remaking of the Church*, p. 108). A first prerequisite is to eliminate certain
presuppositions that have so far made every ecumenical dialogue between Romans and Anglicans—at popular level—stillborn. Such presuppositions include the assumption—no longer universally held—that
Leo XIII's bull was final. The bull's supporters rely on the necessity
for a "sacrificing priesthood"—unknown in the early Church—as the
criterion for validity of Anglican orders. The English Reformation
thrust was against an ecclesiastical mentality that could so compla-
cently permit the ordination of hundreds of priests year after year, in
order to keep going the (very profitable) late medieval Mass-system.
Bearing in mind how tiny was the total population of England in the
sixteenth century (about three and a half million) compared to today,
certain representative facts and figures are startlingly relevant. H.
Maynard Smith records that before the Reformation bishops ordained
a hundred or two hundred priests at a time. The episcopal register of
York shows that 262 priests were ordained there in 1510–11 alone. It
must be remembered that most of such ordinands were "chantry
priests," that is, ordained solely to recite the office and say private
Masses for the intentions paid for through the chaplaincies or chantries which provided their employment. The normal clergy attached to
the cathedrals and country parishes were quite separate. This meant
that there was a sort of roving "proletariat" of priests seeking their
daily bread but not always finding it. A bizarre situation of clerical unemployment even arose and Maynard Smith described how, at St.
Paul's Cathedral, London, on the eve of the Reformation, "groups of
priests hovered about the doors hoping for chantries and chaplaincies,
but idle all the day because no one had hired them" (*Pre-Reformation
England,* pp. 38–39).

John Jay Hughes adds a few more statistics. "As late as 1547 there
were fifty-two priests holding endowed chantries in St. Paul's, in addi-

tion to all the other cathedral clergy. There were forty-five such chantry priests at York Minster at the same period . . . and forty-eight at Lincoln Cathedral. The large but by no means exceptional parish of Newark-on-Trent boasted fifteen chantries at the end of the Middle Ages" (*Stewards of the Lord,* p. 45). There were altogether thirty thousand priests in England in 1530 (according to Maynard Smith). If the same proportion of priests to laity existed in England today, there would be half a million priests. This puts in perspective the enormity of the Mass-system and its economic and social implications. The reformers were attacking a practice more than a principle, since it was the system which had produced the theology. If the system could be brought within reasonable limits and into conformity with earlier Church practice, a reformed theology could be worked out. But the fact that so many purely private Masses were being said was responsible for the emphasis on the (theologically false) notion that it was the priest alone who sacrificed. They were priests', not people's, Masses. This, however, was to stray far from the early Christian practice and belief concerning the Eucharist. And yet medieval Catholic theology, at its best, was capable of meeting all legitimate Protestant objections. Unfortunately it chose not to do so. Rather it was Catholic theology at its worst, or most badly phrased, that was championed, perhaps because this best supported the widespread loss of orthopraxis in Catholic circles. It was the system of the German nominalist theologian Gabriel Biel that was most heavily relied on. The whole tragedy of the misunderstandings leading to a split in Christendom which was far from inevitable is perhaps summarized in a key paragraph from Hughes:

> By the standards of his day Biel's explanation of eucharistic sacrifice was restrained and sober. His theology of the mass can be explained in an orthodox sense. But by jeopardising the uniqueness of Christ's sacrifice it tended toward conclusions which are irreconcilable with the New Testament. . . . It was Biel's theology, and worse, which dominated the daily life of the church in the first half of the sixteenth century. These were the ideas used to explain the practical mass system: the vast multiplication of masses and the commerce in stipends. Prominent amongst these ideas was the assertion that in the mass the priest offers Jesus Christ to the Father as a propitiatory sacrifice for our sins. The English Reformers, with their firm if one-sided grasp of biblical truth, and their knowledge of the Fathers, saw that this was impossible: Christ had offered himself to the Father once and for all on Calvary. Any suggestion that this offering could be repeated struck at the very heart of the gospel.

This emphasis on the uniqueness of Christ's sacrifice was completely
Catholic. Cranmer saw this and called his book A Defense of the
True and Catholic Doctrine. . . . Cranmer was right in what he
asserted, though wrong in what he denied. Important contributory
causes of his error were the closely inter-related bad eucharistic
theology and practice of the age in which he lived (*Stewards of the
Lord,* pp. 186–187).

All this makes it easier for Catholics to appreciate the thought
behind Article XXXI of the Anglican Thirty-nine Articles, which is
seldom recalled by Catholics in its historical context and is frequently
misquoted. Misunderstanding piled on earlier misunderstanding to
keep alive the unnecessary recriminations of centuries ago. The article
in question states that "The Offering of Christ once made is that perfect redemption, propitiation, and satisfaction, for all the sins of the
world, both original and actual: and there is none other satisfaction
for sin, but that alone." It goes on to say (and the exact wording must
be very carefully noted): "Wherefore the sacrifices of masses, in the
which it was commonly said, that the Priest did offer Christ for the
quick and the dead, to have remission of pain or guilt, were blasphemous fables, and dangerous deceits."

If the reformers were attacking what all now consider to have been
an undoubted abuse, what is the modern, official Catholic view of the
Mass? It can best be seen in the revival, by the 1970 order, of the traditional eucharistic prayer—rather than the consecration—as being
"the center and climax of the whole celebration. . . . In so doing the
Order returns to the oldest tradition of eucharistic celebration. For
centuries, roughly up to the eleventh, Christians were not concerned
about 'the moment of consecration,' and, until the addition of the ele-
vation of the host at the end of the twelfth century, they were largely
unaware when it occurred. . . . The whole eucharistic prayer was
regarded as effecting the eucharist and this meant that the early
church had a much wider and, as one may think, a deeper understanding of it. They saw the prayer as not just bringing about the presence of Christ but as making the great thanksgiving-memorial that
made the great redeeming actions of Christ present and enabling the
community to enter into them. They did not at all sharply distinguish
'real presence,' 'sacrifice,' and 'communion' (as was common in the
later Middle Ages); they saw the eucharistic prayer as affecting the
whole *opus redemptionis*" (Crichton, *Christian Celebration: The
Mass,* p. 84).

"Priesthood," moreover, is not, as between Christian churches, an exclusively Roman Catholic concept. But, at popular level, the "priest" —the man who says Mass and runs the parish—tends to dominate Catholic life. If the word were to be changed back to the earlier term "presbyter" Catholics would feel they had lost something not only valuable but also unique to Catholics as having been present in the Church since the very beginning. In fact, however, the tradition on which this belief depends is, once more, medieval in origin. It was not until the Middle Ages that the terms "priest" and "presbyter" became interchangeable, even though "priest" and "presbyter" do not actually means the same thing. In the New Testament, moreover, the term "priest" is never applied to the apostles or to their successors in the Christian hierarchy. The Jesus of history was not himself a priest. He never referred to himself as such, nor did anyone else in his lifetime. Priesthood is, as it were, retrospectively conferred on him by the (unknown) writer of the Epistle to the Hebrews which is an interpretation of subsequent developments in the light of the Resurrection experiences. Jesus took every possible precaution not to be identified with the priesthood of his day, a member of whose elitist ranks was a performer of sacrificing or sacerdotal functions. This is the Greek origin of the word "priest"—*hiereus,* or in Latin, *sacerdos*—and is not to be confused with the rank of *presbyteros* (elder), which was the term used for the apostles and their successors whose main function, as was constantly emphasized, was pastoral rather than sacrificial. The word "priesthood" *is,* nevertheless, used in the New Testament to connote a sacrificial/sacerdotal function; and it is none other than St. Peter ("the first Pope") who does so in his first Epistle. He attributes the character of priesthood to *all Christians.* Such an attribution was logical since all Christians, men and women—for Christ had abolished all distinction in spiritual matters between the sexes, as Paul pointed out —were to join in the one Christian sacrifice by sacrificing *themselves.* It was not indeed to be a sacrifice to the death, but consisted in "offering up your bodies as a holy sacrifice truly pleasing to God" (Rom. 12:1). And at each Mass the celebrant asks those present to join with him in the most important part of what he is doing: "Pray, brethren, that my sacrifice *and yours* may be acceptable to God the Father Almighty." The celebrant is, in other words, the person who presides over his fellow priests at this sacrificial memorial of the Last Supper. The medieval pattern of a multiplication of Masses and a separate (clerical) priesthood of great power has disappeared forever. The whole notion of the episcopate-presbyterate has been transformed by an entirely new emphasis. This comes out clearly in the sacrament whereby "holy orders" are conferred and which underwent radical reform in 1968. The episcopate had been restored to its position of priority by the Vatican Council and are now clearly seen to receive "the fullness of the sacrament of Order" as a gift of the Holy Spirit. The order in fact is specifically spoken of in these charismatic terms which at long last remove the whole concept of Holy Order out of the legal and juridical sphere. The idea of power is foreign to the new rite. The accent is now, as it originally was, on service. The episcopate-presbyterate serves the Church by its pastoral ministry and preaching of the word. To sacrifice is no longer thought of as the only or principal function of this "priesthood," even though it is a very important one. The revised ordination rite brings the various elements into perspective. The anointing is now carried out so as to make quite clear what it symbolizes. It crystalizes the meaning of the ordination prayer and of the laying on of hands, which is the principal sign of the giving of the Spirit (on whom all depends). The accompanying prayer-formula is: "May our Lord Jesus Christ whom the Father anointed with the power and the Holy Spirit keep you that you may sanctify the Christian people and offer sacrifice to God." The cultic function of priesthood is not suppressed but equally is not, as previously, overemphasized. The solemn clothing with sacerdotal vestments has been replaced by much simpler action. The handing by the ordinand of the empty paten and chalice has been discontinued, along with its accompanying formula: "Receive the power to sacrifice to God for both the living and the dead." Now, the ordinand is given the *people's* offering of bread and wine (in paten and chalice) which are to be used in the Eucharist that will follow. Here the accompanying formula is: "Receive the gifts from the people to be offered to God. Be conscious of what you are doing. Be as holy as the actions you perform. And model your life after the mystery of the Lord's Cross."

A complicated jungle of history is reduced to basics by some observations on the liturgy of pre-Reformation days, that is of the "unreformed church": "That the Church should have realistically reformed her liturgy in the fifteenth century (or even earlier) goes without saying. But it did not do this. . . . At times there seems to have been a sense of expectancy that things somehow or other, perhaps even spontaneously, would change for the better; or that the armed force of Emperor Charles V would ultimately prove decisive. It did not however.

The Church was forced to face the issues, even to the point of waiting four hundred years to solve them" (McNally, *The Unreformed Church*, p. 135). Thus "today the eucharist is a joint field of study for theologians of different confessions, who are able to find a wide measure of agreement. It is no longer a matter of controversy, but a subject for common study" (Sewell, *The Vatican Oracle*, p. 114).

Such common study was given great impetus by an historic visit to Pope Paul VI by the then Archbishop of Canterbury, Dr. Michael Ramsey, in March 1966. The "Anglican-Roman Catholic Joint Preparatory Commission" was set up and held the last of three meetings at the end of 1967. The result was the Anglican-Roman Catholic International Commission which issued important joint, agreed statements on the Eucharist in 1971, and on the Christian Ministry in 1973. The degree of agreement reached by the teams of theologians from each communion was astonishing, but the statements did not represent the official joint view of the two churches. They were only blueprints which awaited official approval. The third and most important statement of all came in January 1977, and was on the subject of Authority in the Church. This was thought to be the most difficult theme so far tackled and the leader of the Catholic team, Bishop Alan Clark of England, admitted at the press conference introducing the report that it had originally thought that no agreement could be reached. But it was. And Bishop Clark felt able to go on to say that "For some time there will be a degree of symbiosis between the two churches. We will live alongside each other but grow into each other."

The logical termination of this symbiosis would be the recognition of what is envisaged by the now popular phrase "a Pope for all Christians." For the 1977 agreed statement foresaw Anglican acceptance of the Pope's universal Primacy provided this was understood in the agreed sense. Bishop (later Archbishop) H. R. McAdoo of Ireland, leading the Anglican team, explained that the Pope, in this context, would be seen as the *primus inter pares*. He would occupy a position not unlike that of the chairman of the board of a diversified corporation—a position which, as the documents put it, "precludes the idea that the Pope is an inspired oracle communicating fresh revelation or that he can speak independently of his fellow bishops." The statement went on to clear up certain misunderstandings which Anglicans had had in the past about papal authority and to put into perspective exaggerations previously made from time to time by Catholics. It pointed out that many Catholic scholars today did not think that the New

Testament references to St. Peter supported all the claims that had
been formerly made for the See of Rome. Such expressions used in the
past as the "divine right" of the Pope had "no clear interpretation in
modern Roman Catholic theology." The doctrine of infallibility, moreover, was "hedged around by very rigorous conditions." The First
Vatican Council, the 1977 document reminded Christians, "intended
that the papal primacy should be exercised only to maintain and never
to erode the structures of the local Churches." And again, "Primacy
fulfills its purpose by helping the Churches to listen to one another, to
grow in love and unity, and to strive together towards the fullness of
Christian life and witness; it respects and promotes Christian freedom
and spontaneity; it does not seek uniformity where diversity is legitimate, or centralized administration to the detriment of local Churches."

Perhaps more importantly, the agreed statement laid paramount
stress, in discussing authority, not on any one human person or purely
ecclesiastical group, but on the authority inherent in the community of
God's people:

> The Spirit of the risen Lord, who in-dwells the Christian community,
> continues to maintain the people of God in obedience to the Father's
> will. He safeguards their faithfulness of the revelation of Jesus
> Christ and equips them for their mission in the world. By this
> action of the Holy Spirit, the authority of the Lord is active in the
> church. Through incorporation into Christ and obedience to him,
> Christians are made open to one another and assume mutual
> obligations.
>
> Since the lordship of Christ is universal, the community also bears
> a responsibility towards all mankind, which demands participation
> in all that promotes the good of society and responsiveness to every
> form of human need. The common life in the body of Christ equips
> the community and each of its members with what they need to
> fulfill this responsibility; they are enabled so to live that the author-
> ity of Christ will be mediated through them. This is Christian
> authority; when Christians so act and speak, men perceive the
> authoritative word of Christ.

As Bishop McAdoo remarked after this statement had been issued,
the theologians had finished their work. It was now up to the official
Churches to take matters further if possible. The Archbishop of
Canterbury, Dr. Donald Coggan, met the Pope a month later (in
April 1977) and issued a hopeful declaration, praising the very aus-
picious agreed statements, and the International Commission as a

whole. "We now recommend," they said, "that the work it has begun be pursued through procedures appropriate to our respective communions, so that both of them may be led along the path towards unity. The moment will come shortly when the respective authorities must evaluate the conclusions."

At the present rate of progress that moment may not even come this century. It may never come at all. The fault does not lie all on the Roman Catholic side. Anti-Roman Anglican prejudice based on ignorance is still surprisingly strong. Both Churches, moreover, show little inclination to take the initial step toward the only sort of unity and united action that can have any impact on a world undergoing revolutionary change. And that is relinquishment of its privileged status in whatever regions such status still exists. Some indication has already been given of what this would mean for the Roman Church. For the Anglican Church (in England), disestablishment is the requirement; but it is in no way contemplated at the moment. It would be materially impoverishing but spiritually humbling and therefore enriching. Pride is also a major stumbling block on the Catholic side to the sort of unity which would make possible the reentering of the revolutionary world in pilgrim garb and thus revolutionizing the revolution. This fact came out very strongly in a surprising context.

The papal commission which, as already mentioned, met in the late sixties to advise the Pope on birth control issued a majority and a minority report. The minority report (favoring no change in the existing ban on contraception) laid much stress on the Roman Catholic Church's claim to the exclusive guidance of the Holy Spirit in disputed matters. It argued that for the Church to be seen as changing its mind on the licitness of contraception would damage this apparent possession of a monopoly of divine truth. It recalled that the Lambeth Conference of the Anglican Communion had, in 1930, occasioned a papal encyclical by way of reply. For the Anglicans had declared that birth control, by whatever method, must be a matter of conscience. Pius XI, in reply, had issued his letter *Casti Conubii,* stating that it was the (Roman) Catholic Church "to whom God has entrusted the defence of the integrity and purity of morals . . . in token of her divine ambassadorship . . . and through our mouth." The papal Birth Control Commission's minority report was therefore horrified at any possibility of a shifting of ground, as if it were "now to be admitted that the Church erred in this her work, and that the Holy Spirit rather assists the Anglican Church."

Perish the thought!

The reasoning behind the minority report may seem petty and childish. But it corresponds to the thought of enough Catholics in Britain, America and other Western countries today to ensure that the progress of ecumenism can be no quicker, in real terms, than the preferred speed of the slowest and most anti-ecumenical group of members on either side. Ecumenism cannot be imposed. Only with gradual realization that *"what* is right" is more important than *"who* is right" can ecumenism be revived into any genuine sort of activity. According to Raymond E. Brown, "the side which takes the first bold step will be recognizable as the most Christian" (*Biblical Reflections on Crises Facing the Church,* p. 83).

CHAPTER 15

Special Cases

Christian ideology has contributed no little to the oppression of woman.

SIMONE DE BEAUVOIR

Since the fourth century after Christ, there have been three anti-Jewish policies: conversion, expulsion and annihilation. The second appeared as an alternative to the first and the third emerged as an alternative to the second.

RAOUL HILBERG

---

1. Women

Ecumenism is an area of Church thinking which has thrown certain special cases, or categories of problem, into noticeable relief.

In November 1978, for example, the General Synod of the Anglican Church voted against the ordination of women. A previous synod had stated that there was no theological principle which would be violated if women were made ministers. And in November 1978, there were substantial majorities for ordaining women among the bishops and lay members of the synod. It was only the (all male) clergy who, by a majority of 149 to 94, managed in effect to "veto" the proposal before the assembly. The vote was thus based on personal (male) preference rather than strictly theological grounds (in view of the theological consensus previously recorded). But there had also been much lobbying beforehand and one argument that had been given wide airing was that it would be ecumenically damaging for relations with the Roman Church if the Episcopalian (Anglican) Church were to move toward the official recognition of female orders (such as already existed in America). Was it a male conspiracy? Or was it a responsible act of Christian churchmanship? What is the Roman view? What, first of all, is the prehistory of the male-and-female element in religious development?

In the earliest known societies the female, not the male, was the symbol of life and fertility. The oldest divinity known to have been worshiped by the human race was the Mother Goddess. Documentations of the myths concerning this goddess in Oceania, Africa, Asia, the Middle East, and both North and South America, are supported by the findings of archeology. Principal among the discoveries are those of tiny statues depicting the *magna mater,* some of which have been traced to the year 60,000 B.C. By the time Christianity had come along, however, God had become male, and society was male-dominated. The Catholic Church inherited and preserved this domination with the help, to a great extent, of the image that was gradually built up of the Virgin Mary. She replaced the primitive goddess model but retained many of her earlier characteristics as popularly conceived. Superimposed hereon was the crucial virtue of submissiveness for which Mary was then to become the supreme exemplar for Christian women. Thus, based on Our Lady, as Catholics call her, there developed the myth of *The Eternal Woman,* condemned forever to inferior tasks and worthy of salvation only through childbearing. The myth was fortunately balanced by healthy and reasonable devotion to Mary as the mother of Jesus and first recipient of the gifts of the Spirit which would one day be available to all God's people. As long as the balance was preserved, all was more or less well. The celibate male clergy of the Middle Ages, however, armed with the anti-feminist theology of even the greatest of the Scholastics (such as Aquinas himself, Duns Scotus and many others) commended the "purity" and "submissiveness" of Our Lady as the perfect ideal. The very pedestal on which Mary was placed took all Christian women, her all-too-human, would-be imitators, right outside the scope of real life. This was left for the males of the *societas Christiana* to run as they pleased.

Women, by and large, did not complain until modern times. Now "Women's Lib" has become a Christian controversy—or at least a part of it. But the Church has yet to make its decisive act of reparation for the position it imposed on women in the past. Even scripture was misread—or at least misused—in the course of this process. It is now well-known, for example, that the Book of Genesis contains not one but two quite separate and different accounts of creation. It is the earlier creation story, found in Genesis 2 and known as the "J document," which has been used as the basis for Christian thinking about women. The "P document" account appearing in Genesis 1, and written several centuries later, has been glossed over and its implications either ignored or misunderstood. And yet the later account makes it clear that woman was not brought into being as an afterthought to the creation of man. God's plan was of complete sexual duality with dominion over the earth being given to man and woman jointly: "Let us make mankind in our image and likeness and let *them* have dominion. . . . Male and female he created them" (Gen. 1:26–27). Christianity, however, preferred the more primitive "Adam's rib" version and took this convenient theory into its medieval economic system.

Simone de Beauvoir, in a famous book, charts the course of events. Through St. Paul, the anti-feminist Jewish tradition was affirmed. Adoption of Greek philosophy supplied support for the idea of feminine inferiority. The (false) Aristotelian idea of fixed "natures" was taken over by St. Thomas Aquinas so that woman's place was fixed forever by her "nature." The early Fathers had identified woman primarily with sex, and therefore with sin and uncleanness. Male guilt, in other words, had been transferred to the female. Since the "flesh" was held to be accursed, certain consequences logically followed: "The flesh that is for the Christian the hostile *Other* is precisely woman. In her the Christian finds incarnated the temptations of the world, the flesh and the devil. . . . Since the Middle Ages, the fact of having a body has been considered, in woman, an ignominy" (*The Second Sex*, pp. 184–85). A woman's body after childbirth was unclean and had to be purified in the Catholic ceremony, continued until very recently, called "churching." (Considering their unhappy position in the Judeo-Christian scheme of things, it is hardly surprising that Jewish men should have thanked God for not having created them as women. In orthodox Jewish circles, the same prayer of thanksgiving is still offered.)

Subservient womanhood was highly appropriate to the needs of a patriarchal Catholic Church. Perpetuation of the family kept the patrimony intact. Clerics, however, were forbidden to marry because their wealth would be inherited by their descendants and thus lost to the Church. Man meanwhile "owned" woman and demanded virginity as a condition of marriage. Unmarried women could serve the Church as dedicated virgins. If they became nuns, the convent received their dowries. Virginity was so highly praised that prostitutes were treated as outcasts. But their trade, as an institution, was accepted as an evil that was necessary for preserving good order in the Church-dominated society of the age. Both St. Augustine and St. Thomas agreed that the suppression of prostitution would mean the disruption of society. The setting of a double standard in morality was thus, in essence, a class affair. (The Church always sides with the Establishment where possible.) In the Middle Ages, moreover, "canon law admitted no other matrimonial regime than the dowry scheme, which made women legally incompetent and powerless. Not only did the masculine occupations remain closed to her, but she was forbidden to make depositions in court, and her testimony was not recognised as having weight" (ibid., p. 121). The Church acted on the principle that "there must be religion for women; and there must be 'true women' to perpetuate religion" (ibid., p. 127). "True women" meant passive ones; women who knew "their place" because they remained faithful to their "nature." It is probably superfluous to add that none of these attitudes toward women can be shown to be consistent with or based on any of the actual sayings, still less the deeds, of Jesus himself. (His view of prevailing social attitudes toward women, on the other hand, was a passive one.)

If, however, the Church erred in the past, was it not merely following the social conventions of the day? The argument, though ignoring the fact that the Church was itself the chief molder of such conventions, is often heard. What is the modern view? How has the Church reacted to the twentieth-century trends? Pope Benedict XV supported votes for women feeling that women would be more likely than men to support conservative and religious parties in political contests. As everyone knows, the status of women in "Catholic" countries lagged far behind that of those in other countries. (This, ironically, makes it possible to argue that women themselves wished no change in the status quo.) The campaign for equal education, however, was the most important test. Pius XI opposed coeducation as implying "naturalism and the denial of original sin," in his 1929 encyclical Divini Illius Magistri. "The Creator," said the Pope, "has ordained and disposed perfect union of the sexes only in matrimony and, with varying degrees of contact, in the family and in society. Besides there is not in nature itself, which fashions the two quite different in organism, in temperament, in abilities, anything to suggest that there can be or ought to be promiscuity, and much less equality, in the training of the two sexes." (The Pope seems to have feared equality more than promiscuity. Or his rather muddled phraseology may have been an unconscious reflection of traditional double standards on the subject.)

What of the Church's recent views on the matter? Whole books could be—indeed have been—written on the subject. (One of the most provocative was Mary Daly's The Church and the Second Sex in which the author sees women emerging as a force to be reckoned with

—everywhere except in the Catholic Church.) The test case for many has centered on whether women may be admitted to the ministerial priesthood. The expression "ministerial priesthood" is important since Christian women are already members of the sacrificial type of priesthood along with all their fellow Christians. (The special biblical word to distinguish this common kind of priesthood of all believers from the "presbyterate" has already been commented upon.) To the actual question "Can women become presbyters?" Rome gave the official Catholic answer on January 27, 1977, when the Sacred Congregation for the Doctrine of the Faith issued its *Declaration on the Question of the Admission of Women to the Ministerial Priesthood*. Its answer was "No." And the reason given for this answer is that "Jesus Christ did not call any woman to become part of the Twelve. If he acted in this way, it was not in order to conform to the customs of his time, for his attitude toward women was quite different from that of his milieu, and he deliberately and courageously broke with it." There is such profound and widespread disagreement in the Church on the validity of this argument—especially in the United States—that, while it will hold the line for the time being, it will not do so forever. The Jesus of history was, generally speaking, a social conformist. In particular he accomodated himself to the secondary role played in religion by women. He did not know the future either for himself or for his followers. He prayed in the Garden that he would not have to die, unless it was the will of his Father. He himself had spoken only about preaching his word to the House of Israel. It was the Spirit that took over after his death and formed the infant church which, after much debate, decided to admit Gentiles without demanding their circumcision. Among the early hierarchical orders was that of "deaconess." But perhaps such arguments, for nowadays, are largely unreal. Pedants just bandy them about after dinner for intellectual exercise. The world is starving for justice and Christians have it in their power to supply a soul to the revolutionary march of man-and-womankind. "Male and female created he them" but not to discriminate against each other for, in Christ, as Paul insists, there is no longer Jew and Greek, male and female; all are one. Many Christians and Catholics feel forever bound by the present. Others manage to lift their eyes above the hills. A few years ago Michael Novak wrote, "For myself, I envisage a time, perhaps generations from now (for symbols sometimes come to express reality fully only in the slow ways of organic life), when the Eucharist will commonly be celebrated by two central figures, equal in symbolic power although different in their relation one to another, one vicar of Christ and the other representing the church, both together celebrating the oneness of Christ and his Church" ("Dual-Sex Eucharist," *Commonweal* 103, December 17, 1976, p. 816).

The two central figures, of course, are man and woman.

2. *"Non-Christians"*

For Catholics, ecumenism concerns only the divisions between one sort of Christian and another. For most Catholics (despite the Council) the position of Protestants is readily identifiable. They are "outside the Church." What about those who are not Christians at all? It is only recently that the Roman Church has encouraged its sons and daughters to study non-Christian religions. For we must, in future, live in one world, and a religiously pluralistic one at that. It was the final realization of this which prompted the Council fathers to pronounce so unambiguously in favor of religious freedom, despite the bitter opposition of "traditionalists." No less bitter, but more broadly based, was the opposition to the initial moves which ended up with an official statement by the Council on the subject of "Non-Christian religions" —the declaration *Nostra Aetate*. The reason for this was that the original intention—coming from Pope John XXIII himself—had been to issue a statement on the Jews. It had been intended that this statement should be one of reconciliation and should be included in the decree on ecumenism; but such a course was later thought inappropriate. A statement, on its own, extending the hand of friendship from the Catholic Church to the Jews, was even more strongly opposed.

The opposition came from two quarters: from Catholic Arab bishops fearing that anything friendly said about the Jews would be taken in Arab countries as Catholic support for the political State of Israel; from Catholics, of whom there is a very large number, sharing in one degree or another in anti-Semitic sentiment. To gild the pill it was thus decided to dress up the intended declaration on the Jews as a general declaration on "non-Christian" religions by the brief inclusion of Muslims, Hindus and Buddhists. But the declaration—an historic one—has come to be considered as the final breaking of silence by the Church on the subject of that particular religion and race which Roman Catholicism had actively persecuted so long and so vehemently in the past.

Opposition from a determined minority of the Council Fathers went on at each stage right up to the final voting. In the process the declaration underwent considerable watering down from the form in which it was originally drafted. The Church failed to "condemn" anti-Semitism and succeeded only in "deploring" it. Though exonerating Jews from being guilty of Jesus' crucifixion, it failed, in the final form of the text, to exonerate them from the crime of "deicide." Yet it was for this alleged crime that they had suffered so many horrors at the hands of Christians throughout history. The thesis of a necessary divine punishment for the Jews had been going on since the third century when it was explicitly formulated by Origen: "We may thus assert in utter confidence that the Jews will not return to their earlier situation, for they have committed the most abominable of crimes, in forming this conspiracy against the Savior of the human race. . . ."

Such "theological anti-Semitism" showed itself in every subsequent century. The guilt of the Jews was a constant sermon topic especially in the East where the Jews were more numerous. Gregory of Nyssa (fourth century) called the Jews "murderers of the Lord, assassins of the prophets, rebels and detesters of God, they outrage the Law, resist grace, repudiate the faith of their fathers. Companions of the devil, race of vipers, informers, calumniators, darkeners of the mind, pharisaic leaven, Sanhedrin of demons, accursed, detested, lapidators, enemies of all that is beautiful." Not all of the epithets stuck but the Jews always remained "accursed" in the eyes of respectable Christians. St. John Chrysostom, the famed orator whose name meant "Golden-mouthed," kept the ball rolling: "Brothel and theatre, the synagogue is also a cave of pirates and the lair of wild beasts. . . . Living for their belly, mouth forever gaping, the Jews behave no better than hogs and goats in their lewd grossness and the excesses of their gluttony. They can do one thing only: gorge themselves with food and drink." (St. John was declared patron of preachers by Pope Pius X in 1909.)

When the early Christian community (which had originally been Jewish) was transformed into a Church-State and finally an ecclesiastical empire, theological anti-Semitism became translated into specific anti-Jewish regulations. The similarity of these (as they intensified between the fourth and fifteenth centuries) to the steadily worsening anti-Jewish measures of the Nazis has been startlingly demonstrated by Raoul Hilberg (*The Destruction of the European Jews*, pp. 5–6). John XXIII's attempt to make amends was, correspondingly, an explicitly post-Holocaust gesture. Though the Vatican

Council theoretically cancelled theological anti-Semitism, its effects remain. These invade even the political arena. The Holy See refuses to extend diplomatic recognition to the State of Israel. The official reason given is that Israel is still "at war" inasmuch as its frontiers are still a matter of international dispute. Considering that the same thing could theoretically be said about the Republic of Ireland ("recognized," of course, by the Church) vis à vis its border with the six counties of the North, this reason is widely regarded as spurious and based on a mere technicality. The real reason in practice is fear of reactions among powerful Christians (and others) in Arab countries if the Church were to recognize Israel. The Church moreover is financially tied to that bloc of nations in which oil is a staple product. The third and most important reason for the refusal to recognize Israel is the theological one. For the Church to acknowledge the triumphant return of the chosen people to their promised land would be a reversal of the constant refrain of Catholic theologians over the centuries as to the "accursed" state of the Jews. Such factors explain, in part, the delay of nearly ten years before the Vatican issued any "guidelines" for the actual implementation of *Nostra Aetate*. These guidelines, even though now issued, "fail to recognize the central role which the land of Israel occupies in Jewish religious thought. Despite the assertion that the authors desire to understand Jews as they understand themselves, the failure to make any mention of the burning question of Jewish survival in Israel and elsewhere in the post-Auschwitz era raises a basic question of credibility for the guidelines" (Drinan, *Honor the Promise,* p. 202).

The majority of Catholics—at least in Britain and America—are still, overtly or subconsciously, anti-Jewish. Given past conditioning they could hardly fail to be so. *Nostra Aetate* and the succeeding guidelines, however, broke some new ground. There can now be a real hope that Catholics will eventually behave as Christians toward Jews. It could even be one of the crucial tests of Catholic sincerity in the twenty-first century search for "one world." But much groundwork remains to be done in these last years of the present millennium. The well-known Rabbi Marc C. Tanenbaum—national director for interreligious affairs for the American Jewish Committee—highlights the danger area: "Any definition of contemporary Jewish religious experience that does not provide for due comprehension and acceptance of the inextricable bonds of God, people, Torah, and promised land, risks distortion of the essential nature of Judaism and the Jewish people, and would constitute a regression in Jewish-Christian understanding" (*Catholic Mind,* May 1975).

CHAPTER 16

Clerico-Capitalism

Thou shalt not lend upon usury to thy brother.

DEUTERONOMY 23:19

When the Pope explained that we need money and are a poor
Church, he meant exactly that: We, the managers, want to
improve investment performance, balanced of course against
what must be a fundamentally conservative investment
philosophy. It wouldn't do for the Church to lose its principal
in speculation.

EGIDIO CARDINAL VAGNOZZI

IMAGINE FOR A moment that it is the year 2025 and that you are walking into the Vatican by the "tradesman's entrance." This is still, as it
was way back in the 1970s, St. Anne's Gate. The Vatican is of course
no longer a sovereign state but many of its former administrative
offices survive. Their clerical staff, male and female, are augmented by
specially trained workers from every part of the globe. They mostly
work for love rather than money. They operate harmoniously together
despite some feeling on the part of the whites that their minority status
occasionally brings discrimination. (Whites are rarely employed, for
example, in the Pontifical Secretariat for the Relief and Rehabilitation
of Western Peoples.) The whole place has long lost the funereal atmosphere of fifty years earlier and now bustles with the same sort of
activity as a modern university campus. The young have, to a great extent, taken over. Many live in the commune that was once a little-
known papal farm near Castel Gandolfo.

In this year 2025—the Holy Year of Inter-World Reconciliation—
the effects of Vatican IV are beginning to bite. The world revolution
that few thought would actually happen left the Vatican stunned. But
the resourceful English Pope, Basil I, passed on to his American
successor a viable and fundamentally refurbished instrument with
which to try and serve some of the world's six billion people. That

Pope had, in turn, retired, and been succeeded by a thirty-two-year-old
Indonesian who is currently commuting from a temporary Los Angeles
office by daily ninety-minute subway ride to hold reconciliation services in the Chicago area. The Pope travels incognito and mostly
unrecognized, but will shortly be back at "head office" in Rome where,
at a brief ceremony, she will officially open the new wing of the building you are about to visit.

To reach it you walk straight ahead along the Via di Belvedere,
through the Belvedere Court and on past the Public Records Office
and Central Reference Library (formerly the Vatican Secret Archives). Ahead of you is an open space which looks remarkably similar
to what it did in the previous century. But just beyond the Summer
House of Pope Pius IV a vast complex has been completed underground so as to disturb as little as possible the gardens above. The
summer house, long ago aptly named the "Science Academy," has
been cleverly adapted as the entrance down into this new complex
which houses the Sacred Congregation for the Supervision and Advancement of Applied Pharmacology. The title is a bit of a mouthful
and shows that the twenty-first-century Vatican has not lost its pen-
chant for elaborate and, sometimes, euphemistic descriptions of its various administrative and experimental departments. This congregation
is actually a vast laboratory devoted to birth control research and the
production of contraceptive drugs that "will conform to the Church's
moral precepts as formulated by the legitimate development of traditional teaching and of such chemical makeup as will reduce and, if
possible, eliminate all dangers to the physical and psychological health
of individuals." The laboratory is affectionately known around the
Vatican as "the papal pill box."

This is not fantasy in bad taste. It is admittedly fanciful; but it may
help one to imagine the reactions of men of a former age to the idea of
a Vatican bank, under the shadow of St. Peter's, as part of the
Church's heavy involvement in world investment, shareholding and
trade. To have suggested to the Catholics of the eighteenth century
that such a bank would one day exist would have been profoundly
shocking. Had not that most enlightened of pre-Revolutionary Popes,
Benedict XIV, issued an encyclical in 1745 (*Vix Pervenit*) laying it
down that to reclaim anything but the exact amount of a loan was a
sin? He was only reaffirming the traditional teaching of the Church
for over a thousand years that the charging of interest on a loan was

absolutely forbidden as being contrary to Divine Law. The prohibition was restated in various Church Councils: Arles (314); Nicaea (325); Carthage (345); Aix (789); Lateran (1179); Lyons (1274); Vienne (1311). This last declared that anyone who maintained that the practice (of "usury") was not sinful should be punished as a heretic. Such punishment was no joke at that particular date, after a century of the Inquisition at its worst, complete with torture and imprisonment and death by burning (because the Church could not permit the shedding of blood) for unrepentant heretics. It was only in the nineteenth century that an official change of mind finally came about as a result of individual Catholics having, for so long, been acting in contravention of Church law by their carrying on of normal trade naturally involving the taking and receiving of interest on money lent or invested. But many had done so with a troubled conscience. Moralists had anguished and argued endlessly over the matter and different confessors had given different advice to their penitents. The parallel with the birth control controversy of today is striking. Over the question of interest on money, the Church was being so rapidly overtaken by events that some sort of decision became inevitable. Refuge was sought, among other things, in the fact that *Vix Pervenit* (like *Humanae Vitae*) had not been an infallible decree. The Sacred Penitentiary, in answer to anxious inquiries, finally issued (in 1830) a series of decisions stating that the faithful who lent money at *moderate* rates of interest were "not to be disturbed" (in conscience) provided they were willing to abide by any future decisions of the Holy See. It may be noted that this was merely a compromising and pragmatic way out of the dilemma. No theological judgement was made, then or ever, on the actual morality of moneylending at interest on the theoretical level. Will the Church avail itself of a similar let-out over contraception? Since sex, not money, is involved, it will be more difficult.

At the moment we are concerned with money and must return, in imagination, to that same Via di Belvedere mentioned above. The year however, is 1980, not 2025. Housed in a nearby building is the Vatican bank, though any such actual name is sedulously avoided. Indeed the very existence and whereabouts of the bank would be probably undiscoverable to outsiders. Only an intimate of the Vatican could steer him there. It is not, perhaps understandably, there for all to see, with a prominent front door on the street and under some such superscription

as "Vatican National Bank."* Those privy to its location, however, use
it regularly to deposit and withdraw funds, and for almost all normal
banking facilities. Priests chafe in the queue as they listen impatiently
to the nun in front of them arguing some point with the teller. Changing travelers' checks there can be advantageous as the rate of exchange
is sometimes better than in the banks of the Rome outside the Vatican.
Such business, however, is not the main concern of this unusual bank.
Its operations are very much larger. But they are mysterious. The average Vatican official, in fact, if you asked him about the Vatican
"bank," might deny that any such thing existed. Technically he would
be correct. (Some have even been known to deny that there is a "bar"
off the sacristy inside St. Peter's.) The Vatican itself is coy about the
activity of its bank which is never referred to by anything but its official name: the Institute for the Works of Religion. The only official
reference to the "Institute" in the *Annuario Pontificio* (Vatican Year
Book) is the statement that "its function is to provide for the custody
and administration of capital destined for works of religion." Basically
the institute manages the large sums, stocks and shares entrusted to it
mainly by religious institutes, or orders, with appropriate profit to the
Holy See. These religious institutes (such as Benedictines, Jesuits,
etc.) have long had their "mother houses," or generalates, in Rome.
Their money was once kept in various banks around the city. But such
an arrangement was thought to be dangerous in wartime. Pius XII
then hit on the idea of the Vatican's having a bank of its own to protect the funds of such institutes as well as making possible the building
up of cash reserves for the Vatican itself for the purposes of its charitable and relief work. It was thus that he set up the "Institute for the
Works of Religion" on June 27, 1942. Initial deposits were small but
by the end of the war deposits and disbursements were running at an
annual rate of about twenty-five million dollars. This was due largely
to the major fund-raising activities (mostly American and Canadian)
designed to finance the Pope's aid and charitable ventures which, as
the war came to an end, were considerable. The present "managing
director" of the institute is an affable and engaging giant of a man
from Cicero, Illinois (home town of Al Capone), Bishop Paul Marcinkus. His brief is wide and he has a large say in the general invest-

---

* In fact its "main branch" is housed on an upper floor of the Nicholas V
Tower whose door at street level is well guarded, with all visitors being
carefully screened. It is untraceable in guide books and ordinary reference
manuals. Its present director, Bishop Marcinkus, is one of the most powerful
men in the Vatican.

ment policy of the Holy See. He is the fortunate possessor of business flair, natural authority and personal charm.

Thus, the present Roman Church, is very much engaged in the same sort of capitalistic endeavors as the remainder of the Western world. It seeks the best ways and means to enable money to make more money in order to further its overall and ultimate aims. Nevertheless, the institute, or "bank," is neither the only nor, on paper, the most important cog in the Vatican's financial machinery. Responsibility for overall coordination of this rests on the narrow and slightly stooped shoulders of Egidio Cardinal Vagnozzi. Courteous and cautious, he is one of the most conservative of all the Curial Cardinals, and his career includes long stints as papal representative, first in the Philippines and then in Washington. To meet him (if you can) you must leave the Vatican itself and step across the road to a building in the Palazzo delle Congregazione, facing the outer perimeter of the great Bernini colonnade. This contains the offices of the "Prefecture of the Economic Affairs of the Holy See" and the Cardinal President sits behind an elegant desk at the end of a long room overlooking St. Peter's Square. Cardinal Vagnozzi is, in his own words, "the eye of the Pope in the material and economic sphere of the Holy See." He looks at one shrewdly through his steel-rimmed spectacles and before answering any question peers down thoughtfully at the papers in front of him. No other man knows so much about every aspect of Vatican finances as he. In some other context his title might be that of "Auditor-General." He is willing to give plenty of general information. But no actual figures. The exact wealth of the Holy See—and the Roman Catholic Church as a whole—is a closely guarded secret. And yet Vagnozzi's Prefecture has been in a position—since its establishment in 1971—to summarize annually the exact state of the "patrimony" and the progress of assets and liabilities of all the various administrations of the Holy See as to both final balance or estimate for each year. Before 1971 no such summary was possible. There was a mass of separate balance sheets each drawn up according to different criteria. Now the individual balance sheets all follow a uniform pattern. After being vetted by the Prefecture, they enter into the confidential consolidated balance sheet which is presented directly to the Pope. Why is this overall balance sheet not made public?

It would be dangerous, the Cardinal explains. Its contents might fall into the hands of the Communists or other enemies of the Church. They would misrepresent the figures and make trouble. Undeserved criticism would come from the mass media or other "unsympathetic observers." This would never do. The Prefecture itself, however, makes constructive criticism about all aspects, administrative and other, of Vatican finance, even though it has no control over the Institute for the Works of Religion. The Vatican bank is expected to keep its own house in order. As regards the Vatican's investment policy, the Prefecture makes general comments but not day-to-day decisions.

Vagnozzi's department, though it may worry about "enemies" outside the Church, has enemies right inside the Vatican. But not for any sinister reason on either side. The Cardinal is a conservative. So are most Curial bureaucrats. However, the idea of a new (1971) department being set up to centralize papal records and accounts was not popular. Directly or indirectly almost every other Vatican department would be affected. And in every social entity—the family, the local community, the corporation, the nation—no area is more sensitive than that which concerns money. The benevolent smile fades in seconds when a person's pocket is threatened. Here lies part of the reason for the tragic shadow, still largely unknown, which flickered over the final years of Paul VI's pontificate: his growing unpopularity among rank-and-file members of his own Curia. This involves a short but not irrelevant digression.

The Vatican may be a prestigious sovereign state and nerve center of the world's largest religion. But it is also a village. And like all villages, it thrives on gossip. Vatican gossip is retailed and snapped up round the clock, seven days a week. In and out of one or other of the entrances to the city-state (mostly St. Anne's Gate) tramp the men— and a few women—who work inside the walls. The cafés of the adjoining streets have long since become part of the village. Vaticanians patronize them for "breakfast"—at all hours—coffee breaks, aperitifs, snack meals, long lunches, post-prandial sessions over wine and *grappa* (their offices are closed in the afternoon) and sometimes to transact "business" of one kind or another. The gossip flows freely whether the rumor mongers be monsignori or mechanics, printers or prelates. One *trattoria* near St. Anne's Gate is a favorite with papal personnel and much favored by Vatican-watching journalists. If you can understand Roman Italian you can pick up a lot by merely eavesdropping from behind your newspaper. You can even hear some of tomorrow's headlines originating in the most unexpected quarters, as you sum up your fellow patrons in the bustling café. Who, for example, is that excited, plump Italian lady, jabbering and gesticulating as she answers the questions of the bearded man in slouch hat and mackintosh? It turns out to be the wife of a Swiss Guard whose "beat" is on the corridor outside the private papal apartments. She is telling her companion—a resourceful American reporter—the latest "news" about the Pope's health. This was the chief topic of conversation during most of 1978. And for several years up until that time every conversation began and ended with Pope Paul. His unpopularity grew as he continued to "modernize" things. He was feared by the bureaucracy as a dangerous liberal while the rest of the world had long written him off as a hopeless conservative, or, at best, an ineffectual ditherer. The flavor of Vatican opinion in these years came through much more clearly in the remarks, sometimes throwaways, sometimes Freudian slips, of the Vatican employees of the middle and lower ranks, than from anything you could hear from the men at the top. For the latter were necessarily "discreet" to the end—sphinx-like in their safeguarding of eternal enigmas; but their private views were often known, or shrewdly suspected, by their subordinates. And so the gossip would weave its everlasting web.

The main charge against Paul VI was that he had actually gone ahead and presided over the implementation of every single decree of the Vatican Council. The fact that such implementation was often merely formal did not deter his critics from within. Where, they asked, would the modernization stop? In 1967 the whole Curia was "reformed." In practice the reform was little more than a series of mergers and changing of names. But then, in 1971, came the setting up of the Prefecture for Economic Affairs. The Pope wanted to know exactly how much money the Vatican had, where it came from, and what was being done with it. Paul was seldom more in earnest than when he wrote in his (1967) encyclical *Populorum Progressio* ("The Development of Peoples") : "It is unfortunate that in (industrial) society a system has been constructed which considers profit as the key motive for economic progress, competition as the supreme law of economics, and private ownership of the means of production as an absolute right that has no limits and carries no outstanding social obligations." The Pope, aware of the Church's image as being immensely rich, was also aware of how damaging this was to some of his own most treasured ambitions. These included bringing real help (not just financial "aid") to the third world. He wanted his Church to be on constant pilgrimage and at the service of the poor. This, for him, involved not the liquidation but the drastic redeployment of the

Church's possessions and investments. Vatican civil servants, no longer safe behind the cloak of secrecy and smokescreen of muddle, began to mutter. Perhaps it was true, after all, that Montini, as some liked to say, had begun to listen to Communists and Freemasons?

It was bad enough that the Pope wanted to meet the Italian government halfway in their demands that the Vatican should, as a "foreign investor," pay tax on its holdings within Italy. More radical were Paul's ideas about the need to diversify and change the whole character of the Vatican's very considerable investments in real estate and industry—mostly, up until 1969, Italian. Such investments had made the Church at least appear to be, among other things, a rich landlord, owning, it was reliably thought, large areas of the Monte Mario (a Roman residential area with escalating land values) and having a substantial stake in such small goldmines as Rome's Hilton Hotel.

The responsibility for the Vatican's investments and financial deals belongs largely to one of the most fascinating but also most mysterious of all the departments tucked away within the formidable framework of the "Roman Curia." This department was formerly known as the Special Administration. After the curial reforms of 1967 it became the "extraordinary section" of the Administration of the Holy See's Patrimony. The latter was itself a new body, taking in, as its "ordinary" section, the former Administration of the Holy See's Properties. Its functions can best be described as being akin to those of a revenue department. It has its offices in St. Peter's Square. The main task of the "ordinary" section is to supervise the collections, church tax receipts, securities, portfolios and other holdings of the papacy. The task of the "extraordinary section" is to manage a substantial part of the Vatican's colossal investment portfolio. It was set up as the "Special Administration" in June 1929, to administer the capital (about $2.4 billion) that Mussolini handed over to the Holy See, on the signing of the Church-State Concordat. This sum was given in compensation for the loss to the Church (sixty years earlier) of the Papal States. After all the talk about the need for papal temporal sovereignty in order to be politically independent, it turned out to be chiefly a matter of money. (Restored sovereignty would bring back the ability to operate freely in the money markets of the world.) The Papal States, moreover, had once produced considerable and regular revenue for the Church. Without them, after 1870—having refused on principle the offer of a handsome annuity from the new Italian state—the Church in Rome faced bankruptcy. This unprecedented and undignified position was intolerable. For a thousand years, the Church had, despite periodic crises, been devising ways and means of remaining solvent. Money became a central preoccupation of Church thinking. The Faith could obviously survive without money; but the "Church" could not. And the "Church" mattered.

Despite the bans on usury, the Church was in the moneymaking business long before any other institution now existing in the world. It was Pope Gregory (Hildebrand), already mentioned, who rescued the Church from insolvency. From the eleventh century onward it never looked back. Succeeding Popes spent prodigious sums year by year but the income kept pouring in at even more prodigious levels. The beginnings of the Church's future international fund-raising system is traceable to the twelfth century. The primary source of income was the *census*—a tax based on population. Later, special contributions were levied from the income of the clergy. The Popes varied their demands according to their needs. In 1199, 2.5 per cent of clergy income was demanded. The collections, consolidations and accounting were handled in a new department that had evolved in the papacy's Lateran headquarters. This was called the *camera*. The ease and speed with which large sums could be raised says much for the power of the papal voice. In 1228, Gregory IX needed funds for his war against Frederick II. He instructed the clergy of England, France and Italy to pay over to him 10 per cent of their ordinary income for that year. If all else failed the Pope could borrow sizable sums, simultaneously writing himself a rescript exempting him from the Canon Law provisions against usury. The tax on the clergy—and there was, of course, an enormous number of "clerics" in the Middle Ages, forming a huge professional class, in each country—remained the basic source of papal revenue. The clergy, in turn, got their money from the people. The sale of indulgences was always kept separate and did not become rampant until the fifteenth and sixteenth centuries. Indulgences were sold direct to lay people by papal licensees. There was also "Peter's Pence" which, in the Middle Ages, was an annual sum paid direct to the Pope from crowned heads, based, theoretically, on the tax of a penny per house. (Today, the tax is the combined collection of local funds made direct to the Pope for charitable purposes and it amounts to about $1.5 million a year).

Extravagant though many of the Popes were, the local churches were rich enough, chiefly through their land and property, to meet the papal demands. In mid-thirteenth century England, for example, more than half the arable land belonged to the Church. Many people really did think that they could buy their way into heaven, and to refuse a priest (let alone the Pope) such sums as he demanded was considered grievously sinful. In a strange sort of way this same sort of mentality still survives. "Services" by laymen, for which papal titles are awarded, often have something to do with the provision of money. For many, a cheque or financial offering is still the easiest way of preserving a link with the Church. Catholics, moreover, of a certain type—and there are many of them—would rather spend their time raising money "saving" a cathedral than actually praying in it. (It seldom occurs to them to ask if the cathedral is really worth saving in the first place.) In Germany, the Church gets 90 per cent of its revenue from a tax levied by the state. In order not to pay, a citizen must renounce his religion. Most people do not do so even though a majority of those same people hardly ever go near a church. Money is their only link. The clergy, as a result, enjoy a surplus of money (as well as a surplus of time) and can freely indulge the well-known Catholic mania for building more and more ecclesiastical "plant."

This was also a medieval preoccupation. Church building, in fact, was virtually the basis for Europe's economy. It accounted in part for the fact that the Church was the principal provider of employment. Kept busy year in, year out, were almost every kind of person from the most sublime artist to the most humble laborer. There seemed no money to rescue the people from the misery and hovels in which, mostly, they lived, any more than there seems enough today to relieve world poverty and starvation. But there *was* money then for fabulous cathedrals just as there *is* money now for supersonic planes and space rockets. It is all part of the System. Commerce is the key. Money can always be "found," to make more money, for *some* people. This, in turn, will make for them even more money. In the Middle Ages the Church was not a mere beneficiary of the great money-making system then evolving. It was its very creator. "In terms of economic history, the papacy functioned in medieval Europe as a kind of primitive venture capital firm. . . . The banking and mercantile activity generated by the *camera* made capitalists not out of churchmen but out of goldsmiths and traders." So says James Gollin (*Worldly Goods,* p. 429) in one of the best recent books on Catholic finances, and to which any summary must in great part be indebted.

The Crusades provide a good example of "overseas investment" by the medieval Church. The sums paid over by the Popes to kings and noblemen to go on crusade eventually made available to Europe the priceless riches of the Middle East. New trade routes were opened. In true medieval manner the strangely combined pursuit of piety and lust for loot gave a new and highly commercial meaning to the term "holy war." An important by-product of the new traffic with the East was the flooding of Europe with sacred relics whose marketable value became considerable. The bulk of the profit, however, accrued to local churchmen and churches rather than to the central coffers. As a secondary by-product, new devotional "cults" sprang up all over Europe associated with the relics and the legends surrounding them. Shrines proliferated and theology—particularly with regard to the Mother of Jesus—was profoundly affected as a result.

Surprisingly, however, the Church did not become really rich until the Renaissance and Counter-Reformation period. But from then until modern times the mystery shrouding Church finances has correspondingly increased. So dubious were some of the transactions of Renaissance Popes in selling ecclesiastical offices for lump sums that no documents on the subject have ever been released from the Vatican archives. To "spoils," and the revenues of vacant sees, moreover, the Popes added, directly to their own privy purses, the proceeds from the sale of indulgences. When, during the eighteenth-and early nineteenth-century age of revolution, the Church was being threatened as an institution, the papacy redoubled its efforts to remain financially viable, despite the territorial ravages wrought by Napoleon. In the year 1815 it had to make a fateful decision. The revolutionary impetus had been checked. Its violent phase had passed. The Pope, having lost his worldly dominions, had the chance to associate himself with ordinary people in their aspirations of self-determination. Instead his Secretary of State, the adroit Cardinal Consalvi, argued at the Congress of Vienna for the restoration to the Pope of the Papal States. The price was papal support for monarchy and reactionary government all over Europe. "Morally, Consalvi's bargain was degrading. It allied the popes with all the ruling opponents of human freedom and betterment on the continent, and this 'alliance between throne and altar' made the Catholic Church part of the official machinery of oppression" (*ibid.*, p. 433). One of Consalvi's fears was that without a territorial basis, and therefore with no subjects to tax, the Vatican would go broke. To maintain its territories, however, the revolutionary forces within the restored Papal States themselves had to be brutally repressed by the papal gendarmerie. It was a sad chapter in Catholic history, the more so because its lessons were not learned. When Rome fell to the new Italy in 1870, the Pope did not rejoice at being freed from the curse of "mammon" but sulked for sixty years. The year 1929 brought back token sovereignty and a tidy cash settlement. From that moment on a new chapter in Vatican finances opened. The Special Administration took over the funds supplied by Mussolini and invested them shrewdly. The operation was run for nearly thirty years—almost single-handedly—by a lay financial expert, Bernadino Nogara.

A brother of the director of the Vatican museums, Nogara was himself an engineer and banker. As director of a branch of the Banca Commerciale Italiana in Istanbul he had specialized in the arbitration of gold. He had been reluctant at first to accept the Vatican financial post offered to him by Pius XI but did so, it is thought, when the Pope agreed to the conditions he asked for. These were that his investment-making was not to be restricted by any religious or doctrinal considerations, and that he was to be free to invest Vatican funds anywhere in the world. Nogara thus felt free to engage in currency speculation and otherwise to "play the market" even though this is a form of business activity specifically prohibited in clerical and religious affairs. As the Pope himself was his client, however, and asked no questions, no one else did either. Nogara, during notoriously troubled years, managed to increase the value of the Vatican portfolio by half as much again and produce income simultaneously. Pius XII, after initial doubts, was delighted with him. Few people, however, will ever know what exactly went on inside the Special Administration during those three momentous decades. To this day most of its big deals are put through by word of mouth. The telephone is used much more freely than the mails. What is known is that the Special Administration could rely on its valuable connections in the international money world: the Rothschilds in Paris and London; Credit Suisse; Hambros Bank in London; J. P. Morgan; and the Bankers Trust Company of New York. One of the latter's vice-presidents, Andrew P. Maloney, was also economic adviser to the Holy See mission to the United Nations. The Special Administration, when it wanted to buy or sell shares on Wall Street, would call Bankers Trust, New York, direct, rather than go through the Rome branch. By such means, most of its secrets have been well guarded.

Such secrecy, however, and the inevitable legends that arose as to massive Vatican wealth, greatly worried Pope Paul. The image of a rich Church was totally opposed to his own model thereof. Nor did he like the idea of lay control in money matters since this put the Church on a par with any other capitalist contender in the international free-for-all for whatever pickings were going. Paul brought financial matters back into full Church control by his 1967 reforms and, in the following year, ordered the sale of a substantial part of the Vatican's considerable holding ($350 million) in the mammoth Italian company Società Generale Immobiliare. The sale was effected by the Sicilian financier Michele Sindona. *Time* magazine reported (November 28, 1969) that Sindona negotiated privately with the Pope himself. The point is of minor importance. What matters is the principle guiding Paul. Why was he so insistent on pulling the Vatican out of the Italian market? It was not only because of the new state tax. The Pope was willing to come to terms over this. Another reason has been suggested. "The Vatican might feel that to be involved in building luxury hotels, residential quarters for the very rich, selling the pill to the Italians or sanitary appliances to the Hungarian communists, was not quite in keeping with the image of herself the Church wants to project" (Pallenberg, *Vatican Finances*, p. 191). Some such ideas were evidently in Paul's mind. Società Generale, after all, controlled about fifty Italian companies (apart from the Rome Hilton). And the Vatican had had the controlling interest. The guiding theory here had been that if the Vatican did not have controlling interest it could not influence the sort of business engaged in by the company in question. But in a fluid situation things can easily get out of hand. The Vatican sold a substantial block of its Immobiliare shares to the Parisbas Transcompany of Luxembourg which is controlled by the powerful Banque de Paris et des Pays Bas. The latter, in turn, belongs to the French branch of the Rothschild empire. With the proceeds, and with other funds entrusted to him, Michele Sindona entered into wide-ranging reinvestments on behalf of the Vatican. The Holy See retained 5 per cent of Società Immobiliare but divested itself of such Italian companies as (in 1969) Condotte d'Acqua, (in 1970) Panatella, and (also in 1970) Serono. (The latter firm were manufacturers of contraceptive pills.) It diversified into such "foreign" companies as General Motors, General Electric, Shell, Gulf, IBM, and some airlines. The story of the rise and fall of Michele Sindona, however, is a saga of its own. With his fall (in what came to be called *il crack Sindona*) the Vatican is thought to have lost massive sums amounting to 10 per cent of its total financial wealth.

Pope Paul, in short, was attempting in the last years of his pontificate to do the impossible. He wanted to reshape, if only minimally, the curial mind toward Church money. And not just the curial mind. Complacency about Vatican wealth and (at least apparent) grandeur stretched well beyond Rome. Paul trimmed ceremonial and introduced considerable practical economies. But the slightest moves toward rationalization of the whole framework came up against the dog-in-the-manger attitude already remarked in the job-jealous, unimaginative and often time-serving, middle-rank curial officials and their numerous hangers-on. Paul, at all events, put on record his view on the principles involved, in the course of a startling general audience on June 24, 1970. He began bravely enough by quoting a well-known saying of his predecessor, Pope John: "The Church presents herself as she is, as she wants to be, as the Church of everybody and particularly as the Church of the poor." But the passage that followed should be read carefully and in full to see how Paul faced up (or perhaps did not face up) to the heart of the dilemma facing him and, in one form or another, facing the whole Catholic Church today:

> One could easily demonstrate that the fabulous wealth, which now and then certain public opinion attributes to her, is of a quite different nature, often insufficient to the modest and legitimate needs of ordinary life, to the needs of so many ecclesiastics and religious and of beneficent and pastoral institutions. But we don't want to make this apology now. Let us instead accept the desire which today's men, especially those who look at the Church from the outside, feel for the Church to manifest herself as she should be: certainly not as an economic power, not appearing to have great wealth, not engaged in financial speculations, not indifferent to the needs of indigent persons, institutions and nations. We notice with vigilant attention that, in a period like ours which is completely taken up by the acquisition, the possession and the enjoyment of material goods, one feels that public opinion, both inside and outside the Church, desires to see the poverty of the Gospel and that it wants to recognize this even more where the Gospel is preached and represented in the official Church, in our own Apostolic See. We are aware of this exigency, internal and external, of our ministry. And just as, by the grace of God, many things have already been accomplished to renounce temporal power and to reform the style of the Church, so we shall proceed, with respect due to legitimate *de facto* situations, but with the confidence of being understood by the faithful, in our effort to overcome situations which do not conform with the spirit and the good of the true Church.

The spirit and good of the Church was obviously not served by the Vatican's continuing to have a controlling share of Immobiliare. It was not that this company necessarily did bad things. But it *was* Italy's largest real estate and building company. And apart from the Vatican's vital controlling interest, the company was run by men enjoying the confidence of the Vatican. It could easily be said—and was—that the Vatican thereby occupied so crucial a position in the whole economic situation of Italy that she could hardly be thought impartial in her moral directives to the country and in her political stance (as the most powerful ally of the Christian Democratic Government). Surely the Church should hold its investments—if at all—with no invidious strings attached? Pope Paul obviously thought so, though cynics stress his awareness that Italian business was entering a decline and that much brighter markets—especially in the Eurodollar area—were available elsewhere.

It will also be noticed that Pope Paul referred to the Roman Catholic Church as "the true Church." (A subconscious admission that ecumenism was indeed a delusion despite the brave noises coming from high places?) He held out total poverty as an ideal but seemed to say that the Church had to exist and could not do so on air. He proposed no radical reform of the essentially "capitalistic" structure of the Church's central administration. For the Church to take Jesus literally and sell all to give it to the poor would mean the end of the Church (as a type of multinational corporation with employees to pay and property to keep up). But it would not mean the end of Christianity as a Faith. Pope Paul was willing to modify the Church's investment portfolio and try to make sure that Vatican money supported "good" causes while simultaneously enabling the Holy See to extend its charitable work especially in the third world. The latter was a genuine concern of a Pope who never stopped agonizing on behalf of the world's needy. But he did not feel he could liquidate the portfolio altogether and take the Church outside capitalism into a politically "uncommitted" situation. To some, however, it would have been a supreme act of faith had he taken such a step. To others it would have been a tempting of providence amounting to folly. It would, admittedly, have been a revolutionary action.

There did remain the rather tame alternative of making some gesture with regard to the material treasures of the Vatican in its museum and elsewhere. These are pricelessly valuable but arguably unsalable except perhaps at a knockdown price to the Italian State with no one (least of all the poor) gaining any long term advantage. The Vatican,

moreover, pays for its day-to-day upkeep by admission prices into the
Vatican museum and galleries and by the sale of stamps (including
special issues to dealers and collectors). Would there, nevertheless, be
any value in a quixotic symbolic act on the Vatican's part? A suggestion to this effect was made at the 1971 Roman Synod of Bishops. It
had curious results. A certain cardinal proposed that to help to feed
the hungry, the Church should sell some of its treasures and that Rome
itself should give the lead. The realists of Rome, however, took a more
robust attitude. There, the cardinal's suggestion fell on shocked and
stony ground and was soon discreetly buried without trace. The only
question that most interested people was how such a proposal could
have come to be made in the first place. In an atmosphere always alert
for plots, various theories went the rounds. But one explanation gained
particularly wide credence because of the eminent source from which
it sprang. This was the explanation given by the late Cardinal Wright,
the powerful American Prefect of the Congregation of the Clergy.
(This Vatican department handles particularly large sums of money.)
Wright would tell his guests (or fellow guests) at luncheon and dinner
parties that the poor cardinal who had made the suggestion was a sick
man. His sickness (according to Wright) went through phases. Most
of the time he was quite all right. But at certain times his sickness went
through the sort of phase that made him say things he didn't really
mean. He had evidently been going through one such phase when he
made the proposal about the Church (and the Vatican) engaging in
an exemplary gesture with regard to some of its wealth. Reassured by
the mighty Wright that "the sick man" had only spoken so radically
during a moment of temporary mental aberration, worried Catholics
left his presence much relieved.

The unsolved dilemma about Church wealth was inevitably inherited by Pope John Paul II. His immediate predecessor, John Paul
I, had been greeted at the beginning of his month-long pontificate
with a challenge (still relevant) thrown down by Italy's influential
journal *Il Mondo* (August 31, 1978). An "open letter" asked the new
Pope to impose order and morality on the Vatican's financial dealing
which, it alleged, included some "speculation in unhealthy waters." *Il
Mondo*'s editor, Paolo Panerai, went on to ask, "Is it right that the
Vatican operates in markets like a speculator? Is it right that it has a
bank whose acts help transfers of capital (out of Italy) and tax eva-
sions by Italians?" The reforms of Pope Paul, it was claimed, had not
removed the basic contradiction. "Believe us, Your Holiness," *Il*

Mondo had continued, "we understand well the exigencies of the Vatican, the need to have financial autonomy to sustain its apparatus, to spread the faith in addition to pious works. We believe that is right. But don't you think, Your Holiness, that to achieve those objectives there are other ways than the most unscrupulous channels that capitalism offers?"

Panerai added that the Vatican was heavily involved in money and stock markets and Bishop Paul Marcinkus of the Institute for the Works of Religion "is the only bishop who sits on the board of directors of a lay bank in one of the fiscal paradises of capitalism; the Cisalpine Overseas Bank of Nassau." The open letter was even accompanied by an (unsigned) report called "The Wealth of Peter" claiming that the same bishop also looked after Vatican investments in different parts of the world through the Continental Illinois Bank of Chicago. His Institute, it was stated, held deposits estimated at two billion dollars and its seven thousand accounts included some in which Italian businessmen transferred sums abroad in contravention of Italian currency laws. The report's estimate of the losses involved in the Sindona collapse was eighty million dollars, though other estimates have put these as high as the billion mark. Such facts and figures naturally embarrass and annoy the Vatican and, even when denied, are inevitably damaging. It is for such reasons that the present Pope has come to revise the traditional Vatican view in favor of secrecy at all costs over matters of money.

CHAPTER 17

The Metamorphosis of "Mission"

The rich must live more simply that the poor may simply
live.

DR. CHARLES BIRCH

Don't let the world around you squeeze you into its mold.

ROMANS 12:2

"FOR THE Church's mission, it is a novel experience to be facing the
new nations. With a few exceptions, missionary activity has gone hand
in hand with colonization for almost two millennia." No matter how
we interpret the underlying relation between the two orders, it is self-
evident that political expansion and the Church's expansion in the
world have covered the same ground, geographically and chrono-
logically" (Bühlmann, *The Coming of the Third Church*, p. 42). In
relatively modern times the colonial realms of Spain and Portugal supplied the principal vehicles for the spreading of Catholicism. Then
came the great century of Christian expansion between 1815 and 1914
which was unequaled at any time in history. Christianity became part
of the established order of things within the ambit of British, French,
Belgian and German colonies and protectorates. The end of such
colonialism has set the Church free to develop its true and proper mission.

The earlier idea of mission has, in other words, been metamor-
phosed. The new phenomena for the missions are exemplified by such
developments as "Africanization" of all missionary endeavor on the
African continent. The Western Church is now willing and anxious to
hand over its colonially structured outposts to indigenous peoples on
the spot. Indeed the Church is no longer a Western Church though it
was until the beginning of this century. At that time 85 per cent of all
Christians lived in the West. By the end of the century only about 42
per cent of all Christians will be living in the West. The rest—*and
about 70 per cent of all Catholics*—will be living in the southern hemi-

sphere, that is, Latin America, Africa and Asia. That the majority of Christians will be living in the underdeveloped and hungry two-thirds of the world makes the dilemma posed by revolution that much more stark. Few people have brought this fact more dramatically home to Catholics than the Capuchin missionary, Fr. Walbert Bühlmann, whose works are cited below.

The third world, though in a state of ferment and uncertainty, is the principal future "home" of the Church. Though the "traditionalist" approach to Catholicism may survive until the end of the century in the West, it may have no application to the Church of the future—if only because of the total shift in center of geographical gravity which will have come about. The third world Church—the "third Church" as Bühlmann calls it—will impose its own cultural, social and political norms. This Church, however, will be more truly "Catholic" as it absorbs local customs in a way which the centralized and uniform "Latin" Church was never willing to do in the past. The confusion of uniformity with universality was ever a bar to genuine "Catholicity." Yet such a system, backed by colonialism, survived the Church decline as a great spiritual empire; it only began losing ground after the second World War.

At Bandung, Indonesia, in 1955, the Afro-Asian bloc of nations was formed. This signaled the beginning of *political emancipation*. Many hectic developments followed. One was the end of the Portuguese empire. This vitally affected the Church, but is likely to prove only the first of many shock waves for the old missionary order of things.

There were portents of emancipation on other fronts as well. At Algiers in 1973, the nations of the Third World decided, by pledging themselves to mutual collaboration, to break away from the world market price system. This was the beginning of *economic emancipation*. (Paul VI, meanwhile, had already embarked on his confused and confusing attempts to cleanse the Church of its "clerico-capitalist" image.)

It was not, however, until the Synod of Catholic Bishops held in Rome in 1974 that the Western Church recognized openly that her dominance of the "universal" Church had come to an end. On that occasion the Third World bishops forced onto an unwilling synod the discussion of local control of local Church destiny. This was the beginning of what Bühlmann has called *ecclesial emancipation;* and Cardinal Höffner (of Cologne) afterward remarked that the 1974 synod had been a lesson in humility for the Western Church. Now, we can "recognize that all that happened between Bandung 1955 and Rome 1974 'had to' happen, that Europe 'had to' lose its hegemony in order to pave the way for a greater world and a greater Church and in order to accommodate that brotherhood of all mankind which we hoped for and must work for since it accords with God's plan for humanity" (Bühlmann, *Courage Church*, pp. 106–7). (This virtually captures the Church-Revolution syndrome in a nutshell.)

The future depends on the seriousness with which Catholics take the words of an "encyclical" from their first Pope, Peter: "You are a chosen race, a royal priesthood, a people set apart to proclaim the wonderful deeds of God." Such words were first addressed to God's people in one particular place—"the Church" as far as that locality was concerned. Now they are addressed to *all* God's people, "the Church" in each and every particular locality. Old customs, cosy habits, parochially limited concepts, and allegedly exclusive possession of the complete truth have largely vanished for Catholics. They have, once more, become "pilgrims." No one is exempted from this new call to mission for there is not a square yard of territory that is not now, "mission" territory in some sense of the word. The Catholic cannot convert the heathen unless he has converted himself. To convert himself the modern Catholic, particularly an elderly one, needs a frighteningly large amount of humility, for his instinct is to deny that there is any need for fundamental change in himself or his Church. But he will stay (mentally speaking) "at home" with the old ideas only at his peril and at the risk of making himself even more isolated and unhappy, humanly speaking, than he is already. Salvation—and spiritual happiness—lie in successful exodus. The Church faces *diaspora*. For her, on this earth, there will never again be a secure or "promised" land. She is destined forevermore to be on pilgrimage. Therefore she, in the person of all her members must swim against the tide.

This is precisely what the Church has practically never done in the past. She always swam *with* the tide—the tide of military conquest and political settlement. Even her greatest missionaries followed this plan. But there was one particularly sensational exception: St. Francis of Assisi. One cannot improve on the description given by Walbert Bühlmann:

Francis swam against the tide of his time. Europe had by then become the Christian west, but there was a danger that it would be content to perpetuate its own introverted existence. On the west it was hemmed in by the ocean and on the south and east by Islam. Nobody then gave a thought to mission except Francis. An irresistible impulse urged him to go among the Saracens. His first attempt was frustrated by a storm that hurled him onto the coast of Dalmatia. On his second attempt, when he was trying to get to Morocco by land through Spain, he fell ill. His third attempt at last succeeded: he reached Egypt on a crusader ship and there, in evangelical simplicity, accomplished his masterstroke. Deaf to all advice to be prudent he left the camp clearly unarmed, walked across no-man's-land and entered the Sultan's camp. There he talked to him about the love of God and won his friendship. For the first time the Sultan had found a Christian who was not an enemy but a friend. Nowadays there are some specialists who say that the history of Islamo-Christian relations could have been different if the example set by Francis had been followed by others. Francis was also the first founder of a religious order to insert a chapter on mission in the Rule, a chapter which had its effects immediately. Members of his order found their way as far as Tibet and Peking before the sea route was discovered. Francis did not found his community in order that his brethren might live a sedentary cloistered life, sheltered and well cared for in monasteries, but in order that they might go out into the world. He was the first to confront the most daunting aspect of that world—the Saracens; and he did it without any inhibitions. At that time Christendom sent crusaders out *against* the Saracens; Francis sent his brethren out *among* the Saracens. Intuitively he re-lived the biblical spirituality of the Exodus, which Vatican II has recently recommended once again to the whole Church (*Courage Church,* pp. 136–37).

Without any inhibitions! How the outlook of Francis contrasts with that of today's painfully constipated products of hothouse Catholicism! And how swiftly and surely the latter are driving their younger brethren outside organized religious structures altogether only to proclaim smugly, when this process has taken place: "Typical of the modern generation. They've lost their faith!"

Yet Francis was something more than a mere uninhibited troubadour for Christ. He was a rebel against the social morality of his day. Such rebels, men and women, are the real heroes of Catholic history. They have never been lacking in any century, though their lives are often obscure compared to their more illustrious contemporaries. Their "rebellion" took the form of working, often wearing themselves out, where others preferred not to work: in unpopular and often suspect circumstances and in "doubtful company." They did, and do, consort, with the lowly sort of types with whom Jesus consorted (and was criticized for so doing). Their concern is with history's "outsiders"— such as lepers in the time of Our Lord; slaves in medieval days; homosexuals today: people very often, whom "respectable" Christians have written off as sinners or in some other way "untouchable."

In the course of traveling, however, one finds these heroic Catholic rebels working quietly away in obscure corners of the world. I met many charming Catholic priests and bishops in South Africa. Their jobs were straightforward enough in the "white only" areas. But outside Capetown, I met a lonely Irish priest, typical of many, working in one of the black townships. Such places, something between prefabricated housing developments and prison camps, are depressing. But this priest was happy. He knew "his," and "his" knew him. Though pleased with the verbal protests of leading members of the hierarchy against the injustices of the overall system, his was another kind of job. He reminded one of the sixteenth-century Dominican missionary, Bartolomé de las Casas who opposed the Church thought of his day on the issue of slavery. For his courage he was ridiculed and silenced.

The missionary task of the Church in other parts of Africa is usually very different. In some of the countries which have recently become independent, the Church is often the only effective protest against a new brand of injustice. I learned more about this in Ghana from the officials (who were frightened of their own shadows) than they ever dreamed they were giving away. They eventually deported me. It was at a time when (in 1977) the dreaded head of state, General Acheampong, presided over a ruthless but spectacularly inefficient and corrupt military "government." The people were starving. There was an attempt to overthrow the government. Everyone was jittery. The Catholic Church produced one of the few effective voices of protest. As a visiting Catholic journalist I was a persona non grata. (Acheampong was subsequently ousted and executed, though the basic troubles remain.)

In African countries with a strong "Catholic" past due to colonial structures the missionary Church has had to face yet another type of changing situation. The principal examples are Mozambique and Angola. Here, until recently, the "mother country" was Portugal. As a result of a concordat signed with the Vatican in 1940, the Church had extensive privileges in these vast areas. Its bishops were kept and paid like provincial governors; the journeys of the missionaries to, from and through the colonial territories were at state expense (bishops and priests always traveling first class); missions were considered as educational props for the colonial government and were supported as such. "Converts" were baptized in shoals. The Church, in fact, had a clearly defined role and its bishops, all Portuguese, carried it out rigidly. They saw themselves as ecclesiastical auxiliaries in the state's task of keeping "peace and order." They thus condemned all "terrorists" and every kind of activity described by the state as "subversive." The best of the white priests, and all the black Christians, felt cruelly betrayed. (Non-Christians looked upon the Church, with its magnificent buildings and elaborately maintained diplomatic representation, as a rich, foreign political power.) Finally, in protest at the behavior of a Church dominated by the demands of Portugal's (then Fascist) government, the famous missionary order of the White Fathers withdrew all its missionaries from Portuguese Africa.

In 1973, however, the Pope made the first break in the former Vatican policy of supporting such colonially structured local Church organizations. He nominated an Angolan to a key bishopric and intimated, though as yet timidly, that he favored a new deal and a new approach. After the inevitable coup in Angola, however, the success of the Church in "hanging on" depended only on such goodwill as had been accumulated by those missionaries who had had the courage to stand outside official Church-state policy: to swim against the tide, to be rebels. It had been a grueling vigil and even now it is not possible to say if their private Calvary will have achieved lasting results. Some bitter lessons have meanwhile been learned.

Such lessons have shown that every Catholic today must, to some degree and depending on the type of injustice most closely concerning his own particular social milieu, be a rebel for Christ's sake. This is not at all the same thing as saying that he must be a revolutionary. Some people, on the other hand—in fact very many people—say he *must* be a revolutionary, for all the conditions are present, they say, in many parts of the world, to justify the Church in siding with revolutionaries. But the Church is holding back, and is likely to go on doing so unless and until the whole world situation changes even more radically. The great question is "Will the Church wait too long?" Some attribute its hesitation to the humiliating lessons of the past. Franco's violent revolution against Spain's legitimate government, for example, was supported by the Church. Does the Church now regret such support of revolution? There has been no official admission in any such direction. Too much has happened since then. One veteran of civil and other disorders over many years is a Quaker heroine called Kanty Cooper. As a non-political peace-worker she has found her way into situations others could never have penetrated. On revisiting Spain in the forties she found no one she had helped during the civil war but made an interesting observation about her general experiences: where the Right won, she observed, it built churches; where the Left won, it built schools; when Franco won, he built banks.

The gospels make it clear that Christians are called to be peace-makers and witnesses of a Jesus who is Lord and who was raised to eternal life. Christians were not called to be agents of revolution. But as the Church, in the past, and for many centuries, has justified the killing of tyrants and spoken of "just war" and "just defense," concerned people persist in asking why there cannot be a "just" revolution. In 1967, Paul VI, in *Populorum Progressio,* stated clearly that the revolutionary solution was only a source of renewed injustices and provoked new disasters: "We cannot," he said, "fight against real evil by means of even greater evil." He made a specific exception, however, "in the case of clear and prolonged tyranny, seriously affecting the fundamental right of the person and dangerously harming the common good of the nation." Where, if anywhere, do such conditions exist in today's world? How if at all, should the Church be reacting in face of them? How far has it laid to rest the bogeyman "enemies" of yesterday?

How "fit," in fact, is Catholicism's anatomy to cope with the revolutionary world of the third millennium?

PART FOUR

PROGNOSIS

CHAPTER 18

Iron Curtain Raiser?

The future of Polish Catholicism will depend on the outcome
of the struggle between the forces of laicisation and those of
religious renewal. Particularly important in this contest is the
attitude of the postwar generation, its aptness to relate the
religious faith to contemporary conditions and the ability to
pass the new religiosity on to their children.

VINCENT C. CHRYPINSKI

Many Marxists, but also many self-critical modern
theologians, are aware of the fact that concern for the
future—that longing for liberation and radical change once
found in Christianity—has been taken over almost exclusively
by Marxism.

MILAN MACHOVEČ

THE ELECTION IN 1978 of a Polish Pope produced an instant assumption in some quarters that the Catholic Church was once more about
to throw itself into a mighty trial of strength with the Communist
world. Nothing, of course, could have been further from the truth.
The presence at the Vatican of Karol Wojtyla as Pope John Paul II
has had a dynamic but quite different impact. He has been looking at
man's longing for liberation in every part of the world, aware that
"liberation" from communism is valueless in itself. On one of his several visits to the United States as Archbishop of Krakow, Cardinal
Wojtyla gave a talk to the 1976 Eucharistic Congress in Philadelphia.
He said that "the laws of human freedom are formulated more fully in
the constitutions of new nations, but are these principles really respected everywhere?" The present Pope is particularly insistent that
the Church should concentrate on those Christians who live under an
oppressive regime. This is not necessarily the same thing as Christians
being persecuted for religion as such. Here, a person's material well-
being may be much greater even though his religion, as an institution,

is under fire from the state. What does this do for a person's faith? Going on from Philadelphia during that same visit, Cardinal Wojtyla spoke in Washington of how hardship had helped to reinforce Polish Catholicism. "The atheist character of the government," he said, "forces people consciously to affirm their beliefs." Faith is the key to that larger pattern of liberation which frees the human spirit through the channels of selfless love. The Polish pastor-Pope, after so many years of cohabitation (not confrontation) with Communism, recognizes such faith when he sees it. But he knows that Communism, as a form of Marxism, is also a faith, perhaps, in fact, the most potent in the world at the moment.

The Pope's own country is not only the most Catholic—at least 90 per cent—it is also the most conservatively Catholic country there is. It combines the best and worst features associated with such Catholicism: tenacity to the point of obstinacy; a simple religious family life; unswerving devotion to Our Lord in the Blessed Sacrament and pious veneration of the saints; resistance to theological change and indifference toward ecumenism; strong anti-Semitism, possibly the worst in Europe in the past; courage. Faith in Poland, may be said to have triumphed over all odds. But "religion" as an institution has suffered grievous losses in this and in nearly all Communist countries.

It is at this point that the Vatican steps in with its diplomatic weapons. For Church diplomacy is the auxiliary of "religion," though it may have little to do with faith. But it is considered the only means for dealing with a situation such as that prevailing in the Eastern European countries as far as *centralized* policy is concerned. (The Holy See can never turn itself into a local organization.) The persecuted Church in each country must work out its own salvation in terms of faith and day-to-day existence. It may be helped or hindered by the Vatican whose policy with regard to such countries—a help, say some, a hindrance say others—has come to be called *ostpolitik*.

Is the Church wrong to rely so heavily on diplomatic methods in view of their unhappy consequences before and during the war? Is it in danger, having backed fascism, of going to the opposite extreme in tolerating communism for the sake of only peripheral advantages and at the possible expense of principle? Many would say yes. John Paul II, in fact, has inherited a position which continues to be balanced on a knife edge. Fortunately he is thought to be a man of balance.

The chief architect as of the early sixties of the Holy See's "foreign policy"—including *"ostpolitik"*—was Archbishop Agostino Casaroli,

then Secretary of the Council for the Public Affairs of the Church*
(formerly a department of the Secretariat of State). The Council handles (from the Vatican) diplomatic and other relations with civil governments; oversees, with the Secretariat of State, matters concerning
Vatican representation in various countries through nunciatures and
apostolic delegations; and supervises the Pontifical Commission for
Russia. In recent years, such arrangements have come under criticism
from many quarters. They are thought to be woefully anachronistic in
the modern age. The Holy See, however, still considers its diplomatic
corps fundamental to the work of the Church in the world. Pope Paul
was sufficiently stung by criticism of the principle of Vatican diplomacy as to issue a *motu proprio* explaining its exact scope (June 24,
1969). (A *motu proprio* unlike most papal documents such as encyclicals, allocutions, bulls, etc., is not written for him by permanent
"civil servants" or the equivalent of speech writers: it is characterized
by being issued "on his own initiative".) The Pope did not explicitly
defend his diplomatic corps against such specific criticisms as were
being made, for example: that it deprived local Churches of reasonable independence: that it made the conduct of local Church affairs
dependent on the opinion of a foreigner in the country; that it
reflected an erroneous image of the Pope as a would-be worldly and
political sovereign; and that it violated the principle of "subsidiarity".
(The latter first emerged from Pius XI's social message *Quadragesimo
Anno* in which, in 1931, he wrote that it was "unjust and a gravely
harmful disturbance of right order to turn over to a greater society of
higher rank functions and services which can be performed by lesser
bodies on a lower plane."

The subsidiarity principle was reinforced when Vatican II in its
document on the Church in the Modern World stressed the reliance of
society, if it is to be healthy, on small groups rather than upon a vast
centralized organization. But Pope Paul claimed in his 1969 statement
(entitled *Sollicitudo Omnium Ecclesiarum*) to be responding to the
Council's demand for clarification of the role of papal representatives
round the world. His words, however, were less of a justification than
a restatement of existing conditions: "Papal representatives receive
from the Roman Pontiff the charge of representing him in a fixed way
in the various nations or regions of the world. When their legation is
only to local churches, they are known as apostolic delegates. When to

---

* Now Secretary of State.

this legation, of a religious and ecclesial nature, there is added diplomatic legation to states and governments, they receive the titles of nuncio, pro-nuncio, and internuncio."

Nuncios are papal ambassadors to other countries and are accorded appropriate dignity and protocol. There is great reluctance to see the end to a system of diplomatic service that has the longest uninterrupted history in the world. And yet the main function of such representatives today has become largely reduced to reporting back to Rome on local matters of purely internal Church concern. What of their other aim of fostering good relations with civil governments? The Church's main preoccupation here is to protect her liberty and independent status in as many countries as possible. But what, in concrete terms, can she offer in return? Nothing, obviously, in the form of material gain. But she *can* offer the invaluable advantage of diplomatic recognition. Rightly or wrongly, and surprisingly or not, an enormous number of countries still greatly value the diplomatic recognition of the Holy See. The shakier they are and the more they are criticized for repressiveness, the more they prize the apparent legitimacy bestowed through recognition by the Roman Catholic Church in the form of full diplomatic relations between the two "powers." Similarly the withholding of diplomatic recognition by the Vatican can weaken the position of a country (such as Israel) in its own dealings with other countries. In practice this has led to some extraordinarily anomalous situations in recent years. The Church claims that diplomatic recognition does not necessarily imply approval. But the country recognized invariably claims such approval when this is deemed helpful. The Vatican claims to recognize only such countries as possess borders that have been internationally and finally agreed upon. As already seen, however, the Holy See interprets this last rule in whatever way is most convenient in individual circumstances.

Pageantry and even pomposity surround the working of papal diplomacy in such countries where the Papal Nuncio is automatically given precedence over all other ambassadors. The nuncio then acts as doyen of the diplomatic corps on all state occasions. In countries where such a prerogative is not recognized, the papal representative takes the title pro-Nuncio. There are at the moment about thirty-six nuncios and the same number of pro-nuncios. The Apostolic Delegates, who represent the Vatican only to the local Church in a certain area, number about sixteen. (The numbers vary according to the means of enumeration since some men represent the Vatican in more than one country and even, in some of such countries, as "pro-Nuncio" to one and Apostolic Delegate to the other.) The cardinal principle of the whole system is the maintaining of the best possible relations between Church and State. It is often claimed that incalculable benefits accrue through "discreet" Vatican activity behind the scenes to ordinary people who might otherwise be abandoned. Such people may be groups in various countries who are the victims of political injustice and persecution. But such operations are, by definition, secret and the claims can rarely be verified. It is questionable, moreover, how much people are directly affected by exchanges and negotiations at government-Vatican level. The rights of the Church—which are not necessarily the rights of individuals—are the ones which nuncios and delegates have to bear principally in mind. It is on this basis that, if *ostpolitik* is the acid test for Vatican diplomacy, and Poland is then taken as the crucial country, the validity of the whole system may ultimately be judged. For the maintenance of a civilized and convenient balance between Church and State through diplomatic means is really a preconciliar, even a prewar, concept. Who cares, anymore, about ingenious "corcordats" compared to the *concord* desired by citizens at daily life level? Casaroli has himself pointed to the difference between the two. It is thus that the Catholic Church in Poland is faced with "a growing tendency among the younger generation to turn its back on the endless struggle between Church and State—a tendency to indifferentism" (Bociurkiw and Strong, eds., *Religion and Atheism in the U.S.S.R. and Eastern Europe,* p. 216).

Indifferentism! The universal modern phenomenon among young people in their attitude to religion. The Eastern countries have their own version, the Western countries have another. Institutional churches squabbling with governments for their rights or disputing with each other on abstract points of theology leave young people disillusioned if not revolted by all religion. The extent of such indifferentism in Poland makes it important to get future policy right and to recognize not only past mistakes but also present myths. One of the latter is the romantic picture painted of Polish Catholicism. Poland was still virtually feudal until the outbreak of the last war. As of 1945, hope dawned for the first time that people in the mass might partake of some of the fruits of their own toil and of an equitable share of this world's goods. A mass of literature began to emerge after the war about Catholicism in Poland. On the one hand, Polish Catholicism was glorified. On the other, the story was different. "The critics emphasized negative features such as the backwardness of the Polish Church, apologetic attitudes towards the past, the shallow intellectual content of religious beliefs, sentimentality, and stress on the external, ritualistic aspect of worship unrelated to a moral and eucharistic life" (*ibid.*, p. 241). Quoted to exemplify such conclusions (p. 253) is a 1959 study conducted among Polish youth by the Research Centre of Public Opinion of the Polish Radio. The apparent strength of religion was, it seemed, largely conventional. Of those interviewed 78 per cent were Catholics but, of these, 70.9 per cent did not condemn abortion, 14.5 per cent had no intention of concluding a Church marriage and 9.5 per cent expressed no desire to educate their children in a religious spirit. The search of ordinary people for religious truth seemed to be starting with men looking for God rather than with a predetermined, Church-fashioned image of God being imposed on men.

"The future of Polish Catholicism will depend on the outcome of the struggle between the forces of laicization and those of religious renewal" (*ibid.*, p. 252). Renewal is ever the key. It is an everyday challenge in Eastern Europe, not just a pious ideal. One concrete result is the evidence with which the Polish government has been confronted that Polish Catholics are *believers* and not, as before the war, mere supine subjects of a Church dominated by the landowning aristocracy. The year 1970 was the turning point. After the food riots and the rise of Edward Gierek as the country's leader, the Communist party sought "normalization" with the Church. If the Church did not actively oppose socialism the state would acknowledge the Church's moral and educational role and permit favorable conditions for pastoral activity. Then, in December 1977, Pope Paul himself received Edward Gierek at the Vatican and the Polish leader said that all Poles— Communist and Catholic—were united in promoting "the same goal, the well-being of our country." This was a new kind of communism, but it implied a new kind of Catholicism as well. The incredible fact is beginning to emerge that Polish Catholicism is also part of the New World Revolution. There has been a repetition of what the French Revolution did for the West. But it took more than a century for those adjustments to be made. Even now Catholicism has its protagonists (e.g., Archbishop Lefebvre) of the view that human liberty is a weapon of the devil. In the third great revolution of modern times the Church, under its Polish Pope, seems prepared to fight tomorrow's battles rather than yesterday's.

John Paul II does not underestimate the pitfalls. He is not likely to go overboard in any direction. He has always been a centrist. He has long supported the most representative voice of this group, namely "Znak," which is numerically the largest segment in Poland. Its adherents exhibit a restrained opposition to Communist rule, but avoid getting involved in a mortal struggle with Communism. They do not, however, believe in the possible reconciliation of Marxist and Catholic views as presently understood.

As to the state of Catholicism in the other Eastern European countries, it is impossible to generalize. Since the end of the 1950s, Yugoslav religious policy has become extensively relaxed and the Catholic Church in Croatia and Slovenia is now subject to the least interference in the whole of Eastern Europe. In the G.D.R. (German Democratic Republic) the Church, as in Poland, enjoys normal rights and privileges, relative independence, and is able to speak with its own voice. At the other end of the scale there is Albania which is totally cut off, having proclaimed itself, in 1967, "the first atheist state in the world." Only a tiny Catholic population survives the wiping out of the once healthy Church presence in northern Albania when, soon after 1945, the Italian missionaries were expelled. In the U.S.S.R. itself, the Catholic Church of the Roman Rite has long had a negligible place beside Orthodoxy, though Lithuania, incorporated into the Soviet in 1949, is predominantly Catholic. Hungary (60 per cent Catholic) is a special case largely because of the emotional controversy caused in the past over Cardinal Mindszenty. The 1964 agreement with the Vatican is a good example of the necessarily limited scope of *ostpolitik* however skillfully pursued. At the signing ceremony Archbishop Casaroli said "The Holy See wishes to see in this agreement not the goal achieved but the starting point to further negotiations. . . . There is no lack of good will on the part of the Holy See" (*Osservatore Romano,* September 19, 1964). Made possible, at least, was the consecrating of the first bishops in Hungary since 1951, a development desperately needed for the continuity of a legitimate hierarchy. Above all, the agreement, though only partial, was the first such document negotiated and publicly signed by a Communist government with the papacy, and gave the latter encouragement for negotiations already proceeding with Czechoslovakia and Rumania.

In relationship, however, to the actual faith of real people—to say nothing of the danger of increasing indifferentism—there is something intrinsically unreal about the whole concept of *ostpolitik*. It is, when the frills are removed, nothing more nor less than the weapon for easing tension between two gigantic world powers, the papacy and communism. The Catholics of the individual countries concerned tend to be pawns. The lingering image of the Catholic Church as, in some way, even now, a supranational "empire" holding the sole key to the *societas perfecta* is, by definition, anathema to an equally monolithic concept of world society. Because communism and Catholicism have so much in common they are enemies. A Communist government, when negotiating with the Vatican, sees it as the would-be center of a rival "ideal society." This puts Bulgaria (less than 1 per cent Catholic) on a par diplomatically with Poland (more than 90 per cent) since "the Catholic Church has a similar structure and self-image in all countries, and its ecclesiastical centre, the Vatican, is beyond Communist control" (*Religion and Atheism* . . . , p. 192). When Catholics, in a given country, become and are seen to become citizens who happen to be Catholics, and not subjects of a world religion who happen to be Poles, or whatever, the faith—as *faith* and not as religion—will be faced, admittedly, with a new test. But its adherents will not carry the millstone of belonging, or appearing to belong, to a power-conscious Church with known, or shrewdly suspected, political sympathies (with the capitalist West). The price of making this experiment, and possibly of setting millions of Catholics free, is a dismantling by the Vatican of all such quasi-political structures as its elaborate and expensive diplomatic corps.

Pope John Paul did not rush into any commitment one way or another as to the future of *ostpolitik*, a diplomatic operation much more characteristic of the era of Paul VI, if not of Pius XII. To see the new Pope as a great anti-Communist crusader is to misread his character and career to date. He accepts Communist regimes with much greater realism than any of his predecessors though he is skeptical of the compromise between Church and Communism in Italy itself. This is, for him, based too heavily on expediency. His own relationship with communism at close quarters has always been based on the rights of people. This attitude gains far more respect for the Church than either out-and-out opposition to Communism or a transparently opportunistic approach. He championed the Polish workers who were arrested in the food-price troubles of the early seventies and gained the friendship of Mr. Gierek who allowed him to travel the world widely. Without such travels he could not have become Pope.

He has now reiterated the Church's principle of strict nonintervention in the political affairs of nations and has said that he is not in the

government-changing business. Being neither "soft" on Communism
nor "sold" on capitalism has made him listened to with unusual attention in both East and West. His experiences behind the no longer so
impenetrable iron curtain are entirely different from those of Catholics
in capitalist countries who still tend to look on Communism as the
Church's public enemy number one. Even more intransigent is the attitude of Catholic exiles from Communist countries. Unlike those who
still live in such countries, they cannot be reconciled to Communism as
a way of life with which coexistence does or should work. They are
very bitter in their views on *ostpolitik*. Polish exiles did not take kindly
to the reply made by the Polish bishops in 1971 when faced with a
government offer of "normalization" of relations. The reply acknowledged the revolutionary change in social, political and economic conditions of "our country" since the war, and stated the desire of the
Church "to serve the nation in these new conditions." The Polish
Church disavowed any desire to "fight against the system" or to "assume the role of political" leadership.

This was a notable advance on any previous statement from comparable sources. It represented, in fact, the first major concrete application of a distinction which had been gaining ground since the time of
John XXIII. This Pope's 1963 encyclical, *Pacem in Terris*, was the
turning point. John not only affirmed every man's total liberty of conscience—a notion considered "monstrous and absurd" by Pope Gregory
XVI in the previous century and a cardinal error just before the war
by Pius XI. He also showed his desire to come to terms with Socialism,
Communism and other materialistic philosophies. The vital distinction
was between that "false philosophy" which, he insisted, informed Communism, and many of its practical aspects which might be desirable
in political programs "even when such a program draws its origins
and inspiration from such a philosophy." He gave a new perspective
to Marxist theory as being "subject to practical considerations," while
considering that the practice of Communist states might well contain
"good and commendable elements." The encyclical was issued in April
1963. Two months later, "good Pope John" was dead. *Pacem in Terris*
was his last will and testament.

It was not without effect in the most surprising of quarters, for it
was at that very time that a whole new approach (to Christianity) was
opening up on the Marxist side of the fence. John XXIII's words
seemed to have been spoken at a providential moment and it was this
Pope, and men like him, who were making a sudden and sensational

impact in areas where "hundreds of thousands of Sunday or conventional or fellow-traveling Christians or so-called Christian politicians could do nothing."

The words are those of Dr. Milan Machoveč who, in *A Marxist Looks at Jesus,* points the way to something much more profound than a precarious coexistence between institutional Christianity and institutional Marxism. The latter, through Stalinism, became the political counterpart of a state religion ruthlessly destroying all heretics in its path. In the early sixties however—with Stalinism mercifully dead—Machoveč has been able to trace an astonishing convergence of Marxism and Christianity. The nerve center of "modern" Marxism was Prague where Machoveč opened up a genuine dialogue between Christians and Marxists. Conservative Catholics were appalled and remain, to this day, totally uncomprehending about the entire development. But the Marxists who have been turning toward Christianity for inspiration expect nothing from such "Sunday Christians." They look only to "deeply Christian spirits" such as John XXIII. And they look, on their own side, not among renegades to Marxism but among their most committed adherents to find understanding of Christianity. "The more deeply and rigorously a Marxist understands himself and the vastness of the tasks which lie ahead and therefore the more he is a Marxist, the more will he be able to learn from the Judeo-Christian tradition and to welcome Christians as potential allies and brothers." The same principle works on the other side. "Only Christians like Pope John XXIII or the Czech Protestant theologian Hromadka could create a situation in which Marxists had to start thinking about religion in a more subtle way; for only such deeply Christian spirits could not be denounced. . . . They almost compelled Marxist thinkers to reexamine certain traditional Christian positions, and they achieved this not through harshness but through openness and love. This process is by no means at an end, but the movement has begun" (*A Marxist Looks at Jesus,* p. 31).

The movement has begun. Where will it end? Some think that Latin America will provide the crucial testing ground.

CHAPTER 19

Liberation

We Christians in Latin America have been, and are, seriously
responsible for the situation of injustice that exists in this
continent . . . in practice, don't we seem to have vindicated
Marx, by offering to pariahs a passive Christianity, alienated
and alienating, justly called an opium for the masses?

HELDER CAMARA

If Christians dared to give a thoroughgoing revolutionary
witness, the Latin American revolution would be invincible.

CHE GUEVARA

THE CATHOLIC CHURCH's earthly leader, in framing his "keynote"
thoughts on human rights, said: "We would like to reach out our
hands and open our hearts in this moment to all people and to those
who are oppressed by whatever injustices of discrimination whether it
has to do with economy, life in society, political life, or the freedom of
conscience and just religious freedom." The words were timely in view
of the strong backlash currently in evidence against Church liberalism.
Concluding that there is little they can actually do about their stricken
"neighbors," most conventional western Catholics have taken to passing by on the other side of the equator.

This is not to say that such Catholics would support Archbishop
Lefebvre's proclamation that "we do not recognize the rights of men."
This he said during a sermon at the Church of St. Nicholas du Char-
donnet in Paris, at the end of May 1977, while the literature of *Action Française* was being distributed at the doors of the Church (*Catholic Herald*, London, June 3, 1977). Catholics in general, however, do
not want a rehash of the pre-French Revolutionary world. When given
a chance to endorse democracy, Spain gave a 90 per cent "Yes" to its
new Constitution on December 6, 1978. Suddenly the hollowness of
the Church-State type of system of "protecting" people from themselves was dramatically exposed.

To yet another—very different and very large—group, however, Catholic liberalism, where it still exists, mostly seems like pious talk. This group is concerned with areas where (notably parts of Asia and most of Latin America) Catholics are numerous but where human rights are defiled daily. Until recently the Church has accepted this state of affairs. For a dozen or so years, however, a movement has been afoot which has galvanized Catholic thought and theology toward the unavoidable need for man to be fully liberated in order for his soul to be saved. The greatest danger to this movement comes, ironically, not from extreme right-wing Catholics whose stance attracts more amused contempt than serious apprehension. The chief danger to the possibility of liberating that half of the world's Catholics who live under intolerable dictatorships comes from those living in the West, who may best be termed "moderates." They are, or would certainly like to feel as if they were, "moderates" with an open mind. To many, perhaps the majority, of such people, third world Christian activists are, at best, crypto-Communists, at worst, practicing Marxists. "It is a strange fact," as Bishop Francisco Claver, S.J., puts it (Lane, *Liberation Theology,* p. 51), "that committed Christians in many countries of Southeast Asia who take the social teachings of the Church at face value and, more significantly, try to act on them, are immediately pilloried as Communists or Communist sympathizers. Often by Churchmen, too. It is a sad pass we are in."

Francisco Claver was writing about the proclaiming of liberty for captives. Captives are something he knows about. He is Bishop of Malaybalay in the Philippines, a country where captives abound, having lived since 1972 under the martial law regime of President Marcos. Claver is a somewhat lonely figure since by no means all of his fellow Filipino bishops support his uncompromising stand against injustice. They find it more advantageous to collaborate with the regime, and the Holy See has long had valuable financial interests in the Philippines which is also useful for discreet communication with Peking. Meanwhile as Claver puts it, "we can worry about relatively piddling things like clerical garb, communion in the hands, correct liturgical vestments and gestures, and other such minutiae, but not unjust wages, government by decree, farcical referendums, lack of due process, torture of prisoners. Events that affect people's lives most intensely."

Something has thus come into being which is more full-blooded than mere liberalism. Something radical that aims to cut at the root of the cancer of injustice blocking human beings off from God's salvation by blocking them off from being proper human beings. The phenomenon in question is called "Liberation Theology." Many, if not most, ordinary Catholics in the rich countries have barely heard of such a theology. Few of those who have heard of it have properly understood it. Most of those who understand it dislike it. There is thus, between the northern and southern hemispheres, a moral schism among Catholics. The greatest differences between Christians, "are no longer those between pre-conciliar traditionalists and post-conciliar progressives (who are equally preoccupied almost exclusively with internal pastoral reforms and tend to be politically inactive). The real discrepancy is between those who, fed on North-Atlantic progressive theology, are concerned with internal church reform, and those who are motivated and committed to the prior challenge of the process of liberation. This discrepancy is taking on the dimensions of an abyss" (Assman, *Practical Theology of Liberation*, p. 137).

Despite strong opposition, however, the theology of liberation in one form or another is unstoppable. It will almost certainly assume a dominant role among Catholics during the twenty-first century when, as the demographic forecasts show, Catholicism in the southern hemisphere strides ahead in numbers and influence and the Catholicism of the traditional "West" continues to decay. (See Bühlmann, *The Coming of the Third Church*). (Catholics in Europe and the United States have not yet begun to assimilate the full implications of this inexorable shifting of the world's center of gravity.)

The Western distrust of "liberation theology" springs largely from seeing it only in theoretical and abstract terms. Because it does not apply to the Catholicism they themselves are familiar with, they fail to give it any very deep reflection. Liberation theology sees the mission of the Church as an active sign-sacrament and credible witness of the salvation the Church proclaims. The Church accomplishes this mission not only by passing on the Good News in Word and Sacrament but also by promoting a liberating "praxis" which will create a better world here and now. Such "praxis"—and for once it is a "jargon" word that is indispensable—means more than merely blind application of idealism or theory. It implies that "right practice" which is the counterpart of "right theory," that *orthopraxis* which complements *orthodoxy*. This means that the Church, as the People of God, must be "prophetic" in proclaiming the truth with a clear voice. It feels it must speak out against institutional violence (violence perpetrated by "governments") and it must encourage action movements that will lead, directly and dynamically, to social and economic change at local, national and international levels. Such immediate objectives are also those of Marxists, but where Catholics and Marxists work together they agree to differ—and differ profoundly—on the ultimate and final motives by which they are respectively inspired.

Does it help to be told that liberation theology is the outcome of Latin America's response to the Vatican Council's appeal for an examination of consciences in accordance with the "signs of the times"? It begins to do so only insofar as the actual conditions of life and religion in Latin America are fully appreciated. Most people are appalled when they begin to get an inkling of the truth, including the past contribution of the Church to the present evils.

Catholicism in Latin America is still heavily conditioned by its early history. The colonization of Latin America began in the sixteenth century and the Church was planted in these vast new territories by the then powerful countries of Spain and Portugal. The mother-State helped the Church to become established while the Church agreed to be the State's ally in secular matters. It was the Constantinian formula all over again. No one who wanted to enjoy the rights of full citizenship had any choice but to accept, at least outwardly, the new religion. (With such acceptance, it must be added, came genuine faith in many cases.) Old beliefs, as in Roman pagan days, still lived on but they were suppressed and/or "absorbed" by a Church which was founding a new empire overseas just when its imperial grip on Europe was being shaken. "Even after the Protestant Reformation, the model of Church then prevalent in the rest of Europe (that is, the Catholic part) remained intact in both Spain and Portugal, the two countries promoting the Counter-Reformation and then engaged in founding and colonizing the New World" (Bruneau, *The Political Transformation of the Brazilian Church,* p. 11). This Church model is explainable only by the term "Christendom" in the sense already described, a model which was dominant from the fourth century until the Reformation. Though lost in the old world it was continued in the new in that part—Latin America—which has remained almost entirely Catholic at least in name, to this day. Thus nearly 300 million Catholics are potentially concerned with the effects of liberation theology. Together with Catholics in parts of Asia living under similar conditions (notably the former Spanish colony of the Philippines) the total number of Catholics involved approaches half that of the entire Roman Church.

Though the majority of Latin American Catholics probably live in either subhuman or, in more clinical language, "unacceptable" tions, many live comfortably and a few in almost limitless luxury. The latter are the ruling classes. They either participate in government or influence and support it. Their privileged position, traditionally buttressed by the Church, rests on the very basis of Latin American society since the days of its European origins. Total integration of Church and State was the key to this situation. To take Brazil as an example—and the enormous size of its territory makes it an important one—the settlement of the country was a joint venture of Portugal and the Church. The sword conquered and with the sword went the Cross. The original name of the colony even recalled the true cross, Vera Cruz. "It is impossible to deny that the economic imperialism of Spain and Portugal was bound up in the most intimate fashion with the Church and the religious. The conquest of markets, lands, and slaves —the conquest of souls" (Freyre, *The Masters and the Slaves*, p. 249). Both the Spanish and Portuguese American colonies continued to enjoy the system of Patronato Real, or royal patronage. This was a form of Church-State relationship wherein the State played an active role in the administrative affairs of the Church. It had got off the ground with papal grants especially for Portugal which had long waged a war of "reconquest" of the infidels (principally the Muslims) of Asia and Africa, an excellent "cover" for Portugal's commercial expansion. The subjection of the pagans of the "new world" was looked upon as being somehow a continuation of this "holy"—and very profitable—war. The Portuguese king, in 1515, received from Pope Leo X a special sword and hat blessed by him at Christmas. "In this way did the Supreme Head of the Church proclaim before the whole world the value he set on the war which the King of Portugal alone among Christian Princes had been found to carry on against the infidel by which such brilliant prospects were opened to Christendom" (von Pastor, *The History of the Popes*, VII, 78).

"The church (in Latin America) is indissolubly bound to this history" (*Church and Colonialism*, p. 104). The words are those of a man hailed by many as a "prophet" in the most ancient and biblically authentic sense of the word. He is Helder Camara, Archbishop of Olinda and Recife in the northeast of Brazil and has become one of the world's foremost fighters for God's poor in Brazil and the Third World in general.

"Latin America, since its discovery," says the Archbishop, "has grown and developed under the influence of the Church. All its structures, social, economic, political and cultural, have undergone the influence of Iberian Christianity. The struggles for independence brought about little change in these structures. Today, for the first time, we are witnessing the dawn of substantial transformation" (*ibid.*, pp. 113–14). It is not only possible, moreover, but "objectively correct to talk about 'Latin America' as a real entity. Though divided up into more than twenty nations, it has more shared features than many other population complexes that appear to be politically united today" (Frei, *Latin America: The Hopeful Option*, p. 97). Glaring injustice, widespread poverty, and subhuman conditions exist in almost every one of these countries. The worst are: Argentina (so highly praised by Archbishop Lefebvre), Bolivia, Brazil, Chile, Ecuador, El Salvador, Guatemala, Honduras, Nicaragua, Paraguay and Uruguay. Out of their total population of approximately 180 million, about 160 million are Catholics. The Vatican maintains full diplomatic relations with each of the countries in question. (Though all of them deny human rights, they do not deny Church rights.) The "normal" form of government in each place is by military "junta." Though there is an overall pattern of devastating repression, the degree of horror varies from country to country. The choice of evils makes it difficult to say which state is *the* worst. Could it be Argentina?

Within three years of the seizure of power there by General Jorge Videla (March 24, 1975) about fifteen thousand people had disappeared, at least ten thousand to go to jail as political prisoners (or "subversive criminals" in the preferred, official term) and four thousand to be judicially murdered. Videla's supporters say he is an austere and frugal family man and it is pointed out that, unlike some of the fellow generals who helped him to power, he has not condoned the bombing of synagogues or publicly called for a "final solution" for Argentina's half-million Jews. In May 1977, the bishops, after several formal and informal private protests, finally issued a public statement listing as "disquieting facts" certain specific human rights violations and calling for a return to just law. In Argentina, however, Catholicism is the state religion, and the Church stands to lose its privileges if it protests too much. It must derive such consolation as it can from Videla's declaration that "it is a serious crime to assault our Western and Christian style of life and try to change it into something we do not like."

Next on the list, alphabetically, comes Bolivia, 80 per cent of whose five million people are Indians. Most are Catholics but they speak their own languages and live in such servile conditions compared to the country's rich 10 per cent that Bolivia came to be called the Rhodesia of South America.

In, Brazil, in October 1976, according to an Amnesty International report, two women were being tortured by the police in the small township of Riberao Bonito. A local priest, Father João Bosco Peindo went to protest. He was shot. "It is difficult," says the Amnesty report, "to estimate how common such practices are since victims, naturally, rarely file complaints. However, some idea of the extent can be got from an examination of the police figures for the number of people detained on suspicion alone in São Paolo in the first two months of 1977. There were 28,000 of them." The bishops, the month after this incident, issued a pastoral letter protesting about government abuses of human rights. This represents the Church's tentative "new approach" to try and influence events by moral authority. This however, if carried too far, could mean a drastic cut in state resources for the Church. Thus "today the Church must make a choice between, on the one hand, power and the subsequent neglect of the new approach to influence, and, on the other, adherence to the new goals and no power, which also means, in the Church's view, no influence." There are, nevertheless, some hopeful signs for Brazil's 100 million Catholics. Cardinal Arns of São Paolo, after a cautious and compromising start, has joined the cause of Helder Camara and the many other like-minded priests and bishops. In Brazil, the Church's new role as "the voice of the voiceless" is showing signs of being heeded at last.

In El Salvador—Central America's smallest and most densely populated country—the hierarchy were fairly united in opposition to the institutionalized violence of General Carlos Romero's regime. Romero* was one of the many examples of U.S. backing in Latin America of the regimes, however repressive, which are good for business. Trained by the United States—when he was Minister of Defense and Public Security—Romero built up, in "Orden," his own private army of terrorists who, having cut their teeth on the massacres of farmers and students, now terrorize the country at will. "In God's name," cried the Archbishop of San Salvador in May 1977, "we call in the midst of anguish for peace and unity."

Almost simultaneously, Father Miguel Alanis, a member of the Mexican Catholic Social Action Secretariat, commented on the posi-

* Ousted by coup in October 1979.

tion in his own country. He considered that two recently murdered priests were victims of the "dark mechanisms of repression unleashed in Latin America against priests who besides saying Mass, are committed to the problems of the oppressed majorities."

The catalogue could be continued almost indefinitely with each new description revealing even further horrors. After working alphabetically through the list of Latin American dictatorships, Uruguay is finally reached. This country was singled out by U. S. Senator Frank Church as "the biggest torture chamber in Latin America." It would be hard to find a more total condemnation. Senator Church, however, is better known in connection with his Report on Chile. This country fell to Fascism in particularly tragic circumstances. On September 11, 1973, a military junta murdered the elected President, Dr. Salvador Allende, and seized power. The country at the time of writing was still under a state of siege with a nightly curfew in effect everywhere. The junta's will has become law. Dr. Allende's Popular Unity sympathizers and supporters were hunted down and forty thousand killed. Holiday camps and other abandoned sites became concentration camps. Many thousands went into exile. Violence became more selective as time went on with torture by drugs and electricity, and other atrocities, attested to by many including the English doctor, Sheila Cassidy. "The evidence which various international organizations have collected, among it the large fund of material assembled by the International Commission of Enquiry, will be placed at the disposal of the Chilean people for use in due legal process. The atrocities are of such a nature that they can truthfully only be qualified as crimes against humanity. These crimes constitute a threat to all nations. Fascism must never be solely a matter of national concern. It must be combated wherever it appears" (*Arbitrary Arrests and Detentions in Chile,* p. 152).

The Nazi-style junta in Chile replaced a government which, despite its faults, had carried through most of its ambitious program to transform the country, nationalize its natural resources and monopoly industries, accelerate the land reform, redistribute wealth and make welfare services freely available to all. This threatened the landowning and industrial interests as never before. But it also threatened multinational corporations such as Kennecott, Anaconda and ITT. The last mentioned—the International Telephone and Telegraph Corporation —was particularly deeply implicated and the subject of extensive investigation. The United States was alarmed at the threat to its economic dominance posed by Allende's Chile and the CIA and Pentagon undertook to "destabilize" democracy there and pave the way for the coup. The fact could be neither hidden nor denied after the 1975 Report of Senator Frank Church. Its evidence "showed very clearly that the CIA and the White House had been preparing three years before to use economic sanctions to prevent Allende's staying in power, with the assumption that this would encourage a military coup. . . . The economic chaos which preceded the military coup was thoroughly in keeping with the hopes and plans of ITT and its friends in the CIA" (Sampson, *The Sovereign State,* p. 256). (The Nixon administration spent eight million dollars in three years in its campaign to destabilize Marxist but democratic Chile. The first experiment of its kind was thus duly destroyed from outside.)

The Catholic Church, however, rose to its new challenge. More even than the voice of the voiceless, it became the hope of the hopeless. Spiritual revolution is ultimately irrepressible though many Western Catholics still manage to turn a blind eye to the institutionalized killings and to be unable to see "liberation" in terms of theology. The brutal facts about Chile, however, are now notorious and the junta has been unable fully to exploit its near monopoly of the country's wealth and arms. It has alienated even the middle classes and the forces of resistance become more effective daily. Even the United States government—in 1977—sponsored a United Nations Human Rights Commission resolution condemning the continued violation of human rights in Chile. Campaigns have been launched and fought hard in all parts of the world to free Chilean prisoners, to help the refugees and to pressurize governments to cut off aid, trade and military assistance to the hated junta. But fascism—the ugly and, to some, unusable word—has a habit of surviving. Somewhere, somehow, there is someone willing to sell bodies and souls in return for business. The Church has been active and effectively resistive at local level though its big, centrally placed guns tend to remain muffled. This, at least indirectly, encourages elaborate justifications in some quarters for the "security measures" in so many Latin American countries against the "Communist menace." More restrained is the voice of someone who suffered dreadfully in Chile. "Difficult it is indeed to speak of the rights and wrongs of violent revolution in Latin America," wrote Sheila Cassidy, in the intensely moving personal account of her years in that country. She stayed on after Allende had been overthrown, but was shattered when she discovered, to her horror, how the normal and nice people with whom she was imprisoned and tortured (for giving medical care to a man who turned out to be a guerrilla) harbored so deep and implacable a hatred for the Church which she loved. "In the Latin American context," she concluded, "the hatred of the Church by the revolutionaries stems from the fact that since the arrival of the Conquistadores the Church appeared to align itself with the ruling élite. In the country in particular the priest was paid by the landowner and it seems that here religion was truly the opium of the people, for they were told to accept patiently their conditions of living and work because this was the will of God" (*Audacity to Believe,* p. 312).

With such attitudes prevailing until after even the Second World War, will the Church be able to keep pace with the present terrifying rate of change, not to mention the ever escalating spiral of violence? It is, as Helder Camara has called it in the title to one of his important books, a "Race against Time." By the year 2000 the population of Latin America will have nearly doubled and reached an estimated 640 million. Nearly 600 million of these will be Catholics, more than twice the number of Catholics at that time in Europe and nearly half the total Catholic population of the world. (Bühlmann, *The Coming of the Third Church.*) When, as is far from the case at the moment, Latin American Catholicism is accorded a voice in the whole Church which is in proportion to its numbers and importance, a true Catholic revolution can be confidently expected. "The changes in the church" which currently disturb well-insulated Catholics will seem little more than child's play by comparison.

Meanwhile a mighty battle rages between two vast and diametrically opposed intellectual armies within the Catholic Church. The big guns defending the "traditional" Western theology are at the moment managing to keep the liberation theologians at bay without firing more than the occasional salvo. These act more as ominous warnings than anything else. They have, after all, the Roman arsenal behind them, since the view that Marxism must somehow have infiltrated its way into liberation theology is, though unproven, obstinately held. There are many good breakdowns of what liberation theology actually means (e.g., in Assman, *Practical Theology of Liberation,* p. 11). Such a breakdown can be expressed as follows:

1. *The world:* Liberation theologians believe that the world is meant to be different and that the committed Christian must play an active part in trying to change it.

2. *Sin:* Injustice is a product of human selfishness which must, there-fore, give way to new structures productive of an economic and ethical order based on justice.

3. *God:* The God of Liberation theology is readily identifiable in the biblical tradition. He is a partner with his people in their struggle for social justice. (More controversial is the corollary usually added to this last proposition, namely that this biblical God is most notably manifest in our own age through the processes of liberation.)

4. *Jesus Christ:* It is he who supplies the vital dividing point between means and ends. For liberation is a movement away from sin and to-ward a freedom that is not primarily material but consists of the free-dom of the fully human being in his relationship with God. Thus liber-ation can never be, for the Christian, an end in itself. (Here, for many, comes the parting of the ways between Christians and Marxists.) It is always a means, but an *essential* means, toward the beginnings of sal-vation in Jesus the Lord.

5. *The Church:* Liberation theology helps the Church to be more than merely defensive and negative and enables it to be positive and pro-phetic. This involves an active fight against institutional violence and injustice.

6. *Consummation:* The whole school of thought presupposes an inevi-table, but necessary, tension between historical achievement and apoc-alyptic promise. Between "the already" and the "not yet" lies the dy-namic source of imaginative Christian action for justice. With the exception noted as being possibly "controversial," such a program might pass muster with any reasonably minded Catholic group of nuns, priests and laymen sitting round a room discussing the relevance of their Church to today's world, even though, until refreshments are served, many worthy "glosses" will have been put on the original theses. Why then does the "official" Church in the West virtually reject liberation theology at the moment? The answer is only partly provided by the suspicion that liberation theologians are mostly crypto-Marxists. Some—though a minority—have admittedly proved to have strong Marxist sympathies. They have thus provided their opponents with live ammunition. Their excuse is the urgency of the situation where brutal injustice backed by violence could be effectively met only by violence of another and opposing kind.

Whether they knew it or not they were acting on principles accepted by the Church from the Constantinian age onward. The theory of the "just war" is based on the same principles. But exactly similar situations are largely unknown today in the Christian west which is the heartland of Catholic conventional theology. Hence the comprehension barrier.

More importantly, conventional theologians live in the world of "the already." Liberation theologians live in the world of the "not yet." For many of the former, the Roman Church is objectively or "materially" synonymous with the Kingdom of God (as already established) on earth. Subjectively, or "formally," there may, it is allowed, be certain faults in the Church here and there which remain to be corrected. But such corrections will follow the gradual reformation that is taken to be permanent in the *ecclesia semper reformanda*. No fundamental changes are thought by this school to be either necessary or desirable in a Church which aims, not to change the world, but only to save individual souls. Even if the means for such salvation lie for some in abject poverty, then this must be God's will. The liberation theologian, on the other hand, looks forward to the time when man will be sufficiently free to make a real choice in favor of God and so save his soul through an act of personal love. Such salvation, it is felt, cannot possibly be merited through merely passive membership of an institution which seems to permit excessive material evil for its members ("for the good of their souls") provided the institution itself survives.

Liberation Theology is vulnerable to conventional Western criticism in being presented as inseparable from the revolutionary situation in which it has come to life. Western opponents like to stress the distance between its purely intellectual and theological approach to the intensely human predicament and the largely inarticulate mass of Roman Catholics many of whom hardly ever even see a priest let alone a "liberation theologian." And of course, as is pointed out, they would not understand a word he was saying if he spoke to them in his particular jargon. No—it is asserted—the Church in her perennial wisdom deals with such matters differently. The matter is usually taken out of the control of those nearest to the guts of the problem. The movement is institutionalized. A committee or commission is formed which is supplemented by various "experts" and Rome-vetted prefects, secretaries, monitors or other such officials, and the Vatican, in the name of the Pope, demands the last word.

So it was with monasticism and so it has been with the initiative taken by the Consejo Episcopal Latino Americano (Latin American Bishops' Council) usually known as CELAM. This was set up after the General Conference of Latin American Bishops held in Rio de Janeiro in 1955 (CELAM I). But the Vatican was reluctant to allow a follow-through, sensing the desire for a more radical approach to the subcontinent's harrowing problems. Pope Paul's greatest encyclical, however, *Populorum Progressio* (1967) discredited the ultraconservative Curial view of Church-society interaction. The result was an historic gathering at Medellín in Colombia in 1968 (CELAM II) which was a sensational turning point in the modern Catholic history of Latin America. Even then, however, the brakes were applied by the "curiacrats" in Rome. Everything had to be channeled through the highly conservative Cardinal Antonio Samore, head of the Vatican Commission for Latin America, and former Papal Nuncio in Bogota. But the Pope himself, in his (1971) Apostolic letter, *Octogesima Adveniens,* specifically endorsed a fundamental tenet of liberation theology in calling for "collective action . . . for a just and necessary transformation of society."

The main impetus was continued, but the next major conference scheduled for Puebla, Mexico, in October 1978 (CELAM III) was postponed until early 1979 because of the sudden death of the newly elected Pope, John Paul I. In December it was announced that his successor would be traveling to Puebla. Medellín, whatever could happen in the future, had been a decisive watershed. The bishops chose unambiguously to support the poor—something they had never done before in the whole of Latin American history. They stated boldly that "Latin America faces a situation of injustice that can be called institutionalized violence. We should not be surprised, therefore, that the 'temptation to violence' is surfacing in Latin America. One should not abuse the patience of the people." During the run up to Puebla, however, a conservative counter-reformation was getting under way. In 1972 the Vatican-backed Mgr. Alfonso Lopez Trujillo, Auxiliary Bishop of Bogota, had become Secretary General of CELAM. "A shrewd, forceful man totally committed to the orthodox cause of Rome and Latin America, Secretary General Lopez Trujillo received *carte blanche* from the Vatican to stop the 'nonsense' in Latin America at the conference in Puebla" (*National Catholic Reporter,* August 11, 1978). As a result, liberation theology was translated by the Europeans into their own economic and political language, and was thus tragically misconstrued. The European (i.e. Roman) preoccupation was not with poverty and repression but with its own analysis of Marxism. The preparatory documents for the Puebla meeting were carefully doctored and toned down in accordance with "traditional" norms. The Roman bureaucracy "knew best" even though its revisions were derided in Latin America as so irrelevant as to be blasphemous. The reply to this charge by Pierre Bigo, S.J.—who had been given the invidious task of defending the new drafts—was perhaps made on the spur of an unguarded moment. "The Spirit," he said, "will overcome the hierarchy." A new document was prepared but only five hundred copies were printed and no leading liberation theologians were invited to the Conference. It looked like being a sad betrayal.

Despite everything, however, the long term results of Puebla 1979 (or CELAM III) are still uncertain. Cardinal Aloiso Lorscheider, Archbishop of Fortaleza (Brazil) and president of the Latin American Bishops' Conference, has remained optimistic. Once converted to the directions and principles enunciated at Medellín he never looked back. For him spirit rather than documentation would be decisive in the long run, for Puebla as for Medellín. And this points inexorably forward as far as Latin America as such is concerned. Thus the initial prominence —by the design of Archbishop Lopez Trujillo—of conservative and anti-liberation theologians at Puebla became irrelevant in the long run. It is the rest of the Catholic world that will tip the balance one way or other—an onerous responsibility of which many millions are as yet not even aware. Support for the Latin American church in chains, however, is not lacking. U.S. Catholics were stunned, many shocked, when the colorful president of Washington's Georgetown University, Fr. Timothy S. Healy, stepped boldly into the fray in early 1977 with a spectacular gesture of solidarity with the beleaguered Archbishop of San Salvador (capital of El Salvador).† A year later Fr. Healy commented, "When the government looks the other way and the police and the army and the rich and the powerful are all against the little people, the only voice left is that of the Church. It has made martyrs before. It may, God help us, make more in El Salvador" (Washington *Post Magazine,* September 10, 1978, p. 17).

The Church where it is in a large majority is in a very strong position to influence governments. It is thus that there is greater concern

† Georgetown conferred an honorary degree on the Archbishop, and Fr. Healy presented it to him in his own cathedral in San Salvador.

for it to show its hand uncompromisingly in the Latin American Fascist countries, where it *can* be heard, than in European Communist ones where it mostly can't. The attitude here involved is not "leftist" but realist. The appeal is for a more open-minded examination of liberation theology by western Catholics. If, instead, such theology is rejected outright by the Catholic establishment, then the Church as a force in Latin America might well die at the hands of Fascism or be transformed by default on Marxist lines. The gates of hell would then, within fifty years, have prevailed over half the Catholic Church.

At all events the most sensational happening in the early months of John Paul II's pastorate was his visit to Mexico in late January 1979. (Soon after this, it was announced that the Polish head of state, Edward Gierek, had signified his government's willingness for the Pope to visit Poland in June.) The Pope's welcome to Mexico by the cheering millions (literally millions) was even more tumultuous than anyone had foreseen. His main speech—out of the more than thirty that he delivered in his stay of less than a week—was that which opened the third actual CELAM conference at Puebla itself.

The first half of the speech emphasized the need for doctrinal purity and unity in the Church. The Pope warned against presenting a partial or distorted gospel based on political or social ideologies rather than on faith in Christ and the Church's teaching *magisterium*. The second part of the speech related directly to some of the problems so anxiously being faced by the Church in Latin America. The stand made on human rights was a strong one as far as it went: "We cry out once more: respect man, he is the image of God." The Pope referred to the infringement of rights at various levels: individual, social and political. Infringement occurred "when man cannot exercise his right of participation, or when he is subjected to unjust and unlawful coercion or submitted to physical or mental torture." He went on to say that the bishops could not fail to involve themselves with such issues: "If the Church makes herself present in the defense of, or in the advancement of, man, she does so in line with her mission, which, although it is religious and not social and political, cannot fail to consider man in the entirety of his being."

But what about that "liberation theology" without which so many feel that ordinary people will be lost to the future Church in Latin America as so many millions were lost in Europe in the last century when Rome failed, itself, to read "the signs of the times"? On this point, the Pope seemed to be hedging his bets. "Liberation theology is a true theology," he said, "but perhaps also false if one starts applying doctrines or systems and ways of analysis which are not Christian. . . . Theology of liberation yes, but which one?" The answer, it seemed, had to be supplied by others. The Pope made express mention of the instinct of the people for knowing when the Church was serving the gospel and not some "other ideology."

The Pope's words—the most important perhaps uttered by him in public up to that point—brought both joy and confusion. It was noted that there were some remarkable omissions from the Puebla speech. There was no mention, for example, of the persecution of the Church in some of Latin America's Fascist countries. (Where the Church is being persecuted in Communist countries the fact is invariably mentioned in papal discourses.) There was no praise for the eight hundred or so priests who had been imprisoned, tortured or killed in the previous ten years in Latin America. Nor was there any mention of those many "basic" Christian communities which had become such a vital part of the life of the Church on the continent. In general the world's press represented the Pope's words as an attack on the Catholic "left." This was not, however, how it was seen by the Puebla bishops themselves. Cardinal Silva of Chile and Archbishop Manrique of Bolivia expressed themselves as "very content." What about one of the countries most at the mercy of a brutal right-wing regime—El Salvador? That country's heroic Church leader, Archbishop Romero already mentioned, said he was very happy that the Pope had given his support for the protection of human rights and human dignity. He agreed that unity in the Church was the way forward. One of the most radical of Latin America's bishops is Bishop Proano of Ecuador who said that while he had been depressed about the first half of the Pope's speech, it had to be read as a whole—and the words uttered on human rights were heartening.

Apart from his principal speech, the Pope spoke in a number of other towns and villages. He was booed in a very poor suburb of Puebla when he told a crowd of two hundred thousand of the "simple joys of the poor in their humble shacks." Almost everywhere else, however, he was rapturously received. When the whirlwind tour was over certain phrases of the Pope hung on in people's memory. The poor, he said, were being so exploited in some cases that "even what they had was looted." He called for profound transformation and urgent reform when attacking the "powerful classes who leave land unused" and "hide the bread that so many families need." He told the wretchedly poor Indians of Oaxaca that the Church would champion the expropriation of private land if the common good required it and if done in the proper form. (By some political standards, an exceedingly mild reform measure.)

The reactions of the three hundred and fifty bishops who listened to him at Puebla were inevitably mixed. Both conservative and progressive delegates found ample evidence in the Pope's words to support their own stance. What stuck out sharply was how intensely European, even Polish, was the way in which the Pope's thoughts were conceived and put across. This highlights a perennial "papal" problem. But Puebla was not the end of any road. It was yet another new beginning. A world Pope—a Pope who travels the world and begins to immerse himself in the future rather than the present—may one day throw off the Western approach which, up to now, has characterized all centralized Catholic interpretations of local problems. Latin America is wholly different from anything dreamed of in the philosophies of curial officials and even of the Polish Pope—however enlightened. John Paul, in Poland, is used to a largely right-wing Church and a left-wing government. In South America, largely left-wing Churches are trying to bring hope to the people against right-wing regimes. While the latter permit unrestrained brutality toward their own people (for the sake of the ruling oligarchies and their rich supporters) the position is quite different in Poland. People there are neither brutalized nor commercially exploited.

It is thus a novel situation for the Church to be faced with so stark a dilemma as that which, in the long run, was portended by Puebla, Mexico, during January and February 1979. After CELAM III, it became clear that the Church will have, eventually, to declare its hand unambiguously. Will it stand *with* people, or forever above them? If the former, bland generalizations which seem to satisfy all points of view, will not suffice forever. It may be added that a judicious and diplomatic "rebellion" on the part of certain delegates saved the Puebla CELAM conference from being a conservatively rigged, Rome-plotted disaster. (For rebellion has its place even within the ranks of Churchmen.) After the machinations already noted the conference had opened amidst fears that the insights gained ten years previously at Medellín were now going to be lost by the procedural conspiracy of the reactionary clique at the center. The leader of this group was the conference secretary, Bishop Lopez Trujillo. In the event, however, Cardinal Lorscheider, secretary of the Brazilian Bishops' conference, felt that the result of Puebla would exceed even his expectations. But such optimism was made possible only after the progressive elements (technically "rebels" in terms of the predetermined makeup of the steering committee) had managed to thwart the backstage plan. A proper election produced a new committee all of whose members' credentials were center-progressive. The rest is history, though it should be added that the progressive case was helped by what came to be dubbed "Puebla's Watergate." Bishop Lopez Trujillo's strategy became public knowledge when, to provide the "bombshell" of the conference, a private letter of his was published in the Mexican press. It had been written to an ultraconservative friend of his in the Brazilian hierarchy to enlist his help against the progressive elements which, though as yet underrepresented on the prearranged "committee," were known to be numerous, and could well become effectively vocal. Lopez Trujillo thus laid his cards on the table with his Brazilian confederate (Archbishop Duarte) : "Prepare your bomber planes and some of your sweet venom. We need you on top far more than ever."

Christian rebellion, however, cannot be vindictive. Bishop Lopez, having been caught out, offered to resign from his post as secretary of the Conference, but was "persuaded to withdraw" the offer. All in all it looked as if Pierre Bigo had been prophetic in the remark already quoted: "The Spirit will overcome the hierarchy." His prophecy was, to a great extent, confirmed by CELAM III's final document whose main emphasis was on the attitude the Church should take in the face of violated human rights in Latin America. Jesus was seen not as a political revolutionary but, in line with liberation theology, his sufferings were identified with the sufferings of the poor. Medellín had opened a new era. Priests had thereafter gone in large numbers into the shanty towns, and bishops had forsaken their palaces. Missionaries all over the world had to a great extent followed that lead and gone to live and work side by side with the people. It was unsensational work but potentially of infinite fruitfulness. Puebla itself ended in a sense on an unsensational note that was no doubt appropriate to the gravity of the tasks awaiting the hitherto hesitant Church in the expectant hemisphere of tomorrow. How could such a Church achieve the effects of revolution without using revolutionary means? Only those with unusual Faith could even contemplate such a prospect. When the conference was over, Bishop Aristia of Chile struck a note of optimism tinged with a certain sadness: "Medellín was a leap forward, Puebla is consolidation. We can't move in leaps and bounds all the time."

Without actually naming which of the Latin American dictatorships it had most in mind, the final Puebla document accused certain military regimes of "suppressing political rights and perpetuating inequality. It rejected the pretense that such things were being done in the cause of so-called "Western civilization." In the end of it all, it turned out that the biggest single influence on the two weeks of deliberation had probably been that of a different speech made by Pope John Paul: not the speech opening the conference, but one given a few days later in the Mexican industrial city of Monterrey. To this particular grouping of God's people—that is, "the Church" as far as that locality was concerned—he said: "It is a fundamental right of workers to freely establish organizations to defend and promote their interests and to contribute in a responsible manner to the common good. The dignity of the human person must prevail above all other things."

CHAPTER 20

"Relinquishment" and Rebellion

> The present social order is the most abject failure the world
> has ever seen. . . . This great civilization of ours has not
> learned so to distribute the product of human toil that it
> shall be equitably held. Therefore the government breaks
> down.
>
> C. I. SCOFIELD

> Christ is not interested in poverty for poverty's sake. He is
> interested in man's freedom. What Christ wants is not so
> much a condition of life as an attitude of mind which
> engenders a complete freedom of spirit to put the will of God
> first. We must look for opportunities of sharing and giving.
> The world is crying out for this kind of liberating poverty.
>
> THOMAS LEIGH

DOMINATION BY internal minorities is not, of course, the only reason for the enslavement of the masses in Latin America and elsewhere. Another is the dependence of such masses on external powers. The peoples of Latin America, like many other peoples in the third world, cannot be liberated unless the existing system throughout the whole world is radically modified. Everyone is necessarily involved and the Church can no longer support the "haves" in what they possess, now that it has become evident that the "have-nots" are thereby deprived of part of what is rightfully theirs. The liberation of one part of the world means a corresponding relinquishment by the peoples of the other part. Aid to the undeveloped countries is not only not enough; it actually perpetuates the system, and it is the system which is at fault. "What then should they be doing who are advantaged by the existing system? Perhaps developing a theology of 'letting go.' Accordingly, when the two-thirds of the world not advantaged by the system as it now exists reach out for what is theirs, those who have a firm grip on it (upon far more than they need to be humanly satisfied) will release their grasp rather than continue to blame the victims of the present inadequate structures for the conditions which they experience in their lives" (Neal, *A Socio-Theology of Letting Go,* p. 6).

Not only is aid inadequate (and even counterproductive as it increases dependency), so, often, is reform. Reform is the aim of "progressivists" who, in the sociotheological field, can be as much in error as "traditionalists." For both are at the extremes of a viewpoint that rarely moves out of its bourgeois environment. Herein lies the most unambiguous connection so far noted in this book between the Catholic Church of today and the revolutionary movement of the oppressed against their oppressors. But it is not an obvious connection any more than it was obvious to the self-satisfied and conventional listeners to Jesus who asked slyly, "But who is my neighbor?" They received an unpalatable but unmistakable answer. The potentially good Samaritan of today cannot justify himself by merely doing no one any harm; by proceeding along the road minding his own business. He is aware that two-thirds of his fellow human beings live in subhuman conditions. Somehow or other he must move not just to the other side of the road but to the other side of the world to help his stricken neighbor. He can only do this, without physically leaving his own neighborhood by, in effect, joining the revolution. This does not mean taking to the streets, engaging in violence, becoming a militant activist. The revolution which the Catholic of today can join is of a very different kind. Each individual contribution may, in itself, be very small and will usually have little to do with money as such. It will increase in both size and significance once the principle behind it is fully grasped. What then must the "non-poor" Catholic do to save his soul?

He must relinquish something of what, materially speaking, he has, painful though the very thought may be. But psychologically he must make a far greater relinquishment. The necessity for this is argued for cogently by the author of the work quoted above, Sister Marie Augusta Neal of Emmanuel College, Boston, and a visiting professor at Harvard Divinity School. Though relinquishment, as she points out, has always been called for by the gospel, it has frequently been resisted or cast in individualistic terms because of the absence of a theology of relinquishment. The realization of such a theology, however, makes collective action possible but this necessitates unhesitating and courageous support for radical rather than merely reformist groups, including, if necessary, political ones. It is as hard an obligation for the average well-to-do western Catholic as the test set by Jesus for the rich man in the gospel narrative. But it seems no less mandatory. For the gospel mandates the poor to take what is theirs. But who is to say what this is? Pope Paul VI signaled revolution when, in his 1967 encyclical *Populorum Progressio* (*On the Development of Peoples*) he showed, by reference to St. Ambrose, that when the rich gave to the poor what they asked for, they were only giving what was already theirs. This overturned the Church's former criteria for rights of property based on "private" ownership. In reality there is no such thing, for land can no more, in natural law, belong as of right to any one individual than can the air that people breathe. Such startling truths were not stressed by the Church in the days before it had become as glaringly apparent as it is now that most of the world is starving. It is this which has now committed the Church to a path which is nothing less than revolutionary. It is based on the assertion that no right of ownership supersedes human need. It does not imply that every caring Catholic must immediately sell his land, his garden, his automobile. Such a gesture, in itself, would be futile. But it does mean that he must be prepared for some such sacrifice in some form at some time. For the spirit of such sacrifice lies in being prepared for its actuality, and the revolution demanded by morality is not only slow: it is also permanent. The need for it will never come to an end as long as human beings—and therefore human nature—inhabit the earth.

How can this permanent situation be met? Scripture itself supplies the formula whereby the Church can keep pace with permanent revolution by periodical action in accordance with a predetermined cycle. The starting point for each new cycle is the unexpected one of "Holy Year." For several centuries past the Popes have decreed that after a certain interval of time one particular year shall be Holy Year. Pilgrims are expected to visit Rome and may there receive a special "plenary indulgence" by the recitation of prayers in the four main basilicas. Such Holy Years normally occurred every fifty years, but lately the interval has been shortened to twenty-five years. Each such Holy Year betokens a "Jubilee." The custom originates in a command of Moses to his people that they should, every fifty years, keep a "jubilee." Thus were answered such questions as "Who are the people?" and "To whom does the land belong?" The Book of Leviticus directs that the jubilee should be kept every fifty years because in about that much time new ways are invented to expropriate the people of what is theirs. Scripture demands that restitution must be made to the widows and the orphans. Similarly to be benefited are even the slaves and slave women, the hired laborers, the aliens in the household. Neither are the beasts of burden nor even the cattle to be neglected. For in the year of jubilee "every man comes into his own lands again." Exegetes have long held to a symbolic interpretation of the practice which represents an ideal rather than an attainable reality. "What a glorious task for our time: to make the ideal into a reality" (*A Socio-Theology*, p. 7). It could be done; and future Holy Years could be milestones with relevance and real meaning. For example, 2000 is the year in which the next Holy Year would be due if the Pope decides to declare it such. This bimillennial date *could* climax two decades of assimilation by the Church of the world revolution by showing that its true impact is spiritual rather than material. The complaint of some Catholics that their Church has become "secularized" will otherwise come true. And it will have come true because the Church has failed to spiritualize the world, to canalize it into Christian directions.

Did Holy Year 1975 represent a tragically missed opportunity in this direction? Great controversy surrounded the Pope's decision to have such a Holy Year. What was the point, it was asked, in inviting as many Catholic "pilgrims" as possible to travel to Rome to say certain prescribed prayers in each of four particular churches so that they should gain the Jubilee Plenary Indulgence?

The doctrine of "indulgences" is an old one. Indulgences can be partial or plenary. They remit all or part of the "temporal punishment" due by virtue of an interpretation of the words of Jesus that "nothing defiled may enter heaven." The temporal punishment may be worked off in this world or (in Purgatory) in the next. Alternatively it may be reduced or remitted altogether by one or more indulgences, some of which are "applicable to the souls in Purgatory." Such beliefs have long been a legitimate aid to the devotion of millions of Catholics who realize that, in the final analysis, it is only God who decides on the merit of their penitential actions. But Holy Year was a difficulty to many. It seemed somehow backward-looking and, of course, cynics said its main "promotors" were the tourist-exploiters of Rome.

Pope Paul did his best to meet all criticisms and, when inaugurating the Holy Year, said all the right things at a special Midnight Mass on New Year's Eve in St. Peter's—a magnificent affair. He spoke of the "dynamic idealism of human rights, equality, solidarity and peace." Perhaps more tellingly he asserted that "faith humiliates our ill-founded pride of imagined self-sufficiency and at the same time opens

our heart." It was meant to be a Jubilee of "renewal and reconciliation." It was an eloquent appeal: but was it all that the Church
could and should have done?

It so happens that the previous year (1974) had seen an initiative
which, if supported, could have seen the inception of the kind of
bloodless world revolution that the Church's various top-level, idealistic pronouncements had favored. On May 1 (Labor Day in Europe,
and, for Catholics, Feast of St. Joseph the Workman) a special session
of the General Assembly of the United Nations had adopted a Declaration and Program of Action regarding the problems of raw materials
and development. It had been called a "Declaration on the Establishment of a New International Economic Order." It was an historic
event for those representing the 70 per cent of the world population
who possessed only 30 per cent of its income. For the first time ever
their united voice had been heard, and recorded, to claim what (as the
Pope himself would have agreed) was theirs—namely a properly
human share in the planning and use of world resources. The declaration was specific as to some of the means necessary for the carrying out
of the stated aims. A target was made of the multinational American
and European corporations, and governments which supported them.
Strong meat of course, but what was the vote of the General Assembly? A hundred and ten nations voted for it; only six against.

Some—if not very many—minds may have gone back to an occasion
over eight years previously when Pope Paul had addressed the United
Nations in person. Some criticized him for, on that occasion, giving the
international body unqualified endorsement and not advocating some
alternative. But his words had been clear, "We wish Our message to be
a moral and solemn ratification of this high Institution . . . as an expert in humanity . . . convinced as we are that this organization represents the obligatory road of modern civilizations." Now, in 1974, there
had come this massive vote in favor of a new and more just economic
order for the world. How could it have become, as it did, a dead letter
within minutes of the vote? The answer is that while ten nations ab-
stained from voting, six not only voted against it but also vetoed it.
One of the vetoing nations was the United States, which offered instead a proposal of aid in time of disaster to certain countries. The
Church felt it could only stand by helplessly. The historic vote was
soon forgotten. The rich nations buried it without ceremony. A forbidding task obviously lies ahead if the Church is not in future to miss
another such opportunity of showing that it means what it says, while

explaining very carefully that material redistribution of goods among people is not, as such, its aim or concern. Nevertheless Pope Paul did state, in 1967, that "the earth's goods must be fairly divided." Was he just mouthing a meaningless phrase and reserving only for such things as his prohibition of contraception a rigid determination that his words should be heeded? Was *Humanae Vitae* to be his epitaphal encyclical rather than his great humanitarian and social one, *Populorum Progressio?*

That Pope's great difficulty has been inherited by the Church as a whole. While the idealistic argument of papal socialism can hardly—in view of the way it is expressed—fail to appeal to dedicated Christians who see man as integrated body and soul, its political implication may still be repugnant to some. For they can see the implied need not necessarily to lower their standards of living drastically but to give something more than earthly goods—something of *themselves*—to the overall task of transforming the world. Their Catholicism can no longer be solitary and self-centered. It demands more sacrifice than even the most generous donation to "overseas aid" in whatever form. It demands total inner conversion producing at least potential solidarity with those who may, at any moment, be forced into drastic action to guarantee that very "humanness" that the Roman Pope has commended.

To achieve this, for example, "the Latin American poor seek to eradicate their misery, not to ameliorate it: hence they choose social revolution rather than reform, liberation rather than development, and socialism rather than liberalization" (Torres and Fabella, eds., *The Emergent Gospel,* p. 240). This forces on Western Christians much the same sort of choice faced by the rich man in the gospel. The difference is that individual generosity may not, now, be enough. Collective action, often implying radical political involvement, is the uncomfortable corollary. Only thus can an effective as opposed to a merely symbolic gesture be made by the well-off Catholic. Many Catholics, in all parts of the world, are already heavily involved in effective action. But it cannot be pretended that they have the solid support of conventional Sunday Churchgoers behind them. The latter usually look upon such activist groups as "long-haired" and dangerously "leftist." This is part of the moral schism currently splitting the anatomy of Roman Catholicism. Individuals and groups effectively promoting relinquishment are nevertheless increasing in number and are at work in every part of the world. They are quite often concerned with relinquishment by the

Church, as an institution, of its social and/or privileged position in
given surroundings. This does not, by any means, only apply in European countries with long-standing Catholic traditions. It is operative
also in the mission fields. One whole issue of the *New Internationalist*
(December 1978) was devoted to the efforts of Christianity to make
amends to the world's needy for its own preoccupation with entrenched power. Highlighted, among other subjects, was the traditional role of the Church's religious orders in the sphere of education.
They had usually, in the past, aimed at the training of a high-powered
élite. One particular Indian nun, however, represented a new tendency
which is fighting hard to establish itself widely. Sister Gladys d'Souza
of the Sacred Heart Order works in Bombay. She is seeking to cooper-
ate with the rising generation of Christians "to help build a new
India." Of her Church she says "we are a huge property-owning organization ourselves—and so our alliances are such that we have been
working for the rich." She became involved in a big legal battle on behalf of a group of tenant farmers trying to exercise their land rights.
The local landowner's financial support for the Church, however, enabled him to undermine the position of clergy who were on the side of
the poor and the cause was ultimately lost. Accused of putting across
ideas which were "value-loaded" and "politically biased," she did not,
as do many, try to have it both ways. Her reply was "Education is not
neutral and teachers are not neutral." They were not, it must be admitted, neutral when they were on the side of the Establishment. They
are becoming less and less neutral now, where and when they come up
against human need in the raw. But there is still a very long way to go.

Some choose to fight at home but on a front that has worldwide dimensions. With so many possible examples to choose from, any selection must seem to be made at random. But perhaps an outstanding one
would be the Interchurch Center at 475 Riverside Drive on New
York's Upper West Side. Some call it the "God box," others "Heaven
on the Hudson." Among the activities going on there has been a battle
by a group of American Christians against certain big corporations in
an attempt to reinterpret the demands of the gospel in the twentieth
century. The ground on which the battle has been raging, broad
though it is, is possibly less important than the driving forces behind it.
Another notable factor is the unashamed and uninhibited participation
of some determined nuns in the various campaigns being undertaken.
One of these alleges that powdered baby milk is being heavily
promoted in the Third World to persuade mothers to abandon breast-

feeding in favor of the feeding bottle as a symbol of Western modernity. The result is that babies are fed milk powder overdiluted with unsafe water from unsterilized bottles and thousands of babies die. A Loretto sister (at Interchurch Center), Mary Catherine Rabbitt was asked whether doing battle with a multinational corporation wasn't a bit worldly for a nun. (*New Internationalist*, December 1978). "Why shouldn't I be worldly?" she asked in reply. "That's where I live. What we are doing is not only in harmony with being a nun, it is imperative. We are trying to reinterpret the message of the Gospels in the context of the events of the present." The campaign has attracted wide attention and been sensationally successful. Another of its protagonists is Fr. Mike Crosby, a friar of the Capuchin branch of the Franciscans whose twelve-thousand-strong order has put a third of its manpower to work in the Third World.

Fr. Crosby has summed up the choice for today's Catholics. Should they be dispensers of the opiate which was once, and sometimes still is, the principal constituent of their religion because its consumption by the masses made them superficially happy but fundamentally docile? Or should they proclaim "Christianity the prophet"? For "there is a prophetic voice in the Church. We have to work to be part of it. If we drift away, if we lose the original inspiration, the Church gets coopted and loses its voice. And that is what has happened in this country. We have made a civil religion . . . and coopted Christianity for the service of a political, economic and cultural system." Catholics, in other words, are determined, as of late, to be as full bloodedly American as their neighbors. That "Americanism" once condemned by a Pope, Leo XIII in 1899, is only a shadowy memory from the Catholic "ghetto" days. How ironical that American Catholics were then warned not to accept American freedom and progressivism at their face value for fear of conflict with Catholic power and Church authority. Now, by contrast, they are largely failing to heed the Pope's call for the liberation of the underprivileged lest such an effort should conflict with American commercial power and civil religious authority. Thus the more recent words of the Pope, which sound too much like something out of Karl Marx, fall on deaf ears. Catholics have their own defense against such unwelcome exhortations as that "Capitalism has often bred too much misery. . . . The earth's goods must be fairly divided. . . . From time to time the good of all demands that private property should be taken over by the state. . . . Left to itself the workings of international trade tend to make the rich richer and the poor develop slowly if at all" (Paul VI, *Populorum Progressio,* 1967). They take refuge as if the Catholic "ghetto" had never been abolished. And thus "at the local level, Gordon Allport's assessment of the 1950s still holds true—namely, that the parish is often an 'island of safety' for its members: or, in Glock's categories of religious action, 'to comfort' is a higher expectation for Church members than 'to challenge' " (*Socio-Theology,* p. 26). Helder Camara puts it in yet another way:

> If I am not mistaken, there have not as yet been any decisive victories in the war against poverty in the U.S. The root of the trouble lies, perhaps, in the American bias in favour of the arms race, and in the local wars which could, at any moment, degenerate into a world war. As long as Communism appears to be the greatest of all evils, as long as the average American persists in the illusion that to die in Korea or in Vietnam is to die for the free world—an illusion because two-thirds of humanity do not belong to this free world, living as they do in destitution and sub-human conditions, and being slaves to hunger, disease, ignorance and internal colonialism, to the point that Russia and the U.S. are less far apart than many ingenuous anti-communists think; as long as the American middle class is incapable of realising that the gravest social problem of our time is the ever-widening gap between the rich who get richer and the poor who get poorer; as long as there is no change of mentality, no revolution of ideas, the United States will be unequal to its immense responsibility of being the greatest democracy of our time (*Church and Colonialism,* p. 85).

If "relinquishment" seems too negative or otherwise impracticable, it has its positive counterpart in that quiet, Christian form of "rebellion" already mentioned. Such rebellion is always distinguishable from revolution. The latter, contends Fr. Rolland F. Smith, S.J. ("A Theology of Rebellion," in Marty and Peerman, eds., *New Theology,* No. 6., pp. 135*ff*), ends by denying the human value and liberty that it begins by affirming: "It absolutizes its present or future forms and so becomes demonic and nihilistic." Rebellion, on the other hand, is a continual revolution: "the new system is ever in process of being established and the victory or victories are always still ahead." Rebellious thought, moreover, is connected with Judeo-Christian thought, particularly that theology of hope which looks only forward and sees God as "the power of our future." Here then is the Christian alternative to revolution, for "Rebellion affirms past, future, *and* present, memory, expectation, and activity, faith, hope, *and* love, to overcome the faithless tyranny and hopeless servitude of a loveless world."

CHAPTER 21

The Afro-Asian Wilderness

There is a general consensus among the churches in Asia that
God in Christ is present in the Asian revolution and his
creative, judging, and redemptive will is its essential dynamic.

M. M. THOMAS

African traditional religion is not simply a preparation for
the Gospel as we know it now in the contemporary Church.
Rather it paves the way for the Christianity of the future,
which hopefully will be more universal. It even paves the way
for the era of "the whole Christ" when God will be all in all.

AYLWARD SHORTER

To DESCRIBE Afro-Asia as a "wilderness" in relation to the Roman
Catholic presence therein may sound like an exaggeration. The fact
remains that only just over 2 per cent of Asia's total population of
some 2,133,700,000 people is Catholic. Half of this 2 per cent is accounted for by the Catholics of the Phillipines. The monumental task
of evangelizing the other areas has barely begun. Its impact so far is
minimal—to many, even negligible. We are still in the era of the
"early"—if not primitive and formative—Church, whether we know it
or not. The accepted criteria and methods of traditional Western
Christendom will have little place in the building up of Asia's Christianity of the future. Only now are there signs, in this part of the Third
World, that the "Teutonic captivity" of the past is being thrown off.

The situation for Catholics in Asia, moreover, is wholly different
from that posed by the very special problems of Latin America. Asian
theologians are not concerned with the necessity of liberating people
from the iron grip of repressive governments working in alliance with
an entrenched and established Christian Church. They are proposing,
instead, what they call the "critical Asian principle" as a method of
thinking out theology in their own particular, infinitely variable, situations. It is a process often spoken of as "contextualization," a concept
necessarily prophetic in the true sense of the word (as already

discussed). Contextualization arises out of a genuine encounter between God's Word and God's *world*. Its challenge is restless and dynamic. Its spiritual message is rooted in the historical moment at which it is propounded. It has practically nothing in common with the old, Euro-Catholic principle of imposing fixed and static norms regardless of race, time and place. For the closed Euro-Catholic mind had no knowledge whatever of the vast world that lay beyond its own backyard. Such a world was—and to many still is—a wilderness indeed.

The third important dimension of Developing World Christianity is that which exists in Africa. Again, but for different reasons, the position is quite different from that prevailing in Latin America. African Catholics—about 11 per cent of the total population—are, in their own special sense of the word, "conservative" in their religious outlook. The Western progressivist-traditionalist polarization has little relevance to their particular situation. In an interesting and even humbling sense black Africans are above the pettiness of much Western wrangling over outward forms of Christianity. There is no reason to suppose that progressive European Christianity can be any more successfully adapted to the African scene than could the traditional variety. This fact has at last been recognized in the West now that the old colonial/missionary structure has been abandoned. Indeed the whole theory of "adaptation" of European Christianity to African cultural habits has become discredited. But it was not until 1974 that any official breakthrough on this front actually became visible.

In August of that year, the Vatican's Secretariat for Non-Christian Religions staged a consultation on African Traditional Religion at the Gaba Pastoral Institute in Kampala. The twenty or so Catholic participants at the meeting represented, apart from the Roman secretariat itself, the seven countries of Kenya, Malawi, Rhodesia, South Africa, Tanzania, Uganda and Zambia. Their main consultations were with local experts in African religion and local religious specialists. Amazingly, this was the first ever official recognition by Catholicism that those representing the religious traditions of Africa could be worthy partners in dialogue on a par with those representing the world religions of Asia and the Middle East. The meeting had all the excitement and drama of a new initiative but all the disadvantages of inevitable backtracking by the Vatican (whether admitted or not) and a dangerously late start in an entirely fresh direction. The result was a virtual indictment of the whole missionary/colonial approach of the previous century. (It was not of course a condemnation of individual missionaries who were, in general, courageous and often exceptionally good men and women.)

Perhaps most alarming was the discovery that the misguided attitudes of the past were still operative in the 1970s. For it was found that at every level in the Church there were those whose view of African Traditional Religion was wholly negative. Still warmly approved was that original rejection of African indigenous religion by the first generation of missionaries a hundred years ago. Many questioned whether the term "religion" could even be applied to the beliefs and practices of "pagans." For the early missionaries had tried to create an almost total discontinuity between "pagan" past and "Christian" present. Some of the mistaken preconceptions of the first (late nineteenth-century) evangelizers had not only been obstinately turned into general judgments but were, even now, still in circulation. One of the worst of these was the obnoxious description of "witchcraft" in reference to traditional religious practices. Also noted was the retention of a static rather than dynamic view in Catholic circles of what religion was all about. A small-minded inability to distinguish such essentials as the saving Eucharistic presence from such trivialities as rubrical niceties, was still going on as part of the "governessy" Christian inclination to treat their African converts and pupils as eternal children. The condescending paternalism of the old Catholic empire was still much in evidence. Here and there there were those who thought they were being very daring in championing "Adaptation" and "Africanization." But the former has amounted, in practice (in the years following the Council) to little more than a rather self-conscious effort to supply vernacular liturgical texts accompanied by local musical settings. It has turned out to be a naïvely inadequate cosmetic operation concerned with trying to transplant European Christianity in the inappropriate subsoil of age-old local culture rather than to allow a specifically African Christianity to grow up from its own roots and in its own right. Thus hardly anything had been done (at least up until 1974) to create an African philosophy and theology or to establish typically African Church structures. But the Kampala conference was quickly followed by the Roman Synod of Bishops in the fall of the same year. At this important Synod—whose general theme was "Evangelization"—the African Bishops uncompromisingly rejected the "theology of adaptation" and pleaded for what they called "the theology of incarnation."

"Our theological thinking," they said, "must remain faithful to the

authentic tradition of the Church and, at the same time, be attentive
to the life of our communities and respectful of our traditions and languages, that is, of our philosophy of life.

"Following this idea of mission, the Bishops of Africa and Madagascar consider as being completely out-of-date, the so-called theology of
adaptation. In its stead, they adopt the theology of incarnation. The
young churches of Africa and Madagascar cannot refuse to face up to
this basic demand. They accept the fact of theological pluralism
within the unity of faith, and consequently they must encourage, by all
means, African theological research. Theology must be open to the
aspiration of the people of Africa, if it is to help Christianity to become incarnate in the life of the peoples of the African continent. To
achieve this, the young Churches of Africa and Madagascar must take
over more and more responsibility for their own evangelization and
total development. They must combine creativity with dynamic responsibility.

"It is important to note here that this way of ours must strengthen
the bonds of unity within the universal Church, and in the first place
with the Apostolic See. The grave problems of the hour and the very
nature of the Church itself, the Body of Christ, make this imperative."

In order to become a dynamic force, in other words, Christianity has
to become "incarnate" in the very life of the peoples of Africa. If, for
the Catholics of Latin America, the most significant three words imaginable are "theology of liberation," the corresponding three words for
the Catholics of Africa are "theology of incarnation." It is obviously
true that such people themselves do not go around all day muttering
these three words as the be-all and end-all of life. The words in question are necessarily an inadequate form of technical "shorthand" to
enable intelligent discussion of the whole problem to be conducted on
a general scale. Such is the procedure inescapably imposed by a worldwide Church organization.

The task of future Catholic churchmen will be to break down and
redefine this "theology of incarnation" in the light of the swiftly moving pattern of actual African life. It will be no mean task and those attempting it are virtually starting from scratch. But they have at least
been supplied with a hopeful point of departure, namely the fifth assembly of the World Council of Churches which met in Nairobi in November 1975. The fact that such a gathering should come together in
Africa was significant in itself. Still more significant were the messages
that emerged from its discussions all of which pointed to the conclu-

sion that the Christian churches are today thriving in Africa as almost nowhere else. Missionaries had been pouring in to the continent for just a century—the century corresponding to the crest of the wave of colonial expansion by Britain, France, Belgium, Portugal and (until 1918) Germany. These powers had carved up between them a continent which, in 1875, had been a mosaic of tiny kingdoms, tribes, minirepublics, coastal settlements and the like. Half a century later it had become a series of European-dominated "countries" fattening and enriching the nations of Europe to such an extent that some of these very nations were willing, in 1914, to plunge the world into the greatest slaughter of history in an imperialist war to determine who should be top dog. The missionary Christian churches had established themselves in the wake and under the protection of this great conquest of Africa. But what kind of "Christian religion" had been built up alongside the government buildings and colonially financed schools that came to dot black Africa? It was only in 1975 that a final verdict was pronounced: that Christianity was today thriving in Africa not because the original missionary system had survived but because it was now dead. "The era of 'missions,' in which Christianity in Africa was seen as a plant which had hardly taken root, which needed constant care from outside, which, it was a duty to instruct but to which one would certainly not expect to listen—that era is over" (Hastings, *African Christianity*, p. 1).

The Christian and Catholic Church of the new Africa, if it is to continue to thrive, and start to expand on appreciable scale, must take proper account of one particular factor above all others. It is the same factor which has been noted in different forms and contexts in other parts of this book. It is the factor of revolution. But here, as elsewhere, it is no ordinary or predictable form of revolution. It is a revolution of a special kind that is neither self-evident nor obvious. It is a *cultural revolution*, and one of considerable depth as well as wide implications. Though it has been going on in Africa for some time its indications were at first unnoticed by the foreign missionaries and other Europeans. For they were largely ignorant of African culture; largely unaware, in fact, that any such thing existed, let alone that some of it arguably predated the culture of Europe itself. But in 1972 there was a rude awakening. A regulation promulgated in Zaire was, if not instantly recognizable as such, symbolic of the reassertion of Africa's cultural heritage. This was a heritage that some had said had never existed and some had said had been lost forever. But many others were now saying that it had merely been interrupted by the hundred-year interlude of colonial rule from outside. One way or another the 1972 development in Zaire came as a shock to many. By a new law coming into force in January of that same year all Christian names were forthwith abolished. No little *furore* followed, during which Cardinal Malula of Kinshasa went into temporary exile. But the law was accepted when its true objective was generally understood. It was an effort not only to redress the situation wherein Christian converts had been made by their culturally "superior" white masters, to adopt not only Christian first names, but often European surnames as well; it was also a reminder that people and places in Africa had had their own traditional names long before the European "exploiters" came along and changed them. The return to the old names was part of the resurrection of the old cultural values. The most recent and controversial example of such a change-back is that of Rhodesia to Zimbabwe. "The people want to shift their primary mythical collective symbol of identity from the grave of Rhodes in the Matopos Hills to the walls of the elliptical temple. They want, some more consciously than others, a cultural revolution beyond and below the political revolution" (*African Christianity*, p. 42).

The African cultural revolution is not taken with total seriousness by everyone. But it is taken very seriously indeed by the Christian Church and poses certain acute dilemmas for the Catholic Church in particular due to the inevitable conflict of past rigor with the current need for flexibility and imaginative initiatives. If the Church misjudges the measure of its own inescapable involvement in Africa's cultural revolution the results could be tragic and prolonged. No one knows this better than Catholicism's enemies and critics in Africa, who are watching the Church's every reaction to contemporary developments with intense interest. They are aware that the cultural revolution could either be the stepping-stone to the Church's entry into something like a promised land on that continent—or a snare in which the Church could become fatally entangled. So far the Church has reacted realistically but with caution and within limited spheres. It has begun to establish a new ministerial and pastoral structure for the running and staffing of its "parishes," which of course bear no similarity to parishes in Britain and America. African "parishes" are vast areas within which the true spiritual life of such Catholics who live there is carried on at "sub-parish" level. Here exists the true local church: the praying community which is often prevented from enjoying a fully eucharistic life because of the absence of ordained ministers. Rather than face radical change in order to remedy this situation, the Church now accepts what is rapidly becoming the normal pattern in many areas. The typical Catholic local pastor is a married man (not ordained). He is a member of the local community to whose culture he corresponds and relates. He probably works with a Church council representing his own village and sending representatives to a bigger council covering a wide area. The latter, huge by Anglo-American standards, will be the "parish." Self-reliance is at each stage the keynote. There would not be enough money to support an ordained minister whose only work was the ministry—even if, as is usually not the case, such a minister were available. Will the Church one day return to the early Christian practice of allowing eucharistic services to be conducted by a "president" drawn from the local people, that is, a man—or a woman—who is not ordained in the technical sense of the word? If it ever does, that day is still far off. To many the very question is shocking. Dogmatic theologians will do no more than hesitantly admit the possible validity of such services on the proverbial "desert island" principle. The fact remains however, that hundreds of local churches in modern Africa *are* "desert islands" as far as the officially ordained ministry is concerned. But you make no headway if you put up such arguments in the cold corridors of Curial Rome. (Sooner or later, of course, such married ministers will have to be ordained.)

Despite its cautious accommodations so far, the Church has yet to face up fully to one of the most crucial tests posed by Africa's cultural revolution. For the latter looks far into the past but, at the same time, far into the future. Africa's search for "authenticity"—so dramatically signaled by President Mobutu in Zaire on the issue of "modern" Christian vs. old traditional names—will involve a consensus decision for Africans on the very important matter of polygamy. The Church, too, will have to make up its mind. It would be wrong to suppose that it has already done so, or that its mind has been made up for it by the intrinsic impossibility of admitting polygamy within a fully Christian context. For no such impossibility exists. The Church, as already seen, permitted divorce and remarriage for the first thousand years of its existence. Most Catholics are still unaware of the delicate complexity of Church thought and practice on the subject. The question of polygamy is even less simple. It has never been finally and irrevocably decided—and cannot conclusively be demonstrated from scripture—that polygamy is necessarily inimical to the intrinsic authenticity of orthodox Christianity. The inflexible imposition of monogamy on all would-be African converts has often produced lasting tragedy and unhappiness or, alternatively, has proved to be a fatal stumbling block to the more rapid spread of Christianity. The Church could relent, but it would be a gamble. For Africans themselves may one day conclude that polygamy is no part of their own true "authenticity" in the "post-cultural revolution" world. A short-term advantage to the Church would become a long-term liability. Africa may eventually evolve into a largely monogamous society, particularly considering that polygamy has not prevailed everywhere and at all periods. The Church, which theoretically *could* change its ruling, might only end up by admitting that the hard-and-fast attitude of the nineteenth-century missionaries was wrong, but at the expense of seeing Africa's womanhood of the future cursing it for siding with a "reactionary" and outmoded convention. The dilemma for the Church nevertheless remains and is in no way fanciful or purely hypothetical.

The single most encouraging development in Africa so far is generally thought to have emerged from the transformation of Church music. The intense and inhibited conservatism of the past has been completely discarded. The drum, once prohibited, now symbolizes the quickening pulse of Catholic liturgical worship in Africa. The continent of song, dance and music-making has no longer found Church doors dismally closed to its joyful expression. European hymns are no longer translated with grotesque awkwardness into African languages and "sung" to so-called rhythms that were insultingly discordant to African ears. Imperial-colonial Catholicism has at last recognized the aspirations for religious self-realization. If it does not lose its nerve, it could see a flowering out of powerful Christianity from stems that are already growing and strengthening because they have firm, *local* roots. Of the ninety million or so African Christians, half are Catholic. The numbers are increasing steadily. In the continent as a whole there are more than three hundred dioceses. The process of "Africanization" has greatly accelerated in the last decade or so. Africans have replaced Europeans in the bishoprics almost everywhere. All in all no other continent in the last fifty years has exhibited such growth and diversity in its Christian development. In the last twenty years, pan-African Christian gatherings have proliferated. The most striking Catholic one occurred at Kampala in 1969 when Pope Paul made history by visiting Africa himself—the first Pope ever to do so. "You may and you must," he told the African Catholic Bishops on that occasion, "have an *African* Christianity."

CHAPTER 22

"Religion" and Renewal

Rites are prior to beliefs insofar as religion and magic have
elements which are similar functionally: they originally
formed part of a primitive, undifferentiated attitude, and
separated from each other as experience became more
complex and the requirements more varied.

DR. R. R. MARETT

Allow me to add a word, for those of you who are here with
the charismatic pilgrimage and another for those who just
happen to be present at this huge assembly. . . . There is
nothing we desire more than that the Christian people, the
people of faith, would have an awareness of the presence of
the Spirit of God among us. This should be a renewal . . .
it should reopen the closed lips of the world to prayer, to
joy, to hymns and to witness. . . . The second message is for
those pilgrims present here but who do not belong to your
movement . . . that they too, as devout pilgrims to this center
of the Catholic faith, might nourish themselves on the
enthusiasm and spiritual energy with which we should live our
religion. We should only say this: today you either live your
faith with devotion, depth, vigor and joy, or that faith dies
out.

POPE PAUL VI (Rome, May 19, 1975)

IF CONCERTED REBELLION against injustice is acknowledged to be the
inevitable duty of those seeking first the Kingdom of God and his
righteousness, the Christian may begin to see a possible way out of his
dilemma in the face of revolution. If such a Christian happens to belong to the Catholic Church he can hardly fail to realize the contribution to the fight against injustice which could potentially be made
by the largest organized religion in the world. He may even ask himself
if it is not, in some respects, *too* organized; that is, not loosely enough

constituted to let in such winds of divine inspiration as he feels are forecast by the "signs of the times."

Many feel that such talk is only meaningless, "trendy" jargon. Some, though not all, of such people are withdrawing themselves more closely than ever into that familiar Catholic "shell" where they feel the unique truth of God's revelation will remain secure, and themselves along with it. The Catholic Church is thus in danger of becoming a shrinking ghetto of stubborn souls too pious to risk being sullied by the secular world or too proud to join forces with other seekers after God's righteousness. For such people, it seems, religion is, if not a prison, a haven—a safe and comforting home to which they are gladly returning as to the womb. Though they have been given something of great price by God they have buried it in the sand. Others have caused such gifts—or "talents"—to multiply and become susceptible of being shared. Though it is invidious to make comparisons it is inescapable that Jesus, in his parables, was almost ruthless in dividing off those with real, burning Faith, and those who were content with a counterfeit, outwardly "religious," version of the same thing. He came, in other words, not to promote respectability and power, but dedication and love.

This chapter is largely concerned with certain things that happened, or began to happen, in 1967.

In the course of that year, Archbishop Robert Emmet Lucey of San Antonio, Texas, accidentally came across an idea that nearly gave him apoplexy. It came from a book by Fr. John L. McKenzie called *Authority in the Church,* which the archbishop had not read. When some priests in his diocese used some of the notions of the book as part of a proposed statement, the archbishop had to consider them. One of them presupposed "love as the guiding principle of authority." Such a concept was dangerously false according to the archbishop: love, in his view, had nothing to do with Church authority; this was founded on power delegated by Christ to the hierarchy; Fr. McKenzie's ideas were confused, heretical and completely without foundation (*National Catholic Reporter,* December issues, 1967).

Such an attitude is still alarmingly widespread among Roman Catholic bishops; but the bishops themselves deserve almost as much sympathy as condemnation. They are the victims of Religion—that "religion" which, insofar as it is a man-made System, is dying. It is not yet dead; but it becomes, each day, more deprived of its life force by its lack of relevance to the world of people. Roman Catholicism, as

everyone knows, has suffered huge membership "losses" in the last ten
to twenty years. One reason for this is that the Church no longer seems
able to impose even a minimum of discipline on its members. Yet with
all its shortcomings, the Church has every right to make at least minimum demands on its members. To attend Mass weekly, and on a few
other occasions of the year, to confess one's sins and receive communion at least once a year, are what this minimum amounts to as
regards "outward" observance. Great pains have been taken to facili-
tate the observance of these basic duties. The Catholic who ignores
them does so at his peril. The reason he gives may be that he has lost
"the Faith." But more often than not such an alibi is unconvincing.
Faith is strong today. The connection, however, between Faith and
Religion is no longer clear to many Catholics struggling to love God in
the real world. The truths of Faith have been handed on in terms that
have ceased to be credible to the modern generation. The Roman
Church is in an unenviable dilemma. Should it continue to insist on
the Sunday Mass obligation; to authorize only the "old" theology; to
rebuke society rather than rebel against it? Or should it, having
proclaimed the good news in more prophetic tones than those used
hitherto, leave each man's and woman's response completely free? The
latter alternative is fearsome to a Church used to "counting heads"
Sunday by Sunday to see who is still "practicing." This is a typical response of the Religion-System. It presupposes that Religion is somehow
separate from ordinary life; that a particular place, day or object is
specially "sacred" while other places, days and objects are "profane."
But Jesus himself made no such distinctions; he wished to establish a
new and universal priesthood, a priesthood without "sacred" realities.
He no longer, as had his fellow Jews before him, acknowledged "holy
places." He sanctified all places. With his death the distinction between sacred and profane places was extinguished forever. The early
Church, as long as Jesus remained a living memory, had no churches,
temples or chapels; no sacred clothes, no sacral language, no "holy"
days, no sanctified hours, no privileged persons. All these came later
when man began to devise his own Religion as a vehicle for the Faith
that had been handed down.

This was perhaps a natural and inevitable development; but it came
to mean the devising (for example) of elaborate vestments, ornaments
and regalia that owed their origin to imperial and/or purely secular
influences. Today, as much as ever, men love dressing up. This is one
of the reasons, with interesting psychological undertones, why many
laymen in today's Western Church like to belong to elitist societies and

wear all sorts of uniforms and ceremonial attire. Some even call themselves "knights" of this-and-that and admit only those with plenty of money and/or noble lineage into their exclusive ranks. In one such association of Christian gentlemen no one of Jewish blood can achieve membership. (A disturbing link with the Church of the Crusades!)

The Catholic Church, in other words, has gone very far down the line of man-made "religion." Such religion is not *invariably* a substitute for faith. But its symptoms are very different from those of that deep commitment which eschews all earthly recognition, political gain, financial reward, outward show and social connection. The publican of the parable here parts company with the self-satisfied, middle-class Catholic to whom the former's abject humility is almost ludicrously unreal. The anatomy of today's Roman Catholicism vividly reflects this parting of the ways. In an atmosphere of complacent and passive Church membership, the "religious" man does not find it difficult to talk to God, even if he often has to devise a special and rather stilted language in which to do it (or rely on someone else to do it for him). To accompany the language, other paraphernalia is introduced: music, candles, incense, incantations, relics, rubrics and ritual. The man of Faith, however, barely talks to God at all. God talks to *him;* and man listens. But he may not always hear. At least not at first. And then one day there occurs within him an explosion of the supernatural. He has penetrated the barrier between Religion and Faith after which nothing will ever be the same. It may have happened in a moment, or it may have taken many years. It may well have been accompanied by an agony as intense, relatively speaking, as that experienced by Jesus himself in the Garden. It will have been, in every case, a conscious "conversion" from what went before, even for the person long since baptized. It will be particularly painful for the person who believed that he or she, needed no such conversion. Indeed for such persons it may never come at all for they usually feel, as baptized and confirmed Catholics, that they have all they need already.

Some such dichotomy seems always to have been present among members of the Catholic Church which has, itself, developed in two streams, sometimes joined, sometimes separated. On the one hand, the Church has progressed in a *formal* way, setting up churches, hierarchical rankings, administrative areas, titles and orders. Weaving in and out of such structures has been the second stream from which have emerged from time to time spontaneous but extraordinarily powerful spiritual forces or movements, often among "laymen" and occasionally suspect in the eyes of the "authorities." Without these movements, however, the Church, as a body of "faithful" people, could hardly have survived. The greatness of the Catholic Church—which far out-weighs any such faults as could be enumerated in this or any other book—lies in having allowed these two strains to complement each other even when they have not actually combined.

A particularly interesting feature of those promptings within Christian souls, which seemed to come as a direct inspiration from God rather than through the "usual channels" of Church officialdom, has been the timing of some of their principal appearances. After Jesus had been raised to a new life and his post-Resurrection apparitions had come to an end, his followers went into decline. Though they had been fully instructed by the Master they lacked the fire with which to bring such instructions to life. They were dispirited; deprived of the Spirit. Had they so remained there would have been no "Church" to spread the Good News with which Jesus had entrusted them. But they received the Spirit in dramatic form. The Pentecostal story in the Acts of the Apostles is one of the best known in all scripture. These fright-ened and bewildered men received wondrous gifts from God's Spirit, whom Jesus had promised would be sent. Such gifts, or charisms, were to be given to all, and Paul is careful to make no distinction in kind between extraordinary gifts of prophecy and tongues and the ordinary gifts of "office." So the two strains were then united, though some (such as the local Church in Corinth) seem to have made better use of their own particular charisms, be they to heal, to comfort, to minister, etc. The Christian ministry (*diaconate*) was itself a vital gift and con-sisted in service, not overlordship. Charity, as Paul makes clear, was the greatest gift of all.

Thus did the Church begin. Its origin was "charismatic." Such a theme suffused the early period of Christian development. The Book of Revelation "identifies the 'testimony' or 'martyrdom' of Jesus with the Spirit of prophecy (19:10), while the Spirit and the Bride of Christ, the latter being the Church considered in her present trial, are seen as one in crying 'Come, Lord Jesus, come soon. (22:17 and 20)'" (O'Connor, ed., *Charismatic Renewal*, p. 119). Later texts thus saw the martyrs of the first centuries as being in the direct line of the Pen-tecostal inheritance.

Thus did the Church survive. The post-Constantinian era—as al-ready seen—implied a large measure of spiritual decline even amidst the material splendor of growing political prestige, rising basilicas, and richly adorned and princely bishops. From outside such ranks came, spontaneously, an astonishing "lay" movement: monasticism. This band of humble brothers had to fight a doughty battle with authority before becoming established. And when, after some centuries, they had become too well-established—and too well-heeled—they lost their original inspiration. But in a period roughly corresponding with the second half of the first millennium, they were the wonder of the Christian world. To quote Fr. Bouyer again: "Throughout the monastic tradition of the East (and a good part of that of the West), it will be maintained that the true monk, or spiritual man, is not he who merely conforms to an external rule, but only he who has attained a personal experience of the inner light. By the same token, even if he is a layman, such a one has more right to be a spiritual father than any priest or bishop who knows nothing of this experience" (*Charismatic Renewal,* p. 123).

Thus did the Church revive.

The later Middle Ages, however, witnessed not only ecclesiastical decay but also a curious and rather unexpected lack of interest in the theology of the Holy Spirit despite St. Thomas Aquinas' explanation of how the "gifts of the Spirit" work in man. There were notable exceptions such as the twelfth-century Cistercian, William of Saint-Thierry. But the general trend of Western theological spirituality was influenced by the Augustinian school. This was more concerned with a union of *essences* between God and man than with the mysticism of personal union. This trend was finally and decisively checked by, in particular, the great Spanish Carmelite reformer, St. John of the Cross. For him there could be no certainly authentic experience of life in union with God except by way of something akin to "night"—that dark night which first invades the senses and then the "spirit." The new light, when it finally breaks through, is like nothing previously experienced. His gift from the Spirit was passed on to many.

Thus did the Church rally.

This reform from within, however, did not necessarily find its way into the external fence-mending projects of the Counter-Reformation. These, once completed (so as, in fact, to enclose the entire Catholic Church behind massive ramparts), lasted until modern times. Then came Vatican II. Few Catholics doubt the inspiration of the Spirit behind that gathering. Its principal effect, however, if not its primary concern, still fell within the realm of institutional and structural reform. Spiritual renovation was naturally implied in every document;

but there was little, if any, visible foreshadowing of a particular phenomenon which had become, by the late sixties, one of the chief talking points in Catholic circles. It was only then that the expression "charismatic renewal" was beginning to go the rounds. Within ten years it had become the fastest growing movement in the Church of this or, possibly, any other century. This startling truth seems almost inconsistent with the fact that there has always been charismatic movement of one sort or another in the history of the Church. At no time has the Holy Spirit withheld those gifts which are needed for the people of God to live by. But the intensity with which such gifts have manifested themselves has ebbed and flowed with the ages. After a particularly high tide, the flood is always slow to recede and the aftereffects linger on for a very long time.

Thus does the Church renew itself.

Such periodically intense renewal, however, has never been entirely free of controversy and has often had sadly divisive effects among Catholics. The present wave is no exception. It is not an exaggeration to say that some Catholics despise charismatic renewal with as much fervor as others cling to it. The discord is sometimes the fault of charismatics, sometimes of others. Yet both retain the same basic beliefs. The difference seems to be that one sort of Catholic desires to preserve his belief uncontaminated and so keeps it, as it were, deep-frozen; the other lets it be touched by flame. For the one, faith is on ice; for the other, it is on fire. Given human nature, it is easy to see how such a situation can quickly cause friction. The charismatic may consider his opposite number cold and unresponsive; the latter may consider the charismatic an hysteric or fanatic. To be fully appreciated, moreover, charismatic renewal must actually, vividly, and perhaps repeatedly, be experienced rather than merely read about or observed. This, for many Catholics, would necessitate an unacceptable leap into the unknown. Charismatics, for their part, can be too keen to make converts and are often strangely insensitive to the hesitations of "outsiders." Such tendencies in the past have, on occasion, led charismatics into open heresy with the Church as a whole.

There is a further difficulty for run-of-the-mill Catholics. Charismatic renewal is a form of "Pentecostalism" which, in its modern guise, started (in Kansas in 1900) "outside the Church," in evangelically Protestant circles. There was no such thing as "Catholic Pentecostalism" until the late 1960s. It was then that something out-of-the-ordinary happened to a group of students, sisters, priests and professors at Duquesne University (Pittsburgh). It was the academic year 1966–67, and the members of this particular group felt demoralized. Disillusioned might be a better word. They were disillusioned even with Christianity and, in particular, with the Catholic divisions which had just then reached a peak point in the United States. Pope Paul, however, had neither been unaware of the depth of the divisions nor inactive in trying to ameliorate them. As it happened, 1967 was the fiftieth anniversary of the apparitions of Mary the Mother of the Lord at Fatima in Portugal. Catholics are never bound to believe in the authenticity of such reported visions or apparitions. Some Catholics were skeptical about Fatima. Others were not. In this particular year, "Pilgrim" Pope Paul asked the Madonna to intercede with Jesus for world peace, and also for internal peace for the Church. Though exaggerations, and even abuses, have, over the years, crept into Catholic devotions to the Virgin Mary, the basic and official theology concerning her significance ("Mariology") is less easy to fault. Mary is never elevated to a status on a par with the Divinity. What is often forgotten, moreover, is her special place in history as the first "charismatic" of the Christian era. She was filled with the Holy Spirit in a manner unique among creatures. Such, at least, is Catholic belief and the reason why, since then, all generations have called her "blessed."

Whether by coincidence or not, the Duquesne group came across a book called *The Cross and the Switchblade,* by David Wilkerson. It told of his apostolate among New York vandals and drug addicts and of the prodigious help and conversions brought about among them by the Holy Spirit. It seemed almost like a mass miracle. The book made a deep, though in a sense disquieting, impression on the Dusquesne group. Would it be right—or perhaps presumptuous if not even childish—to pray for some such miracle to relieve the spiritual aridity of their own lives at that moment? Two of the group decided to pray specially for each other. Each day they would recite the prayer "Come, Holy Spirit" in the hopes of receiving from that same Spirit the energy and fervor he had given to the first Christians.

Nothing happened. They nevertheless persevered in their prayers and then, after some months, asked some Pentecostalist friends to pray over them in order to receive baptism in the Spirit. A startling breakthrough came in early 1967 with effects that were immediate and rather overwhelming. They felt new life flowing into them and were overcome by a profound sense of peace and unspeakable joy. They were full of exceptional energy and enthusiasm and of a boundless desire to witness to Christ. Most surprisingly of all they became conscious of receiving "charismatic" gifts as of tongues, of prophecies, of discernment of spirits, and of healing. ("Prophecy" in the spiritual sense does not, of course mean the capacity to foretell events; it rather implies the ability to expound or proclaim divine reality—or pass on a divine command—in persuasive, even inspirational, language.) They were joined by others in a Retreat that was to become famous. The night before it started, one of the girls sensed in the chapel the living presence of the Holy Spirit. Later all experienced the same sensation and remained the whole night in prayer. The next day they felt different. In some way, difficult to explain, they were new men and new women.

Such happenings could well be accounted for by some such explanation as self-hypnosis or group hysteria. The sequel, however, is what is important, since the Duquesne experience proved to be no isolated and freakish occurrence. The movement, in fact, despite lack of leadership or organization, spread very rapidly, first to Notre Dame, Michigan State University and the University of Michigan, and then to other campuses and cities throughout the United States. Catholic Charismatic Renewal is now worldwide and numbers some millions of adherents. It is easily the most significant phenomenon in the Roman Catholic Church today. It might well seem to be God's most timely gift to a theoretically vast and well-organized religion which is having difficulty, by conventional means, in getting its members to come to Church and to obey its other "laws." The Church, however, is no longer a "legal" religion demanding conformism as the price for the salvation of individuals, but at the obvious expense of any sense of solidarity with the community at large. This selfish and self-centered conformism is still favored by some and it often takes a generation or so for Catholics to realize how harmful it can be. In February 1979, for example, the Conference of West German Bishops produced a report that was shocking and upsetting to many. It said that Catholic anti-Semitism in the Nazi period had stemmed from religious motives rather than from the racism of the Nazis, and acknowledged that a strong anti-Semitic tradition had been widespread among German Christians, including Catholics.

It is not, of course, only German Catholics who have, in recent history sold (or at least "lent") their souls to the devil in order to preserve the material props of the Church. In Poland, on the other hand, a curbing of the power of Religion has resulted in a great in-

crease in the potency of Faith. In the world at large Catholicism may
give the impression of being a tired Religion. Fulfillment of its obligations often seems perfunctory. But not, by any means, always. Catholic
Faith is observably being renewed all over the world; and various
phenomena, long dormant except as isolated cases, are now becoming
commonplace. Healing of the sick (and the otherwise troubled or
afflicted) is one example. The revised sacramental liturgy in this field
brings Catholics back to a point lost many centuries ago: healing is
now a "community" affair. For this purpose, family and friends form a
"community" united in praying for the person seriously sick. The
words of scripture take on a new meaning: "If one of you is ill, he
should send for the elders of the church, and they must anoint him
with oil in the name of the Lord and pray over him. The power of
faith will save the sick man and the Lord will raise him up again: and
if he has committed any sins, he will be forgiven" (James 5:14–15).
Healing is also carried out within an even wider community context.
Prayer for the sick person is made by large congregations in whatever
words come to the minds of those who love him. Prayer, at least at
charismatic services, is accompanied by a laying on of hands. It is
sometimes visibly obvious that the human bodies present are somehow
being used as channels for the Spirit's healing power just as electricity
is carried along wires.

The Mass, as clarified in the reformed liturgy, is, for Catholics, the
supreme prayer for healing. One of its prayers is: "Lord through this
sacrament may we rejoice in your healing power and experience your
saving love in mind and body." It is not just a question of believing in
such saving love but of *experiencing* it here and now. Another key
word is "rejoice." The Catholic whose faith is alive and on fire rejoices
in the presence of his Lord, and that of his brothers and sisters. He
wishes to share this joy with them. Sharing is a keynote of Renewal. As
far as possible everything is shared when charismatics come together.
The real presence of Jesus is shared from the moment two or three are
gathered together when, as Jesus promised, he would be there in their
midst. Such presence is almost tangible even to the nonparticipating
observer as he watches the worshipers lift their hands in prayer. Their
outstretched gestures and out-loud prayers seem natural and necessary
expressions of a devotion that is not, as in most conventional services,
held back, perhaps even suppressed, by inhibition. The sharing extends
not only to the prayers said in response to the Mass (if this is accompanying the service) but also to the thoughts, troubles and even the

shortcomings and sins of those present. They share such experiences with one another during a planned interval in the service. Testimony, witness, sorrow, joy, sin, hope: all (and more) are shared. If those participating are spending an evening or a whole day together, they may well share such food as they have brought. Their meal becomes a truly communal one. The sharing of cares implies no production of instant solutions. Charismatics do not give advice to each other. They share their troubles and jointly commend them to that one Lord who is present with them at that moment.

That they frequently, in the course of audible prayer, speak in "tongues" is one of the most difficult phenomena for the uninitiated. Such speaking in tongues is, in kind, the same gift as was given to the apostles at the first Pentecost. It is a question of speaking in a spiritual language rather than in some human idiom other than one's own. It seems to be based on the principle, unconsciously being followed, that certain thoughts, aspirations, sentiments, etc., which the person desires to communicate to God, defy expression in ordinary, everyday words. It is perhaps something like the musician desiring to express something beautiful. He does not do so in words but in music. The charismatic pours out his heart to God and the sounds that come from his lips are something like verbal music, not to be confused with singing since no ordinary words are used. When an entire charismatic congregation is praying in tongues the effect is extraordinary. Something like a rustling murmur, as of wind in trees, begins the process. It gets louder but becomes neither strident nor in any way discordant. The dozens, or hundreds—sometimes it is even several thousand—voices continue in this extraterrestrial harmony, after which, as if at a given but unseen signal, the voices die down and the murmur once more trails off into the same murmuring sound as of wind in trees. The same pattern repeats itself almost exactly at charismatic meetings in all parts of the world. I have personally witnessed them—in some amazement—only in Ireland, Italy, America, and Britain. Others confirm this identical phenomenon elsewhere. It would seem to be universal.

A person does not feel he has become fully integrated into this kind of spiritual Renewal until he has been "baptized in the Spirit." Others present usually lay hands on him and pray. No new "sacrament" is intended nor, obviously, does any such occur. What happens is a personally experienced actualization of the grace already sacramentally received. (If, exceptionally, the "recipient" has not been sacramentally baptized, this charismatic experience is not meant to be a substitute;

but it seems, frequently, to act as an inspiration toward ordinary baptism and subsequent confirmation in the ordinary way.) Baptism of the Holy Spirit has been variously described by its adherents, for example: "A filling with grace and power first recorded in Scripture when the Holy Spirit descended on the Apostles on the day of Pentecost"; or, "The release of the power of the Holy Spirit received in the sacrament of confirmation."

There is no doubt that those who have undergone such Renewal are transformed as persons. There is no doubt that healings occur and that people receive renewed faith, hope and charity. Charismatics, in general, are astonishingly tolerant of opposition when their own Renewal is genuine. The non-genuine and often rather neurotic ones tend to be almost childishly resentful of criticism, and this must count, where it exists, as a weakness in the movement. "Renewal" is meant to, and usually does, free the believer and open him out to new spiritual horizons hitherto undreamed of. Though it is true that no other unorganized movement—it is often more "lay" than clerical in character—has ever developed so quickly in the Church's history, the manner of growth has been even more interesting. From the late sixties onward groups began mushrooming, particularly in different parts of America, without being in any way connected with each other. Each individual growth was isolated and spontaneous. After twelve or thirteen years, organization has come to attach itself to the Renewal. The long-term effects of such organizations are difficult to assess, but this is not of great concern to charismatics themselves. The movement was born to die. When—as a separate movement within the Church—it is dead, its work will have been done, for it will have by that time worked its way into the mainstream of Catholic life. As a result the entire Church could, without any such thing as conscious "conversion" to Pentecostalism, become, in practice, charismatically renewed. In a somewhat similar way the liturgical and biblical movements were, about twenty years ago, offbeat and limited movements. Now, the whole Church has gone in the direction that these movements portended, and the "movements," as separate entities, are dead. One of the world's best-known protagonists of the Renewal is Cardinal Suenens of Belgium who refers to it as "a current of grace, a 'move' of the Spirit. . . . It will disappear as a movement as quickly as possible and enter into the blood and life of the Church." This can happen without Charismatic Renewal's ever becoming, in its own right, anything like a mass movement. It is, moreover, certain to become modified as it works its way further and further into the overall fabric of the Faith. "Even a small amount of yeast is enough to leaven all the dough" (I Cor. 5:6).

There are signs that this leavening process is already beginning to happen in the United States. The charismatic renewal as such seems to be tapering off but its style of devotion, often in modified form, is discernible in the services of many "ordinary" parishes. The process, however, has been slow and subtle. People need time to assimilate "new" things and cannot do so in great gulps. The right mixture is necessary. The assimilation process thus begins to be largely unconscious. Above all, in one overwhelmingly important sense, nothing "new" is actually happening at all. The Holy Spirit, Catholics believe, has been with the Church since the beginning just as a building may have been equipped since its completion, with electric light. But if no one turns on the switches no light burns. Lately, spiritual "switches" have been discovered in innumerable unsuspected corners of the Catholic world-Church and more and more faith has started to burn. Communion between God and man, and between people with each other, has in the process become more relaxed and natural. Christians have begun to reflect how strange it would be to go into their best friend's house and not reach out and embrace that friend; not to accept his hospitality in good part; not to share with him news and views; not, above all, to speak at all but to have downcast eyes and remain in gloomy silence. And they have applied the obvious conclusions to their relationship with God when going to meet him in the company of their fellow Christians. They do not fail to greet Jesus as their best friend, but behave now as the early Christians did. They would not, moreover, think of entering a prayer or eucharistic meeting without greeting each other. "It sounds like a party," noncharismatic Catholics complain. "It is," charismatics reply.

The majority of Catholics, however, are still unconvinced. Many have had no experience at all of charismatic renewal (though this does not always stop them being severely critical of it!). Theologically there is an element of the simplistic and fundamentalist in charismaticism. On the other hand, the Renewal is now a fully clerical-lay partnership and no theological objections have proved conclusive. It is often a matter of personal feeling, temperament and private opinion. The most surprising kinds of people suddenly find themselves carried away into the excitement and consolation of Renewal. Others find it unreservedly repellent to them. Conservatives tend to believe that it is too "liberal" whereas, for example, it is so far notably cool toward the "new theology" and is thought by many liberals to be woefully unaware of social injustice and the concomitant duties of Christians. It appears, however, that as the yeast works its way through the dough, these other factors begin to balance themselves out. But it is much too early yet to chart this particular course with any confidence. One practical danger arises where—and a certain English parish has become almost notorious in this respect—the effect of Renewal, instead of bringing peace and healing, brings divisiveness and rancor. A pastor who is uncharismatic and unfriendly by nature cannot easily respond to the openness required of the genuinely renewed Christian. The criterion always lies in the objective effect of the "movement" on any given group or area. If it is obviously disruptive and disturbing, something is seriously wrong. Not all "charismatics" unfortunately can spot their own hangups and shortcomings. (Fortunately such cases seem to be comparatively rare.)

Despite many misunderstandings and misgivings, the vitality of Renewal is glaringly apparent to anyone who comes into sympathetic contact with it. Preexistent lack of sympathy obviously precludes all possibility of fruitful exchange. It may well be that the Western Church is doing too little to promote active dialogue and dynamic contact between Charismatic Renewal and renewal of other kinds, considering that "renewal" of one kind or another has become the basic test for the efficacy of Vatican II. Though things have come a long way since 1973, words spoken then by the Pope are still important. On October 18 of that year Paul VI met two bishops and eleven representatives who had come to the Vatican specially to evaluate "the Charismatic Renewal." The Pope said to them:

> Certain common notes appear in this renewal: the taste for deep prayer, personal and in groups, a return to contemplation and an emphasizing of praise of God, the desire to devote oneself completely to Christ, a great availability for the calls of the Holy Spirit, more assiduous reading of the Scriptures, generous brotherly devotion, the will to make a contribution to the service of the Church.
>
> In all that, we can recognize the mysteries and discreet work of the Spirit, who is the soul of the Church.
>
> The spiritual lives of the faithful come under the active pastoral responsibility of each bishop in his own diocese. It is particularly opportune to recall this in the presence of these ferments of renewal which arouse so many hopes.

Even in the best experiences of renewal weeds may be found among the good seed, so a work of discernment is indispensable.

It devolves upon those who are in charge of the Church, to whose special competence it belongs, not indeed to stifle the Spirit but to test all things and hold fast to that which is good (cf. I Thess. 5:12 and 19–21) (*Lumen Gentium*).

"Discernment" is certainly vital to distinguish the genuine from the counterfeit. In any exuberant demonstration of religious devotion, such things as fanaticism, hysteria, and self-deception are only some of the dangers that can arise. Discernment, on the other hand, is itself a gift of the Holy Spirit and there can be no conflict between beliefs backed by Church "authority" and those backed by the revelation of the Holy Spirit in some other way. This particular version of supposed "conflict" is illusory. Moreover "the value of a mystical experience is measured not according to the way in which it is subjectively felt, but according to its objective influence" (de Beauvoir, *The Second Sex*, p. 636). It remains true, however, that many Catholics hover on the brink of total renewal rather than trusting to the Spirit in deciding whether to make the great and courageous leap into the unknown. Those who have done it seem never to look back: their total self-giving brings new life in abundance. Those who refuse the call outright justify themselves but often seem unhappy and dry in their spiritual life. They find the stereotype of Religion either a habit they can't quite do without or a duty that becomes increasingly burdensome. In between, there are many who remain on the brink. . . .

This, perhaps, is the situation of the whole Roman Catholic Church today. It stands on the brink of a spectacular breakthrough if it takes up all its options in the developing world of the future. Then, conceivably, the charismatic gift of "sharing" will come into its own and show how ultimately deceptive, by comparison, the Marxist version can be.

EPILOGUE

Pope John Paul's visit to his native Poland in June 1979, was his greatest personal triumph up to that point. It was in fact sensational. To many, its most moving moment was the Pope's visit to the Nazi extermination center at Auschwitz-Birkenau, a modern Golgotha. Four million victims perished there. Two and a half million of these were Jews—a fact surprisingly played down in the English-speaking Catholic press. The emphasis was chiefly on John Paul's impact on the people of present-day Poland and the evocation of that tragic country's tenaciously Catholic past. The Western press, in general, stressed the political implications of the Pope's visit and treated it as little short of an anti-Communist crusade. The Pope himself insisted that the dimensions of his visit were strictly spiritual. Any mention of "liberty," however, inevitably focused attention on state restrictions on the Church in Poland. The main demands of the bishops there are for freedom to build and restore more churches; access for religious broadcasting on state-run television; and an end to state censorship of Church publications. They also strongly oppose job discrimination against admitted believers and state control over episcopal appointments. The Pope supported them on all these points and was much more specific in his support of the liberation of people than he had been at Puebla. In this respect he was perhaps—despite himself—a prisoner of the Vatican whose official mind always distinguishes between Catholic countries such as the Latin American ones where, even if individual human rights are disregarded, corporate "Church" rights are respected; and those (such as Poland) where the official Church is denied any privileged position in the political order of affairs.

Few things stood out more clearly after the Pope's visit to Poland than the strength of Catholic *faith* (as opposed to mere *religion*) in that country by comparison with its weakness in Western Europe where, however, "religion" is given full scope. (This may be one reason for Poland's overriding dread of "Westernization.") Ironically, in fact, at the very time of the Polish pilgrimage, England's Cardinal Hume had some things to say about the "tiredness of the Church in those lands which are rich, which have much, but having much are in danger of losing the one thing that matters." He was preaching at a Mass to celebrate the centenary of the founding by the White Fathers of the first Catholic missions in the African interior. Commenting on the "strength and freshness" of the Church in Africa he thought, "as others have thought, that perhaps one day African missionaries would come to bring freshness back to the Church in the West."

By another irony the papal visit to Poland coincided with the failure of not one but two major "rich-poor" conferences. In late May (1979) a Brussels meeting between European Common Market ministers and ministers from African, Caribbean and Pacific countries ended without agreement on a follow-up in Togo up to the Lomé Convention. An even more deadly blow to the hopes of poor countries came in June of the same year at Manila when the month-old Fifth United Nations Conference on Trade and Development broke up after achieving practically nothing. These doleful developments, coupled with what the Pope was saying and doing in Poland, highlighted more than ever the twin evils today: the two mighty but false gods of East and West. In terms of ultimate moral responsibility for human dignity, was there anything to choose between the physical materialism of consumerist capitalism and the metaphysical materialism of atheist communism? In terms of public reactions among Christians, the melancholy truth seemed to be that while people were naturally excited by the Pope's image as beamed from Poland, they were merely bored by reminders of how little was being done for the Third World by the wealthy West. Reminders of positive Western guilt, seemingly condoned by the Church, in fact, provoke more than boredom. They often provoke positive irritation.

The same reaction must be anticipated in some quarters to any interpretation of Catholicism's current anatomy that is radically critical of certain hitherto accepted positions. It must be stressed, however, that what has been written in the foregoing chapters is no more than just that: an *interpretation*. It is as far from being a supposedly infallible diagnosis as it is meant to be an inerrant compendium of facts and figures set out for purely reference purposes. Such compendia exist in abundance elsewhere. The reader is asked to be as tolerant of the author's provocations as the author would be of the readers' alternative interpretations. It is only thus that the ecumenical aim of unity in diversity can ever be reached. It may be added that the Catholicism described in this book is mainly that which is *implied* by the Second Vatican Council rather than that which has already come to pass. But the aim of the Church today, according to the Pope, is, as already stressed, to make explicit what, during the Council, was still only implied.

The very fact that the gap between these two is still so wide it may make some of the judgments offered above seem extreme. If, for example—as many think—the Polish happening of June 1979 was substantially a Catholic anti-Communist initiative, are some of Chapter 3's interwar verdicts too harsh? Was the Church then passing not so much through a "Fascist phase" as a confrontation with communism making certain "diplomatic" maneuverings regrettably necessary with such countries as Germany and Italy? The best apologia for the Church in that period is probably that of Anthony Rhodes (a highly reliable, non-Roman Catholic, scholar).* But the interwar period cannot be taken in isolation. And the historical section of this book has attempted to restore an overall perspective to the Catholic story that began with Constantine and ended with John XXIII. The immediate pre-Johannine phase was dictated by what had happened in previous centuries. The post-1918 emergence of strong right-wing governments seemed to give a last hope for something like a return to the old ecclesiastical-imperial partnership of throne and altar. Since John XXIII, all has been different. Justice has been put not only before power but also, by that Pope, even before charity itself. Not only that, the need for community has been put before the need for conformity. It is thus much more difficult to be a "good" Roman Catholic today when most of the work is no longer left to God but falls on the individual, seen as a man with a completely free conscience. It is indeed a frightening responsibility.

And what of ecumenism? As the second year of John Paul's pastorate goes by, it may seem questionable to have cited Anglican-Roman Catholic relations as the chief yardstick for general ecumenical prospects, including those with the Orthodox "East." Apart from space limitations, the main consideration has been that if Anglicans and Roman Catholics cannot find a formula for unity, there is little or no chance for any such formula emerging between Catholicism and other, even further-away, forms of Protestantism (taking the word in its widest sense.) Meanwhile the "Uniate" solution (whereby a form of papal primacy can be combined with retention by "sister Churches" of their special traditions) is within the grasp of the Anglican-Roman Catholic bloc; and in June of 1979 the Anglican-Roman Catholic Commission made an urgent plea for the removal of the main obstacle still standing in the way of this, namely adherence to Leo XIII's ruling

---

* See: *The Vatican in the Age of the Dictators,* London: Hodder & Stoughton, 1973.

that Anglican orders were "null and void." The Catholic cochairman of the Commission (England's Bishop Alan Clark) commented afterward that there were two ways in which this could be done. Either Leo's encyclical could be taken to pieces and its findings rejected as wrong; or a new verdict could be arrived at in the light of theological developments since 1896. The ruling contained in *Apostolicae Curae* was not, in other words, irreformable as had formerly been assumed.

It must be admitted, however, that there is a whole "other" world of ecumenical speculation for which no space could realistically be found. For now that Catholic scholars are no longer censored and persecuted for originality and new initiatives, a new era is dawning. It is an era not of "neo-Modernism," for those former controversies, in their original form, have been buried except in the minds of the "neointegralists" who would like to keep the fires of persecution alive. It is, rather a "post-Modernist" era in which Karl Barth is re-presenting Calvin for modern man and Hans Küng is producing an entirely revolutionary synthesis of the whole Christian (including Catholic) belief. But Catholic lay people as a whole are not interested in such speculations, important though they are. In fact they share with their bishops not only a lack of interest in them but, often enough, a lack of comprehension as well.

If theoretical ecumenism is, thus, too theological for some people, practical ecumenism is too "churchy" for others. Many thus believe in an age of renewal based on the guidance of God's Spirit and the real presence of Jesus (as he promised) wherever two or three are gathered together in his name. In such a climate, "ecumenism by committee" could easily be overtaken by events. Catholics and non-Catholics not only desire to receive the Eucharist jointly, but in many cases already do so. The present Pope has reiterated the standing prohibition of such "intercommunion" until formal "unity" has been officially established. And yet the practice is spreading everywhere. Truth, for the person of faith, cannot forever be something imposed from outside. It can flower only from within.

This, perhaps, is the most central and sensitive aspect of Catholicism's multiple dilemma in today's world. It is also the reason why the logic of Archbishop Lefebvre is so embarrassing to the official Roman Church. For so much of it is correct. In London, on June 17, 1979, Lefebvre stated publicly: "We do not want an ecumenical Faith, we want the Faith taught by Jesus Christ." This is exactly what the Pope himself would have said thirty years ago when it was held, without qualification, that the truth resided in the Roman Catholic Church alone. The reversal of direction since then has been constantly advertised by Lefebvre but never admitted in so many words by official Rome. Until it is, however, the Council's "implicit" message can never emerge.

History, as well, is on the side of Lefebvre—at least since the fourth century. Some, indeed, may feel that too much stress has been put in this volume on the sense of power exhibited since that century by a Church claiming exclusive knowledge of the most important matters of life and death. It might appear to imply that no one responded spontaneously to the great message of Christ's Church. On the contrary, this heroic part of the Catholic story is well-known. It is the centerpiece of every Catholic account of Christian history. For that very reason this particular element in the building up of world Catholicism has been intentionally omitted in these pages. Such an omission, far from denying the great surges of faith in every age, presupposes that they are so familiar to most readers as to need little stress. What does need stress, however, is that "other" side of the story which is left out of most Catholic accounts of Christian history—and left out, what's more, in such a manner as to suggest that it is either non-existent or unimportant. It is usually given passing mention only as if it were a mere accidental or incidental cause of the rise of Christianity to a position of ultimately total dominance in Europe. In fact it was the principal one from the fourth century onward and it transformed the original community of God's people into a totalitarian empire-Church in which no opposition to orthodoxy was permitted. Rigid censorship obliterated all but the officially Christian accounts of Christ's impact on the world of the first Christian centuries. This is not to say that the Christian religion, though established in great measure by political, military and economic means, did not, in succeeding generations, produce much genuine faith. But "religion" and "faith" must always be distinguished; and criticism must be expected of an account which turns the conventional picture upside down.

There is yet another front on which criticism may be anticipated, namely the treatment accorded here to the Church of the Middle Ages. The saying is often heard that "the Church of the Middle Ages was the greatest humanizing influence in Europe." This is true. It is also true that the Church was the *only* humanizing influence of that same period. It brooked no rivalry and had no competitors. It exercised a total monopoly of education and complete control over every aspect of the life of the citizens of the *civitas Christiana*. No comparison is therefore possible with any alternative system within Europe itself. But a comparison is possible with the Muslim world as it developed for about five centuries before the age of the Crusades. Here, there arose from the deserts a new world and a civilization so dazzling that it made the corresponding period in Europe seem part of a very dark age indeed. (If there was also plenty of "holy violence" so was there on the Christian side.) Damascus and Baghdad made it seem that the greatness of ancient Athens had been reborn. But the days of Islam, in its most glorious phase, were numbered. Its spirit was broken by the bloodbath of the Crusades. For centuries afterward Muslims could look on Christians only as looters, rapists and murderers. No sooner were the Crusades over than the Mongols, for a hundred years, ravaged the Muslim lands with a brutal ferocity with which history knows few parallels. Pyramids of skulls long remained as monuments to the handiwork of the Mongol invaders. The subjection lasted until relatively modern times. Through it all, another race—the first of all God's chosen people—lived dispersed through a hostile world as outcasts. These people were the Jews. Their story is yet another example of what history itself consists of—the struggle of one set of people to emancipate themselves from the tyranny of another, be it political, religious, intellectual, military, or economic. Though all these elements are important, the economic one is paramount and has been present at the center of every mass movement for change in human history.

Where does today's Catholic stand in this great march of the human spirit—toward the freedom of being its own master? One plausible answer might be that he does not know himself. For his religious training and conditioned view of history has, until very recent years, been so astonishingly narrow, that he is ill-equipped to make some of the painful decisions now required of him. In the past, things were comparatively easy. The Roman Church was the one true Church in the all-embracing sense that all others were in error; and error had "no rights." Catholics were the invariable "goodies" of history according to the prescribed textbooks. The "enemies" were easily indentifiable whether they were Muslims, Jews, Freemasons, Communists, Protestants, or anything else. But now we are called upon not only to believe in human brotherhood but positively to act as brothers. We are called upon to renew ourselves in a manner that is inevitably painful. The Catholic response to this call, however, is not uniformly enthusiastic. Many Catholics find its demands and what is implied by them—to say nothing of being reminded of that "other" side of Catholic history—intensely irritating.

Much, furthermore, of what has been written here may have become obsolete by the time the book is actually published. Events race on. Though it was stated, for example, that Holland had made a promising beginning in courageously experimenting along the lines suggested by Vatican II, that country has come to be faced, in the early eighties, with a serious shortage of priests. Whatever happens next, however, does not invalidate the conciliar experiments which were, in effect, the first attempts to explicate what the Council could only imply behind a barrage of qualifications and loopholes. It merely makes more urgent that reconsideration of the Roman priesthood *as a whole* which is already overdue. The pastoral situation as described, for example, in Africa makes it imperative that married men—already ministers but having other jobs as well—must, sooner or later, be ordained to the full ministry. Many would say the sooner the better. And, bearing in mind Cardinal Hume's words quoted above, Europe and America can hardly lag behind Africa in supplying the faithful with people qualified to minister to their spiritual needs. Stones—in the form of empty churches—will be no substitute for the bread of life. A whole new dimension will thus be added to the (often narrowly considered) questions of clerical celibacy and an all-male ministry when this new and urgent pastoral need is squarely faced.

As for Marxist-Leninism, it may be objected that a too "romantic" view has been taken of it at some points of this "anatomy." Scarcely more so, however, than that taken by John XXIII who looked at the problem in terms of people and not of abstract principles. He could see the social good in a system which was nevertheless philosophically at variance with Church doctrine. Nowhere has it been denied, moreover, that "liberation theology" can put Catholics in danger of being sucked into the Marxist net. But the danger of condemning liberation theology out of hand is to risk repeating in this century—in the "new" world—what happened in the last century in the "old" one. And this was the loss to the Church of many millions of ordinary—mostly working class—Catholics. Dare the Western Church go on being what it once was—the Church predominantly of the bourgeoisie?

The road ahead is forbidding. In 1980 the bishops of the Catholic world will once more meet in synod in Rome. This time they will discuss family life. Their findings may create excitement or show the Church's official mind to be still very far from that of ordinary Catholics on the most basic of pertinent topics. But—as at Vatican II—the Spirit can break through at the most unexpected junctures.

The generally popular but stolidly conservative John Paul II meanwhile plays it cool. His first concern has been to steady, strengthen and consolidate the Church's base within its widest limits. As to the radical changes ultimately inescapable from his desired 'explication' of Vatican II, he will, when the moment comes (if indeed it comes at all during his pastorate), be in a much stronger position to pilot them through than would a Pope of known "liberal" inclinations. History has repeatedly shown that—while progressives may plan and plead for reforms—it is more often the occasional far-seeing "conservative" who actually brings such reforms to permanent fruition. For such a person has the far greater chance of bringing with him the majority of those whom he leads into an entirely new era of their corporate lives. It will take time. John Paul's world travels have only just begun. Within a few years he will have had greater opportunities than any Pope in history to hear at first hand the authentic voice of the People of God.

But will he listen? This is the question which many Catholics have been asking themselves with growing anxiety ever since the "populist-triumphalist" Papal visit to Ireland and the United States in late 1979. Only the future can supply the answer to this crucial question.

BIBLIOGRAPHY
(Books quoted in text)

Arbitrary Arrests and Detentions in Chile. Fourth Session of the International Commission of Enquiry into the Military Junta in Chile. Helsinki: Finlandia House, 1976.

Assman, Hugo. *Practical Theology of Liberation.* London: Search Press, 1975.

Barraclough, Geoffrey. *The Medieval Papacy.* London: Thames & Hudson, 1974.

de Beauvoir, Simone. *The Second Sex.* London: Jonathan Cape, 1953.

Belloc, Hilaire. *Europe and the Faith.* London: Burns & Oates, 1962.

Bigo, Pierre, S. J. *The Church and Third World Revolution.* New York: Orbis Books, 1978.

Bociurkiw, Bohan R., and Strong, John W. *Religion and Atheism in the USSR and Eastern Europe.* London: Macmillan, 1975.

Brown, Raymond E. *Biblical Reflections on Crises Facing the Church.* New York: Paulist Press; London: Darton, Longman & Todd, 1970.

Bruneau, Thomas C. *The Political Transformation of the Brazilian Catholic Church.* Cambridge: Cambridge University Press, 1974.

Bühlmann, Walbert. *The Coming of the Third Church.* Slough, England: St. Paul Publications, 1976; New York: Orbis Books, 1977.

————. *Courage Church.* New York: Orbis Books, 1978.

Callahan, Daniel (ed.). *The Catholic Case for Contraception.* London: Arlington Books, 1969.

Camara, Helder. *Church and Colonialism.* London and Sydney: Sheed & Ward, 1977.

Cassidy, Sheila. *Audacity to Believe.* London: Collins, 1977.

Catholic Almanac. Huntingdon, Ind.: Our Sunday Visitor, 1978.

Catholic Encyclopedia. London: Caxton, 1912.

Catholic Encyclopedia for School and Home. New York: McGraw-Hill, 1965.

Cavallari, Alberto. *The Changing Vatican.* London: Faber & Faber, 1968.

Chadwick, Henry. *The Early Church.* London: Penguin, 1967.

Congar, Yves, O.P. *Challenge to the Church: The Case of Archbishop Lefebvre.* London: Collins, 1977.

Crichton, J. D. *Christian Celebration: The Mass.* London: Chapman, 1971.

————. *Christian Celebration: The Sacraments.* London: Chapman, 1971.

Day, Edward. *The Catholic Church Story—Changing and Changeless.* Ligouri, Miss.: Ligouri Publications, 1975.

Delespesse, Max. *The Church Community: Leaven and Life-Style.* Notre Dame: Ave Maria Press, 1973.

Devine, George. *Liturgical Renewal.* New York: Alba House, 1973.

Dominian, Jack. *The Church and the Sexual Revolution.* London: Darton, Longman & Todd, 1971.

————. *Proposals for a New Sexual Ethic.* London: Darton, Longman & Todd, 1977.

Drinan, Robert F. *Honor the Promise.* New York: Doubleday, 1977.

Dulles, Avery. *The Survival of Dogma.* New York: Doubleday, 1973.

Fessler, Joseph. *The True and False Infallibility of the Popes.* London: Burns & Oates: 1875.

Frei, Edouardo. *Latin America: The Hopeful Option.* New York: Orbis Books, 1978.

Freyre, Gilberto. *The Masters and the Slaves,* trans. Samuel Putnam. New York: Knopf, 1946.

Gallacher, Chuck, S. J. *The Marriage Encounter.* New York: Doubleday, 1975.

Geffre, Claude. *A New Age in Theology.* New York: Paulist Press, 1972.

Goergen, Donald, O. P. *The Sexual Celibate.* New York: Seabury Press, 1974; London: SPCK, 1976.

Gollin, James. *Worldly Goods.* New York: Random House, 1971.

Gontard, Friedrich. *The Popes.* London: Barrie & Rockcliff, 1964.

Greeley, Andrew. *The American Catholic.* New York: Basic Books, 1977.

Grey, F. du Plessis. *Divine Disobedience.* London: Hamish Hamilton, 1970.

Guerin, Paul. *I Believe.* Great Wakering, England: Mayhew McCrimmon, 1977.

Hanu, José. *Vatican Encounter.* Kansas City: Sheed, Andrews & McNeill, 1978.

Häring, Bernard. *Free and Faithful in Christ.* Slough, England: St. Paul Publications, 1978.

Harris, Peter (and four others). *On Human Life.* London: Burns & Oates, 1968.

Hastings, Adrian. *African Christianity.* London: Geoffrey Chapman, 1976.

Hastings, Adrian. *A Concise Guide to the Documents of Vatican II*, 2 vols. London: Darton, Longman & Todd, 1968.

Hilberg, Raoul. *The Destruction of the European Jews*. Chicago: Quadrangle Books; London: W. H. Allen, 1961.

Hitchcock, James. *The Recovery of the Sacred*. New York: Seabury Press, 1974.

Holmes, Derek. *More Roman than Rome*. London: Burns & Oates; Shepherdstown, W. Va.: Patmos Press, 1978.

————. *The Triumph of the Holy See*. London: Burns & Oates; Shepherdstown, W. Va.: Patmos Press, 1978.

Horgan, John (ed.). *Humanae Vitae and the Bishops*. Shannon: Irish University Press, 1972.

Hughes, John Jay. *Stewards of the Lord*. London and Sydney: Sheed & Ward, 1970.

Jungmann, Joseph A. *The Mass of the Roman Rite,* one volume edition. New York: Benziger Bros., 1959.

Kelleher, Stephen J. *Divorce and Remarriage for Catholics?* New York: Doubleday, 1973.

Kosnik, Anthony (ed.). *Human Sexuality: New Directions in Catholic Thought*. London: Search Press, 1977.

Küng, Hans. *The Council: Reform and Reunion*. New York: Sheed & Ward, 1961.

————. *Signposts for the Future*. New York: Doubleday, 1978.

Lane, Dermot A. (ed.). *Liberation Theology*. Dublin: Gill & Macmillan, 1977.

Leonard, George. *Light on Archbishop Lefebvre*. London: Catholic Truth Society, 1977.

Machoveč, Milan. *A Marxist Looks at Jesus*. London: Burns & Oates, 1977.

McBrien, Richard P. *The Remaking of the Church*. New York-London: Harper & Row, 1973.

————. *Who Is a Catholic?* Denville, N.J.: Dimension Books, 1971.

McGinn, John T. *Doctrines Do Grow*. New York: Paulist Press, 1972.

McKenzie, John L. *The Roman Catholic Church*. New York: Doubleday, 1971.

McNally, Robert E. *The Unreformed Church*. New York: Sheed & Ward, 1968.

Marshall, John. *On Human Life,* (eds.) Peter Harris and others. London: Burns & Oates, 1968.

Marty, Martin E., and Peerman, Dean G. (eds.). *New Theology, No. 6.* New York, Macmillan; London: Collier-Macmillan, 1969.

Maynard-Smith, H. *Pre-Reformation England*. London: Macmillan, 1938.

Moore, Maurice J. *Death of a Dogma?* Chicago: Community and Family Center, 1973.

Muller, Alois. *The New Church and Our Children*. London: Burns & Oates, 1968.

Neal, Marie Augusta. *A Socio-Theology of Letting Go*. New York: Paulist Press, 1977.

A New Catechism: Catholic Faith for Adults. New York and London: Herder; Burns & Oates, 1968.

New Catholic Encyclopedia. New York: McGraw-Hill, 1967.

O'Collins, Gerald. *What Are They Saying about Jesus?* New York: Paulist Press, 1977.

O'Connell, Hugh J. *Keeping Your Balance in the Modern Church*. Ligouri, Mo.: Ligouri Publications, 1968.

O'Connor, Edward D. (ed.). *Charismatic Renewal*. London: SPCK, 1978.

Pallenberg, Corrado. *Vatican Finances*. London: Penguin, 1973.

Partner, Peter. *The Lands of Peter*. London: Eyre & Spottiswoode, 1972.

von Pastor, Ludwig. *The History of the Popes,* trans. E. F. Peeler, 40 vols. St. Louis: Herder & Herder, 1898.

van der Plas (ed.). *Those Dutch Catholics*. London: Geoffrey Chapman, 1967.

Prospishil, Victor. *Divorce and Remarriage*. New York: Herder & Herder; London: Burns & Oates, 1967.

Rhodes, Anthony. *The Vatican in the Age of the Dictators*. London: Hodder & Stoughton, 1973.

Rian, Edwin H. (ed.). *Christianity and World Revolution*. New York: Harper & Row, 1963.

Richards, Hubert. *The First Easter: What Really Happened?* London: Collins, 1976.

Roche, Douglas J. *The Catholic Revolution*. New York: David McKay, 1968.

Sampson, Anthony. *The Sovereign State: The Secret History of ITT*. London: Hodder Fawcett, 1974.

Sewell, Brocard. *The Vatican Oracle*. London: Duckworth, 1970.

Torres, Sergio, and Fabella, Virginia. *The Emergent Gospel*. Maryknoll: Orbis Books, 1978.

Troeltsch, Ernst. *The Social Teaching of the Christian Churches,* 2 vols. New York: Harper Torchbooks, 1931, repr. 1960.

Valsecchi, Ambrogio. *Controversy: The Birth Control Debate 1958–1968*. London: G. Chapman, 1968.

Violence in Ireland: A Report on the Churches. Belfast: Christian Journals; Dublin: Veritas, 1976/77.

Wansbrough, Henry. *Risen from the Dead*. Slough, England: St. Paul Publications, 1978.

Ware, Timothy. *The Orthodox Church*. London: Penguin, 1963.

Whitham, A. R. *The History of the Christian Church*. London: Rivingtons, 1943.

INDEX

individuals and groups concerned
with, 241–44; "letting go"
theology, 236; realization of,
237–38

Rerum Novarum (Leo XIII), 47

Research Centre of Public Opinion of
the Polish Radio, 212

Resurrection, 136–39, 167

Rhodes, Anthony, 270

Rhythm system, 79, 81; *see also* Birth
control

Ribbentrop, Joachim von, 42–43

Richards, Hubert, 128

Roman Catholic Church:
ecclesiastical imperialism, 21–32;
fascist phase, 33–43; growth of,
11–48; hierarchy of ranks, 19–20,
63–64; involvement with politics,
33–43; prognosis, 205–67;
readjustment, 109–204; transition
from early Christian community,
13–20; trauma and, 49–108; zenith
of power, 28–29; *see also* Papacy

Roman Empire, 13, 15, 19, 113–14,
154

"Roman Question" of 1870, 35

Romero, Archbishop, 232

Romero, General Carlos, 223

Russian Revolution, 37

Sacred Congregation for the Doctrine
of the Faith, 79, 122, 141, 142,
146, 156, 177

Sacred Council for the Public Affairs
of the Church, 63

Sagnier, Marc, 37

Salazar, Antonio, 39

Salvation, 22, 54, 70, 129, 161, 174,
200, 218–19

Samore, Antonio Cardinal, 229

Saxons, 28

Schillebeeckx, Edward, 131

Schoonenberg, Piet, 133–34

Scofield, C. I., 236

Scotus, Duns, 174

Secretariat for Non-Christian
Religions, 246

Secretariat for Promoting Christian
Unity, 161

Secretariat of State, 63

Serono Company, 193

Sex and sexuality, 74, 78, 140–50;
Church's future priests and, 145;
marriage and, 142, 144, 149, 150,

155, 157; new sexuality morality,
145–47; traditional teachings,
141–42, 143, 147

Shell Oil Company, 193

Shorter, Aylward, 245

Sillon, Le (political group), 37

Silundika, George, 119

Silva, Cardinal, 232

Sindona, Michele, 193, 197

Smith, H. Maynard, 164

Smith, Fr. Rolland F., 244

Società Generale Immobiliare, 193,
195

Sodalitium Pianum, 65

Sollicitudo Omnium Ecclesiarum
(Paul VI), 209–10

South West African People's
Organization, 119

Souza, Sister Gladys d', 242

Spalding, Archbishop, 117

Spellman, Cardinal, 75

Stephen I, Pope, 18

Stephen II, Pope, 28

Stephen VI, Pope, 34

Sturzo, Don Luigi, 35–36

Suenens, Cardinal, 80–81, 264

Syllabus of Errors (Pius IX), 81, 112

Sylvester I, Pope, 16, 18, 28

Synod of Bishops, 71, 196, 199, 247

Szálasi, Ferenc, 39

Tambo, Oliver, 119

Tanenbaum, Rabbi Marc C., 180

Tertullian, 17

Thirty-nine Articles (Church of
England), 166

Thomas, M. M., 245

Togliatti, Palmiro, 48

"Tongues," speaking in, 263

Traditionalism, 59–60, 62

Tridentine (Council of Trent) Mass,
38, 90, 92, 93, 103

Tridentinists, 95

Trinity, 17, 133, 135

Unam Sanctam (Boniface VIII), 29

United Nations, 192, 240

United Nations Conference on Trade
and Development, 269

United Nations Human Rights
Commission, 225

University of Michigan, 261

Urban VIII, Pope, 91